Gesture in French Post-New Wave Cinema

European Connections

Studies in Comparative Literature, Intermediality and Aesthetics

Volume 47

edited by
Hugues Azérad and Marion Schmid

PETER LANG
Lausanne • Berlin • Bruxelles • Chennai • New York • Oxford

François Giraud

Gesture in French Post-New Wave Cinema

PETER LANG
Lausanne • Berlin • Bruxelles • Chennai • New York • Oxford

Bibliographic information published by the Deutsche Nationalbibliothek. The German National Library lists this publication in the German National Bibliography; detailed bibliographic data is available on the Internet at http://dnb.d-nb.de.

A catalogue record for this book is available from the British Library.

Library of Congress Cataloging-in-Publication Data

Names: Giraud, François, 1991– author.
Title: Gesture in French post-new wave cinema / François Giraud.
Description: Oxford ; New York : Peter Lang, [2023] | Series: European connections, 1424-3792 ; vol 47 | Includes bibliographical references and index.
Identifiers: LCCN 2022059049 (print) | LCCN 2022059050 (ebook) | ISBN 9781800796386 (paperback) | ISBN 9781800796393 (ebook) | ISBN 9781800796409 (epub)
Subjects: LCSH: New wave films—France—History and criticism. | Gesture in motion pictures. | Motion pictures—France—History—20th century.
Classification: LCC PN1993.5.F7 G57 2023 (print) | LCC PN1993.5.F7 (ebook) | DDC 791.43/0944—dc23/eng/20230117
LC record available at https://lccn.loc.gov/2022059049
LC ebook record available at https://lccn.loc.gov/2022059050

Cover image: François Giro, *Notation of Gesture* (2022).
Cover design by Peter Lang Group AG

ISSN 1424-3792
ISBN 978-1-80079-638-6 (print)
ISBN 978-1-80079-639-3 (ePDF)
ISBN 978-1-80079-640-9 (ePub)
DOI 10.3726/b21093

Published by Peter Lang Ltd, Oxford, United Kingdom
info@peterlang.com - www.peterlang.com

This publication has been peer reviewed.

For my parents

Contents

Illustrations

Acknowledgements

I would like to express my gratitude to Professor Marion Schmid whose experience and expertise was essential when I first undertook this research project as a PhD thesis in 2015 at the University of Edinburgh. Her support, advice and feedback, along with her capacity for patience in listening to my ideas proved extremely helpful. I am also grateful to her for introducing me to Chantal Akerman's cinema and including me in the interdisciplinary research network 'Film and the Other Arts'. I would like to take this opportunity to thank all the members of the network, especially Professor Hugues Azérad, who has always been very supportive of my project.

I also want to thank Dr Daniel Yacavone and Dr David Sorfa. Their theoretical rigour and thought-provoking questions on my topic helped me improve the quality of my arguments. I am also indebted to Dr Fabien Arribert-Narce for his detailed feedback on my second chapter, as well as Professor Martine Beugnet and Dr Claire Boyle for their enlightening remarks and insights on my thesis. Moreover, I am grateful to Professor Ágnes Pethő for offering me the opportunity to publish parts of Chapter 3 in the peer-reviewed journal *Acta Universitatis Sapientiae, Film & Media Studies* in an article entitled 'Gestural Intermediality in Jean-Luc Godard's *First Name: Carmen* (1983)' (2018).

All my gratitude goes to Elly Grayson, Dr Paul Leworthy and Annie Rutherford, who offered their time to proofread the chapters of my book. I would like to address a special thought to Elly whose constant support gave me a lot of energy to finish this work with enthusiasm. Last but not least, I would like to dedicate my book to my parents Helena and Olivier. Without their love and support, this book would not exist.

Introduction

After the Second World War, in the wake of André Bazin's influential ideas, a young generation of French critics and aspirant directors such as François Truffaut, Eric Rohmer and Jacques Rivette strongly condemned the conventions of the established cinema of *qualité française*.[1] They attacked its stilted codes of representation and obsolete theatrical and literary traditions, including the conventionalism of the actors' poses, attitudes and gesticulations.[2] In reaction against this outdated classicism, the generation of the New Wave praised French *auteurs* such as Jean Renoir, Jean Vigo, Jacques Becker, Robert Bresson and Jacques Tati, who were able to reveal remarkable stylistic potentialities of the body in the mise-en-scène of their films. Influenced at once by American cinema, in which the characters' behaviours lead the mise-en-scène, and Italian neorealism, that stresses the presence of the body in its interaction with the physical reality of the world, the New Wave authors were seeking truth in their actors' body language. From their first short films onwards, they were preoccupied with inventing singular ways of filming and performing gestures.[3] At the end of the 1950s, the New Wave authors created a physical cinema in which gestures became the sensitive expression of their modernist aesthetics. While refashioning Hollywood genres, such as the codes of film noir in Godard's *A bout de souffle* (*Breathless*, 1960) and of musicals in Jacques Demy's *Les Parapluies de Cherboug* (*The Umbrellas of Cherbourg*, 1964), they also invented a modern theatricality, weaving references to Brechtian aesthetics, art history and literature – more specifically the Nouveau Roman – notably in Agnès Varda's pioneering first long feature *La Pointe Courte* (1955), Godard's *Le Mépris* (*Contempt*, 1963) and

1 See François Truffaut, 'Une certaine tendance du cinéma français', *Cahiers du cinéma*, January 1954, pp. 15–29.

2 Jean Douchet, *Nouvelle Vague* (Paris: Cinémathèque française, Hazan, 1998), p. 137.

3 See ibid., pp. 151–3.

Alain Resnais's *L'Année dernière à Marienbad* (*Last Year at Marienbad*, 1961, written by the novelist Alain Robbe-Grillet).

The New Wave revealed 'the new bodies of young actors'[4] like Jean-Paul Belmondo, Jeanne Moreau and Anna Karina, who found a fertile ground for their expressivity in the city. In order to capture the gestures of everyday life, New Wave filmmakers developed modern acting styles in urban spaces – such as the Parisian streets in Varda's *Cléo de 5 à 7* (*Cléo from 5 to 7*, 1962) or the city of Nantes in Jacques Demy's *Lola* (1961) – viewed as places of social interaction, chance, agency and continuously renewed possibilities. In this dynamic environment, attitudes and gestures could drive the narrative without necessarily resulting from the logical succession of action and plot that usually structures classical screenplays.[5] As if echoing Diderot who, in the eighteenth century, encouraged painters to go out of their studio in order to observe movement from life,[6] New Wave authors also left the studio to shoot on location and film the characters in their wanderings, encounters and interactions with the real. By filming the everyday world and gestures in a stylised way, the New Wave forged the audience's imagination to the point of becoming a myth, with a long-lasting influence.[7] At its peak between the late 1950s and early 1960s, and starting to decline in 1962,[8] the New Wave was an ephemeral movement.[9]

In contrast to the abundant literature devoted to the New Wave, scholarship about the post-New Wave has been more sporadic. Critics and scholars usually use two main approaches to outline the developments of the New Wave in the 1960s and 1970s. Either the term post-New Wave is used to name the generation of filmmakers who followed the New Wave

4 Michel Marie, *The French New Wave: An Artistic School*, trans. by Richard Neupert (Malden, MA: Blackwell), p. 109.

5 Douchet, *Nouvelle Vague*, p. 125.

6 Denis Diderot, *Essais sur la peinture: Salons de 1759, 1761, 1763*, ed. by Gita May and Jacques Chouillet (Paris: Hermann, 2007), p. 16.

7 Antoine de Baecque, *La Nouvelle Vague: Portrait d'une jeunesse* (Paris: Flammarion, 1998), p. 149.

8 See Geneviève Sellier, *Masculine Singular: French New Wave Cinema*, trans. by Kristin Ross (Durham, NC: Duke University Press, 2008), p. 2.

9 Baecque, *La Nouvelle Vague*, p. 149.

from the mid-1960s onwards. Or the post-New Wave is regarded as essentially rooted in the sociocultural context of post-May 1968. On the one hand, Gilles Deleuze, Philippe Mary and Jean-Michel Frodon opt for the genealogical approach. The terms post-New Wave ('après-nouvelle vague')[10] or, less frequently, new New Wave ('nouvelle Nouvelle vague')[11] point to the emergence of new authors, considered as the 'heirs' of Truffaut and Godard, including Philippe Garrel, Jacques Doillon, Jean Eustache, André Téchiné, Maurice Pialat and lesser-known directors such as Pierre Zucca.

On the other hand, some scholars consider the political and sociocultural events of May 1968 in France as the dividing line between the New Wave and the post-New Wave. Although Truffaut, Godard, Rivette, Resnais and other artists and intellectuals came together in February 1968 to defend Henri Langlois – the co-founder of the Cinémathèque française – after his dismissal by the Ministry of Cultural Affairs, the political events of 1968 ultimately accentuated the process of fragmentation of the group. According to Ginette Vincendeau, 'May '68 introduced a break with New Wave issues and concerns, with the rise of the political agenda.'[12] The rupture within the original group of the *Cahiers du cinéma* manifested symbolically through the falling-out between its two major figures, Truffaut and Godard.[13] More precisely, the sociocultural, ideological and political context of May 1968 fundamentally influenced the aesthetics of the post-New Wave. According to Jill Forbes,

> [t]he 'post-*nouvelle vague*' is also the period after May 1968 and it would be difficult to overstate the impact of this great social and cultural caesura on the cinema. May 1968 forced filmmakers to confront the influence of mass communications and to

10 Gilles Deleuze, *L'Image-temps: Cinéma 2* (Paris: Minuit, 1985), p. 254; Philippe Mary, *La Nouvelle Vague et le cinéma d'auteur. Socio-analyse d'une révolution artistique* (Paris: Seuil, 2006), p. 239.

11 Jean-Michel Frodon, 'Une nouvelle Nouvelle Vague ?', in *Le Cinéma français de la Nouvelle Vague à nos jours* (Paris: Cahiers du cinéma, 2010), pp. 405–29.

12 Ginette Vincendeau, 'Introduction. Fifty Years of the French New Wave: From Hysteria to Nostalgia', in *The French New Wave: Critical Landmarks*, ed. by Peter Graham with Ginette Vincendeau (London: BFI, 2009), p. 13.

13 See *Truffaut-Godard, scénario d'une rupture*, dir. Claire Duguet (France Télévisions, 2015).

> ask questions about the 'truth' and the 'reality' of the image. It presented filmmakers with the challenge of television and made them consider the politics of representation. It introduced new social actors to the screen and to film making, it called for the reinterpretation of history and, in exposing the problematical absence of the 'people' which in Marxist literature had long been unquestioningly assumed to exist, it forced all those working in the culture industries, but especially in the cinema, to reconsider the nature of this par excellence 'popular' art.[14]

Framed in the context of post-May 1968, the post-New Wave encompasses not only the pioneering *auteurs* of women's cinema like Nelly Kaplan and members of the Zanzibar Group (1968–70) such as Serge Bard, Garrel and Jackie Raynal, but also more established filmmakers like Rivette and Godard who radicalised their methods of filmmaking in the wake of May 1968, in continuation or rupture with their earlier films. According to Forbes, the label of French post-New Wave also includes a category of transnational filmmakers 'who position themselves in relation to French cinema', such as the Belgian Chantal Akerman, the Swiss Alain Tanner, the French couple Jean-Marie Straub and Danièle Huillet who made films mainly in Germany or the Franco-Chilean director Raoul Ruiz.[15]

However, instead of highlighting May 1968 as the boundary between the end of an era and the beginning of a new one, Forbes suggests considering the post-New Wave in its continuity with the New Wave: 'the post-1968 French cinema' (which Forbes uses as synonym for 'post-*nouvelle vague*'), without overtly mourning the end of the New Wave nor denying its legacy, 'built on its achievements'.[16] Post-New Wave filmmakers continued to explore the representation of the body, stylise gestures of everyday life and shoot on location. Albeit in different ways, filmmakers of both eras also tackled political issues. During the New Wave, Godard and the Left Bank filmmakers Resnais, Chris Marker and Varda were preoccupied with urban change, the emancipation of youth, the Algerian war, the politics of memory, the critique of consumer society, social conditioning and, more exceptionally in Varda's cinema – the only woman in a predominantly

14 Jill Forbes, *The Cinema in France after the New Wave* (Basingstoke: Macmillan, 1992), p. 3.

15 Ibid., p. 260.

16 Ibid., p. 3.

masculine milieu[17] –, the emergence of the female gaze. Radicalising the cinematic exploration of similar political concerns in the ideological and sociocultural context of post-May 1968, some post-New Wave authors not only sought to make films about political matters, but also attempted to find ways of producing and shooting films politically: 'The problem is not to make *political* films but to make films *politically*,'[18] argued Godard, by now working with the Dziga Vertov Group.

In the post-May 1968 era, many directors preoccupied with politics reflected on the necessity of reorganising the film crew as a political community, developed self-reflexive and metacinematic strategies to unveil the political nature of representation and reconsidered their relationship with their actors. The practice of filmmaking became a collaborative process engaging a community of artists and technicians, rather than promoting the author's individuality within the market-oriented system.[19] Consequently, 'both a political and aesthetic self-consciousness'[20] lies at the core of films such as Akerman's *Jeanne Dielman, 23 quai du Commerce, 1080 Bruxelles* (1975, see Chapter 2), Luc Moullet and Antonietta Pizzorno's *Anatomie d'un rapport* (*Anatomy of a Relationship*, 1976) and Godard's political works made with the Dziga Vertov Group. From 1967 to 1974, Marker initiated the Medvedkin groups in Sochaux and Besançon, which gathered workers and film technicians who made militant films together and expressed their voices collaboratively. From the mid-1970s onwards, Alain Cavalier also decided to rethink the means of production and the conditions of filmmaking of his cinema. For example, he wrote the screenplay of the road-movie *Le Plein de super* (*Fill'er Up with Super*, 1976) in close collaboration with the actors and shot the film with a reduced crew and a small camera, avoiding the constraints of conventional shootings. Like Rivette, Cavalier aims to stimulate the agency of his actors, who thus become responsible for the narrative and get involved in the mise-en-scène.

17 See Sellier, *Masculine Singular.*

18 Colin MacCabe, with Mick Eaton and Laura Mulvey, *Godard: Images, Sounds, Politics* (Bloomington: Indiana University Press, 1980), p. 19.

19 Forbes, *The Cinema in France after the New Wave*, pp. 14–15.

20 Ibid., p. 20.

As Vincendeau explains, '[...] trends in literary theory (Roland Barthes) and philosophy (Michel Foucault) were dealing severe blows to the notion of the auteur.'[21] At that time, it is notable that the dogmatic vision of the *politique des auteurs* was even questioned and redefined in the *Cahiers du cinéma*.[22] Yet, Forbes argues that '[t]he *auteur* film continued to be a distinctive category within the French cinema and this was a trend which, if anything, was exaggerated after 1968'.[23] Although the crisis of authorship impacted on the cinematic practice of many post-New Wave filmmakers, such a crisis was also strategically staged by some of them in their films, in order to reflect on their marginal position in the film market and reaffirm their authority as artists. As I will discuss in Chapters 2 and 3, self-representation enables directors such as Akerman and Godard to critically reflect on their practice of filmmaking and on their condition as authors working at the margins.

Permeated as they are by the ideological, sociocultural, artistic and intellectual context of their time, post-New Wave films were made in a period of French history marked by the political and economic decline of the *Trente Glorieuses*, a term coined by French economist Jean Fourastié which refers to the economic prosperity of French society between 1946 and 1975.[24] As Kristin Ross explains, French society drastically changed in the years and decades following the application of the Marshall Plan, piloted by the United States after the Second World War in order to fund the economic reconstruction of European countries.[25] Influenced by Henry Ford's systems of mass production and mass consumption, state policies favoured the massive development of capitalism through the accelerated

21 Vincendeau, 'Introduction. Fifty Years of the French New Wave', p. 15.

22 See Jean-André Fieschi, Jean-Louis Comolli, Michel Mardore, André Téchiné, Gérard Guégan and Claude Ollier, 'Vingt ans après. Le cinéma américain, ses auteurs et notre politique en question', in *La Politique des auteurs: Les textes*, ed. by Antoine de Baecque (Paris: Cahiers du cinéma, 2001), pp. 122–42.

23 Forbes, *The Cinema in France after the New Wave*, p. 259.

24 See Jean Fourastié, *Les Trente Glorieuses ou la révolution invisible de 1946 à 1975* (Paris: Fayard, 1979).

25 Kristin Ross, *Fast Cars, Clean Bodies: Decolonization and the Reordering of French Culture* (Cambridge, MA: MIT Press, 1995), p. 4.

modernisation of industries.[26] This fast-growing modernisation introduced new everyday gestures in French society, as Tati's films reveal in an acute way.[27] From the postman of *Jour de Fête* (*The Big Day*, 1949) who tries to apply rationalised methods of mail delivery to Monsieur Hulot in *Playtime* (1967) who wanders in an ultramodernist setting, Tati provides a playful and critical depiction of the impact of Fordism on the everyday gestures of French people. As Ross writes, '[Tati's films] make palpable a daily life that increasingly appeared to unfold in a space where objects tended to dictate to people their gestures and movements – and that for the most part had to be learned from watching American films.'[28]

In response to these rapid developments, new preoccupations with the anthropology of everyday life emerged in post-war French thought.[29] Analysing the impact of capitalism on French modern society, Marxist philosopher and sociologist Henri Lefebvre pioneered the study of everyday life in academia.[30] In addition, novelists such as Simone de Beauvoir or Georges Perec, as well as filmmakers like Tati depicted and criticised the alienating structures propagated by mass consumerism.[31] Such a criticism took a political turn during the events of May 1968, considered by Ross as 'a protest against Fordist hierarchies of the factories and the exaggerated statism that had controlled French modernization'.[32] Bringing out the dissatisfaction of a large part of the French population towards the increasing role of capitalism in the conditioning of everyday life, May 1968 'marked the political end of that accelerated transition into Fordism', Ross explains.[33]

26 Ibid., pp. 3–4.

27 Ibid., p. 5.

28 Ibid.

29 Ibid., p. 4.

30 See Henri Lefebvre, *La Vie quotidienne dans le monde moderne* (Paris: Gallimard, 1968).

31 See Ross, *Fast Cars, Clean Bodies*, p. 13; Simone de Beauvoir, *Les Belles Images* (Paris: Gallimard, 1966); Georges Perec, *Les Choses: une histoire des années soixante* (Paris: Julliard, 1965).

32 Ross, *Fast Cars, Clean Bodies*, pp. 3–4.

33 Ibid., p. 3.

Ultimately, the 1973 oil crisis foreshadowed the end of the triumphant economic success of the *Trente Glorieuses.*[34]

Made in the aftermath of May 1968, the utopian film *L'An 01* (*The Year 01*, Jacques Doillon, 1973) celebrates the end of market economy, mass production and mass consumption. In this emblematic film of the post-New Wave, society refuses collectively to comply with the principles of capitalist society and aspires to think about alternative ways of life. Released the same year, Claude Faraldo's satire *Themroc* (1973) also expresses the rejection of capitalism and authority through the subversive gestures of a working-class antihero (Michel Piccoli) who disrupts social rules. Both films reveal the extent to which the questioning of alienation, conditioning and high productivity became more radical in French culture after May 1968. While Beauvoir, Perec and Tati critically examined the transformation of society and the emergence of new behaviours in the 1960s, post-New Wave films often focused on the crisis of everyday gestures. According to film critic Gérard Lenne, this crisis, which is anticipated by Pierrot's (Jean-Paul Belmondo) self-destructive gesture at the end of Godard's *Pierrot le fou* (1965), corresponds to a more general crisis in French film after 1968, especially after the end of the New Wave.[35]

In French cinema made directly after the New Wave, normative, codified and pre-programmed behaviours are disrupted by unpredictable nervous gestures that contradict the imperatives of efficiency and standardisation promoted during the *Trente Glorieuses.* Made after the watershed of May 1968, the films that I analyse in the five chapters of this book offer a particularly pertinent exploration of the crisis of the characters' ritualised, customary and everyday gestures. In *Un homme qui dort* (*The Man Who Sleeps*, 1974), Perec and Bernard Queysanne convey the feeling of anxiety aroused by the mechanisation and automation of gestures in the private sphere of the main character's everyday life. In *Saute ma ville* (*Blow Up My Town*, 1968), *Jeanne Dielman* and *L'Homme à la valise* (*The Man With the Suitcase*, 1983), Akerman questions the pressure of gender norms

34 Ibid., p. 4.

35 Gérard Lenne, *La Mort du cinéma: film/révolution* (Paris: Les Editions du Cerf, 1971), p. 6.

on the female characters' gestures by filming the progressive malfunction of their daily routines. Within this French corpus, Belgian-born director Akerman occupies a singular position, due to the transnational dimension of her work. Associated with major French post-New Wave directors such as Jean Eustache and Garrel, but also with American avant-garde cinema of the 1970s, Akerman crossed geographical and artistic borders throughout her career.[36] In *Prénom Carmen* (*First Name: Carmen*, 1983), Godard depicts a fragmented and chaotic world in which human gesture appears as a means of reconnecting the scattered elements of the film. In *Roberte* (1979), made in collaboration with writer and artist Pierre Klossowski, Zucca shows how codified gestures are disrupted by the impulsive expression of the characters' and performers' nervous gestures, to the point of disorienting the spectator's interpretation. In Godard and Anne-Marie Miéville's television series *France/tour/détour/deux/enfants* (1977–8), the directors focus on the social and ideological codification of two children's everyday gestures. By referring to the late nineteenth-century technique of chronophotography, they attempt to reveal how gestures can express margins of resistance to social conditioning. In Josée Manenti and Jean-Pierre Daniel's *Le Moindre Geste* (1971) and Renaud Victor's *Ce Gamin, là* (1976), made at the instigation of Fernand Deligny's ideas, two types of gestures are interwoven: on the one hand, the wandering gestures of neurodiverse children and teenagers and, on the other hand, the customary gestures of workers who reiterate the same gestures everyday. Finally, in *Out 1* (1971), made in the context of post-May 1968, Rivette experiments with improvisation and explores radical modes of performance, which not only force the actors to invent their own gestures, but also show their difficulties and failures in doing so.

Although the post-New Wave turns out to be indebted to the gestural innovations of the New Wave, the films under discussion develop a contrasting approach to gesture and speech. Occupying a central and playful place in many New Wave films,[37] the art of dialogue underwent a deep crisis

36 See Marion Schmid, *Chantal Akerman* (Manchester: Manchester University Press, 2010), p. 5; see also Garrel's documentary *Les Ministères de l'art* (1988) that focuses on French post-New Wave cinema and features Akerman.

37 Douchet, *Nouvelle Vague*, p. 190.

during the post-New Wave. By referring to the origins of cinema, some films emphasise the muteness of gesture and reflect on its ontological difference with speech. Coined by Michel Chion, the genre of 'mute cinema' refers to neo-silent films 'where characters express themselves through actions, gestures, and looks'.[38] If mute cinema can be nostalgic about the origins of cinema, it manifests above all a problematic tension, if not a rupture, between gesture and speech.

Anthony Paraskeva uses the phrase 'speech-gesture complex' to consider the discrepancy and dialectical tension between gesture and speech (or the visible and the sayable) in modernism, notably in Kafka's literature, Brechtian and Beckettian theatre and Charlie Chaplin's silent cinema.[39] In post-New Wave films such as *Un homme qui dort* and *L'Homme à la valise*, gestures emerge from the characters' decisive silence and act out their problematic relationship with society. The characters' solitude and refusal to interact with others are expressed through nervous gestures, evoking pathologies of the late nineteenth century, including ambulatory automatism and hysteria. The tension between speech and bodily expression also appears in the autistic children's gestures filmed by Renaud Victor in *Ce Gamin, là*, and through the process of desynchronisation between the voice-over and the image in *Un homme qui dort* and *Le Moindre Geste*. While Godard attempts to revitalise the aesthetics of silent cinema in *Prénom Carmen*, Zucca and Klossowski also explore the muteness of gestures, as well as the difficulty in deciphering their meanings, through the mise-en-scène of *tableaux vivants* in *Roberte*. As Giorgio Agamben argues, the mediality of gestures expresses and communicates something that cannot be put into words, manifesting 'the being-in-language of human beings' and their need or desire for communicability.[40] In post-New Wave cinema, gestures often convey taboos, pathologies, traumas, fantasies and

38 Michel Chion, *Film, a Sound Art*, trans. by Claudia Gorbman (New York: Columbia University Press, 2009), p. 328.

39 See Anthony Paraskeva, *The Speech-Gesture Complex: Modernism, Theatre, Cinema* (Edinburgh: Edinburgh University Press, 2013).

40 Giorgio Agamben, 'Notes on Gesture', in *Means Without End: Notes on Politics*, trans. by Vincenzo Binetti and Cesare Casarino (Minneapolis: University of Minnesota Press, 2000), p. 58.

conflicts that prove difficult to translate into words. The crisis of speech mirrors other sorts of crises, such as the crisis of the everyday, the crisis of authorship, the political crisis resulting from the disenchantment after May 1968 and, in a manner that recalls the preoccupation with nervousness at the end of the nineteenth century, a gestural crisis.

Definition(s) of Gesture in Film: An Interdisciplinary and Intermedial Approach

From antiquity to the present day, gestures have been examined as sociocultural, expressive and rhetorical signs that most often accompany speech. In the field of *chironomia* (i.e. the art of gesture in rhetoric), John Bulwer's *Chirologia, or the Natural Language of the Hand* (1644) and Gilbert Austin's *Chironomia, or a Treatise on Rhetorical Delivery* (1806) – which draws on classical oratory practices theorised by Cicero and Quintilian in Roman antiquity – emphasise the crucial role of gesture in the delivery of speech by establishing a semiological classification of codified gestures. In the twentieth and twenty-first centuries, the semiotic analysis of gestures has developed in sociology, anthropology, cognitive psychology and kinesics. Erving Goffman, Adam Kendon and David McNeill study gesture – an 'instrument of human communication'[41] – within the frame of ordinary social interactions.[42] For Kendon, gesture is a visible action used as an 'utterance' to provide information. Necessarily voluntary and intentional, a human gesture is regarded as an

41 David McNeill, 'Introduction', in *Language and Gesture*, ed. by David McNeill (Cambridge: Cambridge University Press, 2000), p. 9.

42 Adam Kendon, *Gesture: Visible Action as Utterance* (Cambridge: Cambridge University Press, 2004); Erving Goffman, *Interaction Ritual: Essays on Face-to-Face Behaviour* (New York: Pantheon Books, 1982); Erving Goffman, *Frame Analysis: An Essay on the Organization of Experience* (Boston, MA: Northeastern University Press, 1986).

act of communication that intends to convey meaning to another individual or a group of individuals:

> [...] There is always the implication that the actor is deemed to exercise at least some degree of voluntary control over any movement regarded as 'gesture' and what it expresses. Usually 'gesture' is not used to refer to those visible bodily expressions of thoughts or feelings that are deemed inadvertent or are regarded as something a person cannot 'help'.[43]

In this sense, Kendon excludes nervous gestures (e.g. 'clothing adjustments'), since a gesture has to be the deliberate expression of an individual who ostensibly wants to convey meaning.[44] This classical conceptualisation of gesture is only partly shared by other thinkers. Keith Thomas and Yves Citton suggest that a gesture can be a sign (i.e. the result of an intentional act of communication) or a symptom (i.e. an inadvertent expression like a grimace of pain).[45] The immediacy of gestures, their 'pure mediality' to borrow Agamben's phrase,[46] can reflect the individuals' lack of control and self-awareness. A gesture can be revealing and meaningful precisely due to the lack of conscious intention behind it.

Since its invention, cinema has contributed to transforming the classical understanding of gesture as an intentional and voluntary act of communication. In the second half of the nineteenth century, gestures were no longer exclusively considered as the product of will, the manifestation of a stable self and the expression of the symbolical code: they also entered the realms of the unconscious and the involuntary. In continuity with Charles Darwin's research on reflex, involuntary action and gesture in *The Expression of the Emotions in Man and Animals* (1872), Sigmund Freud's attempt to visually perceive the unconscious in gestures,[47] and Aby

43 Kendon, *Gesture*, p. 8.

44 Ibid.

45 Keith Thomas, 'Introduction', in *A Cultural History of Gesture: From Antiquity to the Present Day*, ed. by Jan Bremmer and Herman Roodenburg (Cambridge: Polity Press, 1991), p. 1; Yves Citton, *Gestes d'humanités: Anthropologie sauvage de nos expériences esthétiques* (Paris: Armand Colin, 2012), pp. 28–32.

46 Agamben, 'Notes on Gesture', p. 58.

47 Catherine Cyssau, *Au lieu du geste* (Paris: Presses universitaires de France, 1995), p. 13.

Warburg's study of symptom and *Pathosformel* in art history,[48] the medium of cinema, and more specifically 'the optical unconscious' of the camera,[49] developed means of perception that gave new visibility to the body's impulsive gestures. According to Agamben, cinema emerged in the late nineteenth century when Gilles de la Tourette's research on bodily disorders, and neurologist Jean-Martin Charcot's studies on hysteria revealed 'a generalised catastrophe of the sphere of gestures' that manifested through 'an amazing proliferation of tics, spasmodic jerks, and mannerisms'.[50] Crucially, Charcot made use of different scientific and pre-cinematic devices – such as Etienne-Jules Marey's chronophotography – to observe the facial and bodily reactions of patients.

When commenting on Agamben's thesis, several scholars validate the idea that, between the late nineteenth and early twentieth centuries, silent cinema captured the 'gestural crisis' that was occurring in fin-de-siècle Western society.[51] According to Pasi Väliaho, such a crisis, which affected bodily rhythms, the coordination of gestures and the nervous system, proves notably perceptible and exemplified in Georges Méliès's films. Significantly, Väliaho suggests that the cinematic medium, which has been '"pathological" from its inception as a kind of nervous gesture',[52] modifies the traditional perception of the body through the use of technology that highlights and amplifies the body's nervousness:

> […] The crisis of gestures implicated in the emergence of the moving image can be understood in terms of changes occurring in the history of life, changes that incorporate bodily rhythms such as breathing, the heartbeat and walking, for instance.

48 See Georges Didi-Huberman, *L'Image survivante: Histoire de l'art et le temps des fantômes selon Aby Warburg* (Paris: Minuit, 2002).

49 See Walter Benjamin, 'The Work of Art in the Age of Its Technological Reproducibility. Second Version', in *Selected Writings. Vol. 3, 1935–1938*, ed. by Howard Eiland and Michael W. Jennings, trans. by Edmund Jephcott and others (Cambridge, MA: The Belknap Press of Harvard University Press, 2002), p. 117.

50 Agamben, 'Notes on Gesture', p. 50.

51 Erin Brannigan, *Dancefilm: Choreography and the Moving Image* (New York: Oxford University Press, 2011), p. 66.

52 Pasi Väliaho, *Mapping the Moving Image: Gesture, Thought, and Cinema circa 1900* (Amsterdam: Amsterdam University Press, 2010), p. 73.

> Nervous gestures signal how the body becomes caught in a novel type of medial arrangement in the cinema, as well as the occurrence of a new form of life that the technology of self-moving images implies.[53]

Sociologist and philosopher Georg Simmel's essay *The Metropolis and Mental Life* (1903) examines how nervousness intensified in the urban spaces of the early twentieth century.[54] Similarly to Walter Benjamin, who argues that human consciousness, perception and behaviour became accustomed to being constantly jolted with the shocks of modern life, Agamben suggests that nervousness, resulting from the crisis of gestures, may have become the norm in the twentieth century.[55] In film aesthetics, and more particularly during the French post-New Wave, the nervous gesture proves to be of prime importance, especially when considered in relation to the specific expressive and perceptual means of the cinematic medium.[56]

As many theorists, critics and filmmakers have pointed out, film technology can record and amplify the slightest gestures of the body, not only through the use of certain techniques such as the close-up but also thanks to the device of projection onto the big screen. According to Eric Rohmer, the specificity of cinema lies in its ability to develop its own expressive means; even the rectangular space of the screen conditions the representation, performance and perception of gesture in a way that differs from theatre arts.[57] If the actors' gestures are usually less pronounced in cinema than in theatre, cinematic techniques of magnification, distortion, fragmentation and interruption enhance their emotional and sensuous impact on the spectator. Similarly to Rohmer, Peter Brook compares the performance and perception of gestures in film and theatre. 'The great magnifier, the lens' can grasp the slightest impulses and tremors on the surface of

53 Ibid., p. 18.

54 See Marielle Macé, *Styles: critique de nos formes de vie* (Paris: Gallimard, 2016), p. 145.

55 Agamben, 'Notes on Gesture', pp. 51–2.

56 See Emmanuelle André, *Le Choc du sujet: de l'hystérie au cinéma* (XIXe-XXIe siècle) (Rennes: Presses universitaires de Rennes, 2011), p. 14.

57 Eric Rohmer, 'Le Cinéma, art de l'espace', in *Le Goût de la beauté*, ed. by Jean Narboni (Paris: Cahiers du cinéma, 2004), pp. 42–3.

the body.[58] In contrast to stage actors who need to amplify these impulses with ostensive gestures, film actors have to adjust their own expressivity according to the communicative and expressive means of cinema. In this sense, gestures are not only performed by the actors, but also shaped by the cinematic medium itself.[59] As discussed in Chapter 1, filmed gestures are engaged in a process of exchange with all the media components of cinema, from the soundtrack to the projector.

Furthermore, the cinematic medium also blurs the distinction that is often made between a gesture and a movement. Barbara Formis suggests that gestures are less predictable than movements, which result from automatic reflexes and bodily mechanisms.[60] For that reason, in line with André Leroi-Gourhan's theories that highlight the crucial role of the hand and upper parts of the body in the development of humanity,[61] definitions of gesture usually tend to focus on the hand, arms and face, which are more likely to be directed through intention and will. While the theatre theorist Jerzy Grotowski argues that gestures are mainly peripheral and thus result from the movement of the hands and the face,[62] Bernard Vouilloux asserts that individuals gesture exclusively with their hands and arms.[63]

However, by emphasising the mechanics of the body in an expressive way, the cinematic automaton widens the definition of gesture, showing its humanity or animality, as well as its mechanical dimension, as Jacques

58 Peter Brook, *The Empty Space* (London: Penguin Books, 2008), p. 122.

59 See Jacqueline Nacache, *L'Acteur de cinéma* (Paris: Nathan, 2003), p. 51.

60 Barbara Formis, *Esthétique de la vie ordinaire* (Paris: PUF, 2015), p. 18.

61 As André Leroi-Gourhan demonstrates, human agency originated in the progressive development of the vertical position and the liberation of the hand, which, in the history of humanity, enabled individuals to transform their reality and develop innovative gestural practices, for instance through the production and use of tools and technologies. See André Leroi-Gourhan, *Le Geste et la parole I: Technique et langage* (Paris: Albin Michel, 1964); Leroi-Gourhan, *Le Geste et la parole II: La Mémoire et les rythmes* (Paris: Albin Michel, 1965).

62 See Thomas Richards, *At Work with Grotowski on Physical Actions* (London: Routledge, 1995), p. 75.

63 Bernard Vouilloux, 'La Pesanteur et la grâce du geste. Jean Starobinski dans l'espace des peintres', *Littérature*, 161 (2011), 33–50 <https://www.cairn.info/revue-litterature-2011-1-page-33.htm> [accessed 2 August 2018] (para. 3 of 26).

Aumont notes.[64] Through the intersection of the human body and film technology, the human and the inhuman, cinema builds a different understanding of gestures. If hand and arm gestures occupy an essential place,[65] other gestural categories become prevalent in film, such as human gait, feet and facial gestures, as well as tics and inadvertent motions. Moreover, although cinema tends to isolate certain body parts, Sergei Eisenstein considers that a gesture always involves the effort of the whole body. The performance of a gesture involves the coordination of numerous transitory movements, from the lower to the upper parts of the body. For example, when people grab objects with their hands, their chests, backs, thighs, legs and feet move accordingly with the trajectory of their arms. With the device of slow motion, the moving image makes the complex coordination between all the body parts involved in the execution of one gesture, as well as the subtle transitions from one gesture to another, visible.

Consequently, every bodily motion could potentially be perceived as a gesture. 'What the actor tries to impart – the physical existence of a character – is overwhelmingly present on the screen. The camera really isolates a fleeting glance, and inadvertent shrug of the shoulder,' Siegfried Kracauer explains.[66] According to him, films are able to reveal the most transitory and ephemeral elements of physical reality, such as '[s]treet crowds, involuntary gestures, and other fleeting impressions'.[67] Film stresses all the minuscule and microscopic motions which are made visible through the cinematic lens, especially nervous gestures as Jean Epstein notes.[68] Tics, muscular motions, nervous reflexes, jerks, spasms, and all the movements which were regarded as too insignificant and not deliberate enough to be called gestures, suddenly appear as such on the big screen. The vocabulary used by Epstein to describe gestures in silent cinema – such as hypnosis, tics or

64 Jacques Aumont, 'Avant-propos', in *L'Invention de la figure humaine: Le Cinéma: l'humain et l'inhumain*, ed. by Jacques Aumont (Paris: Cinémathèque française, 1995), p. 7.

65 See Harun Farocki's film essay *The Expression of Hands* (1997).

66 Siegfried Kracauer, *Theory of Film: The Redemption of Physical Reality* (New York: Oxford University Press, 1960), p. 94.

67 Ibid., p. ix.

68 Jean Epstein, *Ecrits sur le cinéma, tome 1: 1927–1953* (Paris: Seghers, 1974), p. 97.

crisis – eloquently evokes psychoanalysis and clinical terminology.[69] When Epstein observes Lilian Gish's nervous and seemingly involuntary gestures on screen, he highlights their mechanical and involuntary dimension.[70]

However, it would be an exaggeration to reduce film performance to a catastrophic choreography of tics and involuntary gestures. Beyond the specificity of its medium, cinema has also assimilated various theatrical and painterly traditions since its invention. In this regard, intermediality is a key concept to consider gesture in film. As Ágnes Pethő explains,

> [a]lthough the idea that film has indissoluble ties with other media and arts is one of the oldest concerns of theorising about the movies, it is the theory of intermediality that has brought into the spotlight the intricate interactions of different media manifest in the cinema, emphasising the way in which the moving pictures can incorporate forms of all other media, and can initiate fusions and 'dialogues' between the distinct arts.[71]

The intermediality of gestures in cinema can be conceptualised in two different ways. On the one hand, through the interrelation between the mediality of human gesture and the expressive and perceptual features of film technology, the cinematic medium spectacularly highlights gestures that pass unnoticed in other media such as painting and photography. On the other hand, the performance of gestures proves intermedial in the sense that it appropriates gestural codes and techniques developed in other arts and practices, such as dance, sculpture, opera and theatre. It is in this respect that Christian Viviani and Roberta E. Pearson examine the migration of theatrical and painterly gestural codes in cinema, especially during the silent era.[72]

69 Ibid., pp. 93 and 97.

70 Ibid., p. 97.

71 Ágnes Pethő, *Cinema and Intermediality: The Passion for the In-between* (Newcastle upon Tyne: Cambridge Scholars, 2011), p. 1.

72 See Christian Viviani, *Le Magique et le vrai: l'acteur de cinéma, sujet et objet* (Aix-en-Provence: Rouge profond, 2015); Roberta E. Pearson, *Eloquent Gestures: The Transformation of Performance Style in the Griffith Biograph Films* (Oxford: University of California Press, 1992).

Furthermore, gesture in film shows not only the dialogue between the arts, but also the proximity between art and life. In his seminal essay on film acting,[73] James Naremore argues that performance – in a film such as Godard's *A bout de souffle*, for example – reveals the theatricality of everyday life. Drawing on Goffman, he stresses the proximity and permeability between film and stage performance and performance within society and everyday life: '"Performance" [...] is understood in its broadest, most social, sense, as what we do when we interact with the world – a concept embracing not only theatre but also public celebrity and everyday life.'[74] Through the construction of a social identity, performance enables one to forge the image of a united and stable self: 'the self is more like an effect of structure – a crowd of signifiers, without any particular origin or essence, held in place by ideology and codes of representation.'[75] Performance is therefore ideologically and socially codified, through gestures, behaviours, speech, costumes, roles, etc. According to Richard Dyer, gestures are 'performance signs' that are 'culture- and history-bound': 'The signification of a given performance sign is determined by its place within culturally and historically specific codes.'[76]

In this respect, scholarship on gesture often examines the notion in relation to cultural studies and semiotics. Although silent cinema reactivated the myth of a universal language of gestures[77] implying 'a universal comprehensibility of facial expression and gesture',[78] Thomas explains that '[...] most modern writing on the subject [of gesture] starts from the assumption that gesture is not a universal language, but is the product of social and cultural differences'.[79] For example, Jean-Claude Schmitt

73 It should be noted that if acting and performance are often used as synonyms, the term acting refers more specifically to the craft of actors who develop certain techniques to play a role in theatre, fiction films and TV shows.

74 James Naremore, *Acting in the Cinema* (Berkeley: University of California Press, 1988), p. 19.

75 Ibid., p. 5.

76 Richard Dyer, *Stars* (London: British Film Institute, 1979), p. 152.

77 See Paraskeva, *The Speech-Gesture Complex*, pp. 26–34.

78 Béla Balázs, *Theory of the Film: Growth of a New Art*, trans. by Edith Bone (London: Dennis Dobson, 1952), p. 45.

79 Thomas, 'Introduction', p. 3.

demonstrates the extent to which the ritualisation of gestures, which were endowed with a strong symbolic value, structured social life and political order during the Middle Ages in Western culture.[80] Far from being natural, human gestures, which are acquired through learning processes and contact with society, result from cultural influence. While in the famous essay 'Les Techniques du corps' ('Techniques of the Body', 1935), the anthropologist Marcel Mauss studies how the most elementary gestures vary from one society to another,[81] the sociologist Pierre Bourdieu argues that gestures – which play a fundamental role in the cultural construction of the body – reflect differences of culture, gender and class.[82] Pointing out the lack of a clear boundary between the performance of ordinary gestures in life and art, Formis claims that adults do not make spontaneous gestures.[83] On a daily basis, people perform acquired gestures that build their identity, social role and sense of self.

However, while being socioculturally conditioned, gestures also express the idiosyncratic nature of human existence. According to Vilém Flusser, it is through intersubjective relationships that gestures, which manifest people's 'being in the world', can free themselves from their conditioning.[84] Furthermore, Carrie Noland argues that individuals have the agency to alter socially acquired behaviours and beliefs, in spite of the pressure of conditioning on their bodies: 'Gestures, learned techniques of the body, are the means by which cultural conditioning is simultaneously embodied and put to the test.'[85] Within the society they belong to, individuals perform socially codified gestures in a singular manner, according to their bodily

80 See Jean-Claude Schmitt, *La Raison des gestes dans l'Occident médiéval* (Paris: Gallimard, 1990).

81 See Marcel Mauss, 'Les Techniques du corps', ed. by Jean-Marie Tremblay (Québec: Chicoutimi, 2002). Electronic edition (first publ. in *Journal de Psychologie*, 32 (1935), 271–93).

82 See Pierre Bourdieu, *La Distinction* (Paris: Minuit, 1979).

83 Formis, *Esthétique de la vie ordinaire*, p. 18.

84 Vilém Flusser, *Les Gestes* (Paris: Hors commerce Cergy, 1999), p. 193.

85 Carrie Noland, *Agency and Embodiment: Performing Gestures/Producing Culture* (Cambridge, MA: Harvard University Press, 2009), p. 2.

features, interpersonal experiences, ways of being, moods and agency.[86] The notion of style makes it possible to consider idiosyncratic nuances within the performance of gesture. In *Gender Trouble*, Judith Butler demonstrates how gender is culturally shaped on the surface of the body and performed through ritualised acts and stylised gestures.[87] A gestural style refers to the singular manner in which an individual makes gestures (even when these are already codified), in everyday life or in the theatrical frame of an artistic performance.[88]

Finally, the correspondence between art and life in relation to gesture can be considered in terms of spectatorship and reception. Drawing on the work of the anthropologist Marcel Jousse, who studied how human beings assimilate new gestures in interaction with reality and other humans,[89] Citton demonstrates the ability of media – such as cinema and television – to instil interpersonal gestures in spectators across different cultures, through the process of empathy.[90] It is in this sense that mainstream cinema, as a globalised industry that fabricates mass-produced and homogenous gestural stereotypes, was regarded by Balázs as 'one of the most useful pioneers in the development towards an international universal humanity'.[91] Largely amplified through audiovisual technologies, the porosity between art and life was already conceptualised by Diderot in his writings on eighteenth-century theatre and painting.[92] According to Diderot, the energy (*energia*) of gestures that circulates between the stage (or the *tableau*) and the spectators crosses the invisible frontier (i.e. the fourth wall)

86 For Noland (2009) and Citton, the notion of gesture, which cannot be reduced exclusively to a non-verbal act of communication, invites us to rethink the concept of agency. See Citton, *Gestes d'humanités*, pp. 28–32.

87 See Judith Butler, *Gender Trouble: Feminism and the Subversion of Identity* (New York: Routledge, 1990), p. 140.

88 See Guillemette Bolens, *Le Style des gestes: Corporéité et kinésie dans le récit littéraire* (Lausanne: BHMS, 2008).

89 See Marcel Jousse, *L'Anthropologie du Geste* (Paris: Resma, 1969).

90 Citton, *Gestes d'humanités*, p. 121.

91 Balázs, *Theory of the Film*, p. 45.

92 See Inès Guégo-Rivalan, 'Energie du geste et représentation: Denis Diderot, précurseur d'une "théâtralité" moderne?', *ATALA Cultures et sciences humaines*, 17 (2014), 337–49.

that separates the stage from the audience. Carrying emotions, affective forces, sensations and ideas, gestures leave a dynamic trace in the spectator's mind and body. In the modern age, Bertolt Brecht's epic theatre, which also emphasises the correspondence between art, politics and social life, breaks the fourth wall through distancing effects in order to enable the spectator to critically engage with the social situation embodied by the actors' gestus on stage.[93] '[A]t once gesture, gist, attitude and point', gestus refers to an overall attitude that intersperses the delivery of the lines and aims to reveal a specific social condition with an educative effect.[94] The intersubjective dimension of gestures thus defines the position of individuals in society, whether they are spectators or actors.

By considering the multiplicity of angles through which gesture in film can be analysed, this book will develop an evolving and interdisciplinary model of gesture which incorporates different ways of conceptualising the notion. The performance of socioculturally codified gestures will be scrutinised through an interdisciplinary lens, with references to sociology, anthropology, semiotics, acting studies and art history. The cinematic expression of performed gestures – and more specifically nervous gestures – will also be examined in light of philosophical and theoretical discussions in film studies. As explained above, nervous gesture is a crucial notion to understand the specific nature of the cinematic medium by contrast to other arts. However, the analysis of gesture will not be restricted to the question of medium specificity. By examining gesture from an intermedial perspective, I will demonstrate how its performance can also draw on various artistic migrations that question the purity of the cinematic medium.[95]

The book begins with an investigation of everyday gestures, conditioning and memory in Perec and Queysanne's *Un homme qui dort*. This

93 Bertolt Brecht, *Brecht on Theatre: The Development of an Aesthetic*, ed. and trans. by John Willett (London: Mehtuen Drama, 1990); Walter Benjamin, *Understanding Brecht*, trans. by Anna Bostock (London: Verso, 1973).

94 John Willett, *The Theatre of Bertolt Brecht: A Study of Eight Aspects* (London: Eyre Methuen, 1977), p. 173.

95 The notion of 'impure' cinema has been coined by film critic André Bazin. See Bazin, 'Pour un cinéma impur. Défense de l'adaptation', in *Qu'est-ce que le cinéma?* (Paris: Les Editions du Cerf, 1987), pp. 81–106.

first chapter explores the complex interplay between the mediality of human gesture and the media components of the cinematic machine: to what extent do the character's gestures mirror the mechanisms and features of the cinematic automaton, in terms of camera movement or editing? Through a different lens, Chapter 2 develops the reflection on sociocultural conditioning and its impact on the performance of gestures in film. The styles of women's gestures in Akerman's cinema are analysed from an interdisciplinary perspective, including anthropological, sociological and gender theories. By comparing Akerman's different approaches to film acting, I examine the extent to which the style of gestures informs her style of filmmaking, especially regarding the quality of framing and the crucial role of sound. Focusing on Godard's *Prénom Carmen*, Chapter 3 also discusses the close relationship between gesture and cinematic form. Inspired by Beethoven's music and Rodin's sculptures, the filmmaker reflects on the gestural ontology of the cinematic image, whilst developing intermedial strategies to strengthen the connection between the gestures of creation, the image and the spectator's senses. Chapter 4 explores a different perspective on the role of gestures in the dialogue between cinema and the other arts. By referring to Klossowski's ideas about body language, and comparing ways of representing and perceiving gestures in painting, photography and film, I analyse how the performance of gestures in the cinematic *tableaux vivants* of Zucca's *Roberte* problematises the tension between code and impulse, which proves crucial to the conceptualisation of gesture in film. Finally, by considering Godard and Miéville's television series *France/tour/détour*, the various film projects involving Deligny, as well as Rivette's improvised film *Out 1*, the last chapter focuses more directly on the sociocultural, political and ideological context of post-May 1968. It examines the tension between the straight lines of the social order and the serpentine lines that animate the singular lives of children, adults, neurodiverse persons, marginal characters, intellectuals and artists, who live either at the centre of society or on its fringes. In this way, the book concludes the reflection on gesture in post-New Wave cinema by emphasising the links between aesthetics and politics.

CHAPTER 1

Everyday Gestures, Automatism and the Archive in Georges Perec and Bernard Queysanne's *Un homme qui dort* (*The Man Who Sleeps*, 1974)

In 1971, writer Georges Perec decided to adapt his novel *Un homme qui dort* (*A Man Asleep*, 1967) in collaboration with Bernard Queysanne.[1] Unlike his first novel *Les Choses* (*Things*, 1965) that describes the materialistic fascination with consumer goods in 1960s French society, *Un homme qui dort* focuses on the marginalisation of a twenty-five-year-old anonymous student who breaks away from society by dropping out of education and taking refuge in his Parisian *chambre de bonne*. One year before he began writing *Un homme qui dort*,[2] Perec was struck by Alain Jessua's long feature film *La Vie à l'envers* (*Life Upside Down*, 1964) in which the protagonist (Charles Denner) believes that he will find the key of happiness by imposing on himself a solitary and austere discipline that regulates his gestures.[3] In Perec's novel, the character's gestures

1 Due to his lack of technical knowledge, the French writer did not plan on making the film alone. Although his friend Queysanne had not read the book, he seized the opportunity to work with Perec and direct his first feature film. From the development to the promotion of the film, Perec and Queysanne showed a strong complicity. See David Bellos, *Georges Perec. Une vie dans les mots*, trans. by Françoise Cartano (Paris: Seuil, 1994), p. 492.

2 In December 1965, Perec explained that the writing of *Un homme qui dort* was in progress. Later, in 1974, he confirmed having written the book in 1965. See Georges Perec, *Entretiens et conférences. Volume I 1965–1978*, ed. by Dominique Bertelli and Mireille Ribière (Nantes: Joseph K., 2003), pp. 51 and 163.

3 In 1967, Perec mentioned *La Vie à l'envers* in the programme 'Georges Perec à propos de *Un homme qui dort*'. (See also Perec, *Entretien et conférences*, p. 179.) David Bellos also points out its influence on the adaptation of *Un homme qui dort*. (See David Bellos, *Georges Perec: A Life in Words* (London: Harvill, 1995), p. 479.)

reflect his detachment from the world. Reduced to automatic bodily movements, they seem to have neither particular significance nor social value. By sticking to elementary practices that are necessary to his solitary and daily survival, such as eating, dressing and walking, he attempts to withdraw from society while paradoxically being constantly in contact with it. As André Leroi-Gourhan explains in his magnum opus *Le Geste et la Parole* (*Gesture and Speech*) published two years before *Un homme qui dort*, elementary practices entail everyday gestures that are social by nature: 'Elementary practices are the individual's vital programs. They include all those daily actions [gestes quotidiens] that affect one's survival as an element of society.'[4] Due to the contradictory nature of his project – surviving in society while hoping neutralising the social dimension of his gestures – the character finds himself at an impasse.

Un homme qui dort is regularly compared by Perec, as well as by his critics, to Herman Melville's short story 'Bartleby, the Scrivener: A Story of Wall Street' (1853) in which the famous formula 'I would prefer not to' symbolises the character's refusal to act in society.[5] While Perec's novel explicitly refers to Bartleby's stillness,[6] the filmic adaptation shows a young man in constant motion, except when, sitting on his bed, he stares at the camera without moving. Most of the time, his gestures betray his vital need to move and, gradually, his profound anxiety. If the character seems alienated and wanders like an ambulatory automaton, if his gestures are repetitive, automatic and mechanised, he paradoxically acts of his own free will and attempts to have absolute control over his body by avoiding making

However, contrary to what Bellos writes, Queysanne did not like Jessua's film. (See Bernard Queysanne and Cécile De Bary, 'Entretien avec Bernard Queysanne – Propos amicaux', in *Cahiers Georges Perec. Vol. 9: Le Cinématographe*, ed. by Cécile De Bary (Bordeaux: Castor Astral, 2006), p. 115.)

4 André Leroi-Gourhan, *Gesture and Speech*, trans. by Anna Bostock Berger (Cambridge, MA and London: The MIT Press), pp. 231–2.

5 See Jacques-Denis Bertharion, *Poétique de Georges Perec. '… une trace, une marque ou quelques signes'* (Saint-Genouph: Librairie Nizet, 1998), pp. 37–8; Jacques Neefs and Hans Hartje, *Georges Perec: Images* (Paris: Seuil, 1993), p. 95.

6 See Georges Perec, *Un homme qui dort* (Paris: Denoël, 1967), p. 136.

spontaneous gestures. His social conditioning is thus replaced by his own ability to condition himself, which is the illusory proof of his freedom.

Although Perec did not seek to convey a political message about alienation in French post-May 1968 society (a recurring topic in 1970s French cinema) or about any other contemporary ideological concern,[7] the writer was aware that the character's anxiety and marginal condition could ultimately reflect the fears of 1970s French society.[8] In contrast to iconic post-New Wave films such as Claude Faraldo's *Themroc* (1973) and Jacques Doillon's *L'An 01* (*The Year 01* (1973), with Alain Resnais' and Jean Rouch's participations), Perec and Queysanne sought to avoid all political references to May 1968 and protest movements of the 1970s.[9] Far from the character's solitary wandering in *Un homme qui dort, L'An 01* is a political utopia that tells the collective refusal of capitalist society by directly alluding to the anti-establishment movements that emerged from the late 1960s onwards – the population suddenly decides to stop everything by common consent. Without being overstated, the political significance of *Un homme qui dort* fundamentally lies in the character's individual failure to obliterate the social meaning of his gestures and to live outside the community.

The cinematographic adaptation of the novel *Un homme qui dort*, which is devoid of dialogue and plot, performed by a silent actor (Jacques

7 During their media campaign in 1974, Perec and Queysanne insisted on the topicality of the story. (See Perec, *Entretiens et conférences*, p. 154.) The character's marginality and his desire to break out from the conventions of society were in the spirit of the times, especially if we consider the works of some post-New Wave filmmakers such as Philippe Garrel (*Marie pour mémoire* (*Marie for Memory*), 1967) or Peter Emmanuel Goldman (*Wheel of Ashes*, 1968). However, in many regards, it seems that Perec and Queysanne's emphasis on the topicality of the film was principally a media argument addressed to critics. In more recent interviews, Queysanne highlighted the timelessness of *Un homme qui dort*, arguing that the film, which already looked old in 1974, was not particularly rooted in the 1970s. See Queysanne and De Bary, 'Entretien avec Bernard Queysanne – Propos amicaux', p. 121.

8 Perec, *Entretiens et conférences*, p. 180.

9 Bernard Queysanne, 'Nous étions inspirés par la ville et la lumière', *Vertigo*, 35 (2009), 78–83 <http://www.cairn.info/revue-vertigo-2009-1-page-78.htm> [accessed 1 April 2016] (para. 19 of 22).

Spiesser), read by an omnipresent voice-over and financed by a very low budget, was a stimulating challenge for Perec, who – as a dedicated Oulipo member – loved working under creative constraints.[10] Queysanne relied on his experience of assistant on Robert Enrico, Philippe Labro and Georges Franju's films to direct his first long feature. More than an exercise in style, the film is a critical examination and cinematic exploration of everyday gesture in its most fundamental aspects. On the one hand, the mechanics of ritualised and automatic gestures, reiterated daily by the character, reveal the interplay between the human body and the cinematic machine. On the other hand, the film stresses the crisis of everyday gestures: the predictable programme of daily life is disrupted by nervous, compulsive and anxious gestures, which crack apart the character's desire for control and self-conditioning. Through the character's gestures, in their interaction with the urban spaces of Paris and the components of the cinematic medium, the film ultimately undertakes a reflection on memory and the archive, evoking the autobiographical projects that Perec developed in the 1970s.

A Cinematic Laboratory of Gestures

The term laboratory is used by Giuliana Bruno to describe city films of the 1920s, such as Fritz Lang's *Metropolis* (1927) and Dziga Vertov's *Man with a Movie Camera* (1929), which scrutinise the 'mechanics of the body' as well as the movements of urban life.[11] Influenced by silent cinema, *Un homme qui dort* also shows the city as a place of experimentation in which the actor's body is examined by the camera. From a phenomenological

10 '*A Man Asleep* is a film made under constraint – the constraint of an unprecedentedly tiny budget.' See Bellos, *Georges Perec: A Life in Words*, p. 520. Founded by Raymond Queneau and François Le Lionnais, Oulipo (Ouvroir de littérature potentielle) is a group of writers and mathematicians, who explore, invent and apply writing constraints.

11 Giuliana Bruno, *Atlas of Emotion: Journeys in Art, Architecture, and Film* (New York: Verso, 2002), p. 22.

perspective, the film reveals the interaction between the human body and what Vivian Sobchack names 'the film's body'.[12] According to the latter, film technology forms a body, which, in its perceptive and expressive potentialities, proves comparable to the human body, albeit made of a different substance.[13] Like the human body, the film's body is characterised by movement: 'From the first, the film's body functions to visibly *animate* perception and expression in existence. Thus, its primary function always already entails *movement.*'[14] Drawing a parallel between the evolution of film technology and the 'development of the human lived-body from infancy to adulthood', Sobchack compares the human body's gestures, which become more and more sophisticated and precise 'with exercise and experience', to the movements of the camera that has freed itself from its initial passivity and stasis to move and 'perform' with assertiveness in the world.[15]

Un homme qui dort shows the interplay between the character's body and the body of film technology (including the camera, the editing and mixing table, and the projector) in urban spaces. Through complex constraints of mise-en-scène, mutual exchanges can be observed between the actor's gestures that mimic the mechanical and automatic features of the cinematic medium, and the film body that is endowed with certain qualities of human gesture, in terms of motility, expression, perception, intentionality and memory.

12 Vivian Sobchack, *The Address of the Eye: A Phenomenology of Film Experience* (Princeton: Princeton University Press, 1992), pp. 164–259.

13 Ibid., p. 247.

14 Ibid., p. 205.

15 Ibid., pp. 250–4.

A Cinematic Approach to Everyday Gestures

From January to July 1973, Perec and Queysanne shot the film with a small crew, mostly on weekends.[16] The writer showed the actor Jacques Spiesser[17] how to perform specific gestures, such as playing cards or biting his nails.[18] As a director, Queysanne used his technical skills to create complex movements of camera with the collaboration of the cinematographer Bernard Zitzermann. The actor Ludmila Mikaël read Perec's text that has the distinctive feature of using the second-person singular in order to address the character.[19] In the film, oral expression is at once absent – the actor does not talk, his gestures are his only mode of expression – and omnipresent through the voice-over. Perec and Queysanne decided to exclude the passages of the novel that explore the character's consciousness and hypnagogic experiences (hypnagogia refers to the intermediary state between wakefulness and sleep) in order to focus on his everyday gestures.[20] In Perec's text, gestures correspond to elementary actions, such as eating, sleeping, walking, shaving, etc. The cinematic adaptation proceeds differently in relation to gesture, since actions are visually transposed – thanks to the actor's performance – into a series of distinct bodily movements. As Eisenstein puts it, the film adaptation of a literary text entails a phase which he calls the 'mise en geste': a character's inner conflicts and motives are transposed into elements of visible action, which are then transposed into 'the actor's gesture and physical change

16 Georges Perec and Bernard Queysanne, *Un homme qui dort* (Paris: La Vie est belle, 2007), p. 40. DVD booklet.

17 Spiesser belongs, with Francis Huster, Jacques Villeret and Jacques Weber, to the new generation of the Conservatoire national d'art dramatique. Far from being unknown, Spiesser is a prolific actor who appears in 1974 in four other films: Edouard Molinaro's *L'Ironie du sort*, Alain Resnais's *Stavisky*, Claude Pinoteau's *La Gifle*, and Costa-Gavras' *Section spéciale*.

18 Perec, *Entretiens et conférences*, p. 166.

19 In the film adaptation of *Un homme qui dort*, the text in voice-over uses the same sentences as in Perec's novel.

20 Perec, *Entretiens et conférences*, p. 160.

of location'. Gestures confer to 'concrete actions and events' an 'idiosyncratic, unique, and inimitable' style, that mirrors 'the individual quality of a character's behaviour as well as the author's perspective on the events'. If an action corresponds to *what* happens in a scene, the 'mise en geste' refers to *how* this action will be peformed by the actor, according to the character's singularity and the author's vision and method of directing.[21]

Perec and Queysanne divided the film into six chapters entitled 'La Rupture' [Rupture] (06:35–21:10), 'L'Apprentissage' [Learning] (21:10–41:24), 'Le Bonheur' [Happiness] (41:24–53:05), 'L'Inquiétude' [Worry] (53:05–61:40), 'Les Monstres' [Monsters] (61:40–67:06), and 'La Destruction' [Destruction] (67:06–69:20), in addition to the prologue and to the epilogue entitled 'Le Retour' [Return], which consists in a long panoramic shot.[22] Such a structure had a significant impact on the directors' stylistic choices of filmmaking. Perec attempted to invent a cinematic equivalent of the sestina, which is a poetic form composed of six stanzas of six lines each.[23] The words that conclude each line are repeated from one stanza to another, but in a different order. During the shooting, Perec and Queysanne planned to film each object, action and set, in six different ways according to the tone of each chapter.[24] As a result, similar sequences of gestures are shown from different angles, for instance when the character prepares his breakfast or eats at the restaurant. Although reiterated throughout the film, the same gestures are perceived differently, according to the psychological evolution of the character from one chapter to another. Even though Perec and Queysanne failed to strictly apply this principle to the editing, the sestina influenced the way gestures are shown and perceived in the film.

21 Sergei Eisenstein, *Mise en Jeu and Mise en Geste*, trans. by Sergey Levchin (Montreal: Caboose, 2014). Ebook.

22 All translations are my own unless otherwise noted.

23 The literary form of the sestina inspired Oulipo writers, including Perec, who applied and reinvented the constraint. See Michèle Audin, 'Mathématiques et littérature: un article avec des mathématiques et de la littérature', *Mathématiques et sciences humaines*, 178 (2007), 63–86 (p. 65).

24 See Queysanne, 'Nous étions inspirés par la ville et la lumière' (para. 7 of 22).

As Lesley Stern explains, '[g]estures migrate between everyday life and the movies, but where the gestural often goes unnoticed in the everyday, in the cinema (where it travels between the quotidian and histrionic) it moves into visibility.'[25] Through processes of 'inflation',[26] the cinematic medium can modify and amplify the perception of quotidian gestures. Silent cinema emphasised the visibility of gestures, which was an inexhaustible source of cinematic research for avant-garde filmmakers. In his theoretical essays, pioneer filmmaker and theoretician Jean Epstein demonstrates the capacity of the cinematic medium to describe and interpret bodily movements in an infinite variety of ways. Epstein compares the process of cinematic reproduction with mirrors which, when facing each other, enable someone to look at his or her body and gestures from different perspectives concurrently – in this respect, the cinematic experience, which provides an unfamiliar perception of the body, can evoke Magritte's painting *La Reproduction interdite* (*Not to Be Reproduced*, 1937), referenced by Perec and Queysanne in their film.[27] Through the use of different shot sizes and camera angles, the cinematic medium has the unequalled capacity to generate a multiplicity of points of view on a character's gestures.

In *Un homme qui dort*, a trifling gesture can suddenly grow out of all proportion. When the character starts to bite his nails in the second half of the film, this mundane gesture first looks insignificant. In a shot of the chapter 'L'Apprentissage', Spiesser, who is located far from the foreground, on the extreme right side of the screen, walks towards the camera and bites one of his nails (see Figure 1.1). The tic goes unnoticed because the mise-en-scène does not highlight it in any way. One minute later, he performs the same gesture while playing cards. The camera moves towards the actor's face, from a medium shot to a close-up (see Figure 1.2). Although the contrasted light conveys an uneasy feeling, the act of biting one's nails could be interpreted as a simple gesture of concentration: the character does look absorbed by his game; the camera angle, which is at the character's level, is relatively 'neutral'. Later, in the chapter 'L'Inquiétude', this gesture

25 Lesley Stern, 'Paths that Wind through the Thicket of Things', *Critical Inquiry*, 28.1 (2001), 317–54 (pp. 328–9).

26 Ibid., p. 326.

27 Epstein, *Ecrits sur le cinéma, tome 1: 1927–1953* (Paris: Seghers, 1974), p. 128.

Figures 1.1–1.3. *Un homme qui dort*: The character bites his nails in three different shots.

is repeated in a compulsive way and isolated in a series of extreme close-ups and high-angle shots, with very expressive lighting (see Figure 1.3). The voice-over insists on the physical pain provoked by this compulsive gesture in order to emphasise the feeling of anxiety that torments the character. While the soundtrack produces an oppressive sound effect, the editing connects the gesture with the mechanised movements of a pinball machine. As a result, the gesture, which first looks insignificant, then relatively neutral and finally highly expressive, is spectacularly transformed by the components of the cinematic medium (i.e. lighting, soundtrack, voice-over, camera angle, field size and editing), making it possible to interpret the same gesture differently.

By traversing different scales – from long shot to extreme close-up – the character's gesture of biting his nails is gradually isolated from its environment and context. As film critic Jean Douchet suggests, gestures can become autonomous in cinema when they are isolated by the camera.[28] In *Un homme qui dort*, the character's gestures are often separated from the rest of his body through extensive use of close-ups. Unlike in theatre, in cinema bodies are rarely integrally exhibited. The camera and editing can fragment and decontextualise gestures. The French term *découpage* refers to a fundamental task in the process of filmmaking, which consists in cutting (*découper*) the sequences into a series of shots and the bodies into a series of gestures.[29] Before the shooting, a director usually writes a shooting script (*découpage technique*), which, for each shot, details all the necessary information regarding the props, the special effects, the lighting as well as the camera's and the characters' positions. Although Perec and Queysanne, who worked with a small team and used an unconventional screenplay,[30]

28 Jean Douchet, 'Le Visage comme révélation, le geste comme signe, le corps découpé comme figure, le corps plein comme opacité', in *L'Invention de la figure humaine*, ed. by Jacques Aumont (Paris: Cinémathèque française, 1995), p. 118.

29 See Noël Burch, *Theory of Film Practice*, trans. by Helen R. Lane (London: Secker & Warburg, 1973), p. 3.

30 In the first version of the screenplay, inspired by Ermanno Olmi's *Il Posto* (1961), Perec and Queysanne wrote the prologue with dialogue in the tradition of Italian neorealism. As they were not convinced by the result, they decided to use Perec's literary text in order to create a duality between the voice-over and the silent image,

did not develop a shooting script,[31] they carefully reflected on the difference between filming a sequence of gestures in three different shots or in a single movement of camera, in a medium long shot or in a close-up.

In accordance with the sestina constraint, the same actions in *Un homme qui dort* were filmed in different ways in order to mirror the character's evolution throughout the film. In the prologue, the character prepares his breakfast, plugs the kettle in to boil water and pours Nescafé instant coffee in his bowl. He is an ordinary student getting ready to sit an exam in sociology in the morning. The camera follows him moving about in his room, frames his body in American shots, and, without fragmenting them much, captures his gestures in the continuity of their movement. At the beginning of the first chapter 'La Rupture', we realise that the directors used the conditional tense to narrate the prologue: if the character had sat the exam, he would have been an ordinary student who revises his course, prepares his breakfast and joins the other students in the examination room. Instead, he decides to stay in bed and not to graduate. Perec and Queysanne represent this breaking point in the character's life by breaking down his gestures, in the same way that the cracked mirror fragments his face in three irregular pieces. In a first close-up, his left hand grasps the instant coffee jar; then in a second close-up, his right hand seizes the electric kettle. His gestures are isolated in close-ups from the rest of his body, suggesting his identity crisis (see Figures 1.4, 1.5, 1.6 and 1.7).

The beginning of *Un homme qui dort* stresses not only the essential role of shot scale, but also of editing in giving meaning to the gestures. In the prologue, the parallel editing integrates the character's gestures in society. The neighbour fills a bucket of water in the corridor, workers are active in the street and crowds of people are walking through the underground station: the city awakens just as the character. His gestures are rooted in a social project, symbolised by his morning preparation for the exam in sociology. At the end of the prologue, the character's gestures converge with those of his fellows. Like the other students, he is shown entering the

in the same way as Sacha Guitry in *Le Roman d'un tricheur* (*Confessions of a Cheat*, 1936). See Queysanne, 'Nous étions inspirés par la ville et la lumière' (para. 5 of 22).

31 According to Queysanne, Spiesser was frustrated by the absence of a shooting script. See Perec, *Entretiens et conférences*, p. 166.

Figures 1.4–1.7. *Un homme qui dort*: The character boils water and makes coffee.

examination room and writing his essay, performing the same gestures and postures. Significantly, the break with society starts when the character silently crumples his friends' messages slipped under his door. Subsequently, the absence of parallel editing highlights his isolation and marginalisation as he reiterates the same gestural sequences in an increasingly pre-programmed way that evokes Henri Lefebvre's description of everyday life in the modern world, dominated by the recurrence of 'mechanical movements both human and properly mechanic'.[32] By stressing the interplay between the cinematic machine and the character's body in motion, Perec and Queysanne aim to explore the mechanics of everyday gestures.

32 Henri Lefebvre, *Everyday Life in the Modern World*, trans. by Sacha Rabinovitch (New York: Harper & Row, 1971), p. 18.

The Mechanics of Everyday Gestures

In the second half of the nineteenth century, Etienne-Jules Marey and Eadweard Muybridge experimented with the photographic medium to study the corporeal movements of animals and people. As will be discussed in Chapter 5, chronophotography is a device that makes it possible to break down the trajectory of a gesture into a series of frames. In 1878, funded by the industrialist and politician Leland Stanford, and influenced by Marey's research on animal locomotion, Muybridge developed a multicamera system to capture the gallop of a horse. For the first time, by showing the mechanical nature of the animal body, the technical features of the photographic apparatus enabled the human eye to scrutinise the mechanics of gestures in detail. For Stanford, who was one of the railway industry leaders, this scientific and artistic experiment was a means to 'consolidate, promote, and naturalise the developments of industrial capitalism',[33] by linking 'the speed and power of the locomotive to the gait and beauty of the racehorse'.[34] The industrial age deeply believed in the mechanisation of bodies. After having tried to animate the horse's gallop by creating an illusion of cinematic movement, Muybridge started to study the human body. Thanks to the use of multiple cameras, he succeeded in capturing the gestures of athletes from different angles at the same time. He documented some elementary and previously unrepresented everyday gestures by examining them from various perspectives. For instance, women, whose body was often eroticised, were asked to perform domestic actions, such as ironing clothes or getting into bed. Considered as a machine, the body was scrutinised in its slightest motions. According to Philip Brookman, 'Muybridge proposed a synthesis of people and machine in his work, reimagining the body and

33 John Ott cited in Philip Brookman, 'Helios: Eadweard Muybridge in a Time of Change', in *Eadweard Muybridge*, ed. by Philip Brookman (London: Tate, 2010), p. 84.

34 Ibid., p. 83.

its movements through industrial systems of cameras, shutters, electrical wiring, batteries, and telegraphic apparatus.'[35]

In the wake of chronophotography, cinema explored the mechanisation of gestures in urban environments. As Bruno points out, the speed of modernity defines both 'the motion of the city' and the cinematic movement.[36] The city and cinema 'are machines of reproduction, bound together by mechanicalism and by the mechanics of the body'.[37] In cities, or in cinema, factories invent new bodies, produced in series and shaped by industrialism, as Lang's *Metropolis* shows. By accelerating, decelerating or even freezing the motion of images, the cinematic machine has the power to manipulate urban and gestural rhythms. In René Clair's *Paris qui dort* (*The Crazy Ray*, 1925), some pictures of empty Parisian streets and petrified bodies anticipate Perec and Queysanne's film, in which the tension between movement and stillness is revealing of the character's crisis. Admiring the ability of an old man to remain perfectly immobile during hours, the student fails to mimic his posture; nervous gestures thwart his desire for stillness. Absorbed by the rhythm of the city and carried away by the movement of the camera, the character cannot stop himself walking.

Un homme qui dort is reminiscent of the city symphonies made during the silent era of cinema.[38] The style of filmmaking – notably the fluid movements of the camera – evokes André Sauvage's *Etudes sur Paris* (1928). In the overture of his documentary, Sauvage films the gestures of workers who bustle along the banks of the Seine. Paris is presented as an industrious city, or to borrow Bruno's expression, as a 'labor-atory'[39] in which the flow of moving images embraces the flow of human activity. In the prologue of *Un homme qui dort*, Perec and Queysanne depict the city as a social machine that starts working at sunrise. Street sweepers clean the avenues, dustmen collect the bins, cars swamp the streets and people rush into the metro entrance and use the escalators. People's gestures and activities necessitate the

35 Ibid., p. 100.

36 Bruno, *Atlas of Emotion*, p. 21.

37 Ibid., p. 22.

38 Perec and Queysanne wanted to structure their film like a symphony. See Perec, *Entretiens et conférences*, p. 155.

39 Bruno, *Atlas of Emotion*, p. 22.

use of automatons. If automatic reflexes and habits always governed our everyday gestures, the externalisation of human movements in the form of increasingly sophisticated machines considerably altered gestures in the age of industrialisation. Industrial machines instilled new automatic and stereotypical gestures that prove necessary to the working order of modern societies.[40] In the prologue, Parisian people, including the main character, potentially repeat the same stereotypical gestures every day. Later in the film, the voice-over insists on the character's ability to repeat basic gestures like an automaton ('gestes d'automate').

Just as Ludmila Mikaël had to articulate Perec's text with a flat and neutral voice, Spiesser had to make gestures in a way that reflects the character's indifference. At first glance, it would make sense to draw on Robert Bresson's ideas on film performance, based on the concept of automatism, in order to analyse how Spiesser performed his character's automatic gestures. Spiesser shares with Bresson's 'models'[41] a certain lack of facial expressivity; he had to avoid acting his role.[42] Bresson's method consists in preventing his models to be conscious of their gestures in order to render the spontaneity of the character's habitual actions and automatic reflexes.[43] As he explains, '[n]ine-tenths of our movements obey habit and automatism. It is anti-nature to subordinate them to will and to thought.'[44] Bresson requires his models to repeat the same scenes numerous times. The mechanical process of repetition conditions them to speak and make gestures without thinking. The director wants to show their 'true natures'[45] by capturing the most spontaneous, 'imperceptible' and 'inward' bodily

40 See Yves Citton, *Gestes d'humanités. Anthropologie sauvage de nos expériences esthétiques* (Paris: Armand Colin, 2012), pp. 64–5.

41 Linking the notion of acting with theatre, Bresson prefers to use the term 'model' instead of film actor. See Robert Bresson, *Notes on the Cinematograph*, trans. by Jonathan Griffin (New York: New York Review Books, 2016), p. 1.

42 Perec, *Entretiens et conférences*, p. 166.

43 Rose-Marie Godier analyses Bresson's method of acting in the light of Pascal's definition of the automaton, which has profound religious implications. See Godier, *L'Automate et le cinéma. Dans 'La Règle du Jeu' de Jean Renoir, 'Le Limier' de Joseph L. Mankiewicz, 'Pickpocket' de Robert Bresson* (Paris: L'Harmattan, 2005).

44 Bresson, *Notes on the Cinematograph*, p. 17.

45 Ibid., p. 42.

movements.[46] 'Catch instants. Spontaneity, freshness,' he writes.[47] Bresson's approach, which aims to reveal the model's existence by looking at his or her unwilled gestures, differs from Perec and Queysanne's intentions.

While, in *Un homme qui dort*, the character is compared to a laboratory rat,[48] Queysanne uses the same analogy to describe Spiesser's performance.[49] In 2009, Queysanne confessed that Spiesser was disconcerted by their method of directing to the point of leaving the set.[50] Perec and Queysanne used him as a soulless machine only able to perform gestures indifferently, just as his character. The latter keeps to the gestures he has learnt, like an automaton whose movements are pre-programmed. As Michel Estève writes about Bresson's films, gestures evoke the characters' inner life.[51] By contrast, the character's gestures in *Un homme qui dort*, which are not supposed to manifest his inner being, are reduced to their most obvious and superficial surface. His automatic behaviour seems to mirror the nature of the cinematic machine, which is an automaton that reproduces the illusion of life. As a result, the character's gestures appear to be 'performed' by the film's body itself, more than they are by the actor.

In *The Time-Image*, Gilles Deleuze defines the two complementary, although contradictory, meanings of automaton. On the one hand, the spiritual automaton is a highly sophisticated instrument of thought (i.e. cinema as a spiritual art) in the tradition of Spinoza and Leibniz; on the other, the psychological automaton, which is deprived of the capacity to think, is able to perform elementary gestures only, like a somnambulist.[52] At the end of the nineteenth century, Pierre Janet and Jean-Martin Charcot studied

46 Ibid., p. 26.

47 Ibid., p. 19.

48 Significantly Oulipo writers compared themselves to laboratory rats, due to the literary constraints that they liked to impose on themselves. See Eve Célia Morisi, 'The OuLiPoe, or Constraint and (Contre-)"Performance": "The Philosophy of Composition" and the Oulipian Manifestos', *Comparative Literature*, 60.2 (2008), 107–24 (p. 116).

49 Perec, *Entretiens et conférences*, p. 160.

50 Queysanne, 'Nous étions inspirés par la ville et la lumière' (para. 11 of 22).

51 Michel Estève, *Robert Bresson* (Paris: Seghers, 1974), p. 81.

52 Gilles Deleuze, *Cinema 2. The Time-Image*, trans. by Hugh Tomlinson and Robert Galeta (Minneapolis: University of Minnesota Press, 1997), p. 263.

the psychological automaton in the field of psychiatry; more specifically, Charcot researched on the case of ambulatory automatism (*automatisme ambulatoire*). Only diagnosed between the late nineteenth and early twentieth century, this syndrome referred to the automatic quality of the bodies of vagabonds who, compared to somnambulists, wandered in a neutral and indifferent state. Philosopher Jean-Claude Beaune describes their mechanical behaviour in his extensive research on the topic.[53] In a pathological way, the vagabonds' behaviours mirrored the impact of the social machine on the conditioning of gestures in the industrial age. Considered as an anomaly and a threat to the social order, the vagabonds' silent and solitary lives were regressive and indifferent to 'the rules of human society defined by affective units of husband, wife, children, parents, relatives, bound by traditions, patrimonies, and other customary memories'.[54] They could stroll without stopping, while looking perfectly normal to others.[55] Like somnambulists, they could forget what they had done during their strolling crisis.[56] In *Un homme qui dort*, although we will not go as far as diagnosing the syndrome of ambulatory automatism in the character's behaviour, his condition evokes some of the symptoms described above. In Perec's text, he is regarded as a 'somnambule' and compared to a (laboratory) rat, a cat, a spider, even a monster; his vegetative or animal life is the mark of his social desertion. Most of all, he is left without any memory during his experience of detachment. The voice-over insists repeatedly on the character's progressive amnesia.

The notion of ambulatory automatism can be analysed from a cinematic perspective. The character seems to identify himself with the camera which, just like him, strolls in the streets of Paris and dollies in or dollies out. According to Balázs, walking is a 'quite specific cinematic gesture'. By contrast, stage actors 'rarely have an opportunity to use the walk as a

53 See Jean-Claude Beaune, *Le Vagabond et la machine: Essai sur l'automatisme ambulatoire, médecine, technique et société en France 1880–1910* (Seyssel: Champ Vallon, 1983).

54 Matt K. Matsuda, *The Memory of the Modern* (New York: Oxford University Press, 1996), p. 126.

55 See Beaune, *Le Vagabond et la machine*, p. 187.

56 Ibid.

characteristic gesture, because of the lack of space'.[57] The movements of the camera enable actors to walk long distances, and can be more or less synchronised with them. Moreover, the camera also looks indifferently at things and people. It is an inhuman eye without memory, without thought, according to Epstein.[58] Bresson describes its 'scrupulous indifference'.[59] In several shots, Perec and Queysanne show the surveillance cameras that permanently scan the streets of Paris. The directors create an analogy between the film camera and the surveillance camera, which both move or pivot as if they were endowed with an autonomous life.

When, in the chapter 'Le Bonheur', the character reaches his goal to live in a complete state of indifference, he and the camera move at the same rhythm, which was not always the case in the first chapters. Throughout the film, the character's gestures and the camera's movements gradually merge. In order to represent respectively the camera's and the character's trajectories, I traced a white arrow and a black arrow on the following figures. In the prologue, the character's gestures lead the camera's movements. His agency enables him to impose himself on the camera (see Figure 1.8). In 'La Rupture' and 'L'Apprentissage', the character's trajectory is often perpendicular to that of the camera which is no longer dependent on his gestures (see Figure 1.9). In 'Le Bonheur', the character's neutral and automatic behaviour sets him on equal footing with the camera (see Figure 1.10). The harmony between both character and camera is translated into synchronised movements. For instance, when the student walks down the stairs that lead to the quay of the river Seine or strolls the upper part of the city, the camera stops when he stops, moves when he moves, and vice versa: their mimetic relationship reaches its climax in this sequence. The symbiosis between the man and the machine results in their fusion. At one point, they both move around a city square, but in opposite directions; while the camera still performs its circular movement, the character vanishes (see Figures 1.11 and 1.12). This surreal scene is symbolic of the process of substitution between the character and the camera. The chapter 'Le Bonheur'

57 Béla Balázs, *Theory of the Film: Growth of a New Art*, trans. by Edith Bone (London: Dennis Dobson, 1952), p. 135.

58 See Epstein, *Ecrits sur le cinéma, tome 1*, p. 128.

59 Bresson, *Notes on the Cinematograph*, p. 20.

includes numerous tracking shots, filmed in the streets of Paris without the actor (see Figure 1.13). The character and the camera's automatic gestures seem to have merged, at least temporarily.

Figures 1.8–1.13. *Un homme qui dort*: The character and/or the camera move in the streets of Paris.

A Paradoxical Automaton

The character's trajectory throughout the film is not only gradual, but also paradoxical. From the beginning, his metamorphosis into an automaton appears to be problematic. What is it that essentially distinguishes the character from Charcot's vagabonds? As Beaune explains, the vagabonds' gestures were regular but uncertain, repetitive but arbitrary.[60] Deprived of reason, willpower, desires, feelings and even pain,[61] they did not know in which direction they walked. Matt K. Matsuda suggests, '[i]n this impulsive vagabond, the reflex, the instinctive primordial imprint overwhelmed the "representative" coordination of the memory-will, the *volonté*, which made individuals responsible members of human society.'[62] Conversely, in *Un homme qui dort*, the character conditions himself voluntarily. As Perec points out, he is the spectator of his own indifference.[63] The voice-over insists on the character's willpower and consciousness: 'Tu veux l'attente et l'oubli' [You just want to wait and forget]; 'Tu découvres, avec presque, parfois, une certaine ivresse, que tu es libre' [It's almost sometimes with a kind of ecstasy that you discover you're free] – as well as on his predictable and ordinary behaviour: 'Tu ne traverses pas quand le feu est rouge, tu t'abrites du vent pour allumer ta cigarette' [You don't cross when the light is red, you shelter yourself from the wind to light your cigarette].[64] When he believes he has fulfilled his dream of automatism, his gestures start resisting his own conditioning. In 'L'Inquiétude' and 'Les Monstres', he experiences a deep crisis that breaks apart his indifference. His programmed motions turn into compulsive gestures exacerbated by frustration, anxiety, fatigue, suffering and loneliness: the mechanics of his gestures goes wrong.

His project is paradoxical by definition. He wants not to want, he desires not to desire, he wishes to leave society, but wanders in society. Certainly the

60 Beaune, *Le Vagabond et la Machine*, p. 157.

61 See ibid., p. 301.

62 Matsuda, *The Memory of the Modern*, p. 130.

63 Perec, *Entretiens et conférences*, p. 180.

64 All translations of *Un homme qui dort's* text in this chapter are quotations of the English voice-over in the DVD *Un homme qui dort* (Paris: La Vie est belle, 2007).

streets of Paris empty as his indifference grows, but most of the time he never stops roaming among the crowd. Like an automaton, he temporarily manages to simulate neutral gestures, but he lives in the illusion of his own indifference. Such illusion is suggested by the often-ironical discrepancy between the voice-over and the image, which highlights the gap between the young man's disproportionate ambitions and the banality of his gestures. When the character plays a game of skill, the 'Foxhunt puzzle', and then prepares a bowl of Nescafé with powder milk, the voice-over says: 'Ici, tu apprends à durer. Parfois, maître du temps, maître du monde, petite araignée attentive au centre de ta toile, tu règnes sur Paris' [This is how you learn to endure. Sometimes, master of time, master of the world, little spider at the centre of your web, you reign over Paris]. Compared to the ordinariness of his gestures, this disproportionate vocabulary creates an adversarial relationship between the text and the image. By producing oppositions between two images, the image and the text, the image and the sound, and the sound and the text, the editing enables the spectator to question the potential significance of the gestures. The ambiguity of *Un homme qui dort* consists in creating a contradictory movement between the character's intentions and the film itself: he wants to dissolve language, but language is omnipresent through the voice-over, which insistently addresses both the character and the spectator; he seeks to be amnesiac, but the film incorporates his gestures into a process of memory; he believes his gestures are indifferent, neutral and meaningless, but, in the eyes of the spectator, they mean his refusal of the world and, ultimately, his distress.

Such discrepancies contribute to confusing the ideological interpretations of *Un homme qui dort*. Does the film depict a conditioned and alienated society, in which surveillance cameras monitor people's gestures? At the beginning of the film, Perec ironically reduces ideologies to an enumeration of academic topics taught to students in sociology.[65] The effects of

65 Perec's text read in voice-over sums up the character's sociological knowledge in these terms: 'Tu ne diras pas sur quatre, huit ou douze feuillets ce que tu sais, ce que tu penses, ce que tu sais qu'il faut penser sur l'aliénation, sur les ouvriers, sur la modernité et sur les loisirs, sur les cols blancs ou sur l'automation [...]' [You're not going to say on 4, 8, or 12 pages what you know you should think about alienation, or the working class, or modernity and leisure, about the white collar workers, or automation].

desynchronisation between the image, the soundtrack and the text counter all doctrines. Rather than denouncing alienating social structures, Perec and Queysanne show the character's ability to build his own prison walls and alienate himself.[66] The film tells not only the story of his indifference, but also of his corporeal resistance to self-alienation. The character, who wanted to erase his past, realises that he cannot escape his memory.

Archives of Gestures

Fundamental aspects of Perec and Queysanne's film – such as the character's failure in his attempt to escape memory and history – evoke Alain Resnais's *Hiroshima mon amour* (*Hiroshima, My Love*, 1959). In both films, the influence of the Nouveau Roman and the formal dialectics[67] of the editing cast doubt on the apparent truth of moving pictures through a process of desynchronisation between the text, the soundtrack and the image.[68] In his correspondence with Jacques Lederer, Perec conveys a genuine enthusiasm for *Hiroshima mon amour*.[69] In May 1960, the latter published a review of Resnais's film in *La Nouvelle Critique* where he praises the way the film makes the audience aware of Hiroshima's impact on history.[70]

In *Un homme qui dort*, oblivion is at the core of the character's quest of a neutral life, and certainly his first motive. 'Tu veux l'attente et l'oubli' [You just want to wait and forget], the narrator says in reference to Maurice

66 On the topic of self-alienation, see Jean Brun, *Les Vagabonds de l'Occident: L'Expérience du voyage et la prison du moi* (Paris: Desclée, 1976), p. 213.

67 Noël Burch theorises such a dialectical approach to film aesthetics in *Theory of Film Practice*, pp. 49–101.

68 See Mathieu Remy, 'L'évidente nécessité de la mémoire', in *Cahiers Georges Perec. Vol. 9: Le Cinématographe*, ed. by De Bary, p. 48.

69 See Jacques Lederer and Georges Perec, *'Cher, très cher, admirable et charmant ami …' Correspondance Georges Perec-Jacques Lederer (1956–1961)* (Paris: Flammarion, 1997), p. 519.

70 Cited in Remy, 'L'évidente nécessité de la mémoire', p. 44.

Blanchot's *L'Attente, L'Oubli* (*Awaiting Oblivion*, 1962). Memory is perceptible in the urbanity of Paris itself, embodied in everyday gestures and symbolically represented by the empty house of the character's childhood. The cinematic medium, and more particularly the camera as 'eye-witness',[71] has the ability to index, incorporate, catalogue, store and archive 'gesturing human forms'.[72] In the early ages of film history, the technology of cinema mediated a collective and intersubjective memory of urban life, by capturing the fleeting gestural traces of anonymous passers-by and city-dwellers. As Stephen Barber explains, '[b]y the opening of the twentieth century, the film city had amassed into a vast accumulation of bodies and gestures, of urban surfaces and movements.'[73] While evoking the origins of cinema, the depiction of Paris in *Un homme qui dort* remains rooted in the context of European post-war cinema. 'In the decades after the Second World War, a primary preoccupation of European cinema was the slow-burning impact on cities and their inhabitants of that conflict's residue,' Barber writes.[74] At the end of *Un homme qui dort*, the memory of the war resurfaces in the character's roaming in the ruins of Paris.

Gesture and Memory

As demonstrated by anthropologist Marcel Jousse, the human body incorporates and archives gestures on a daily basis, through experience and social interactions. Influenced by psychologist and philosopher Pierre Janet and anthropologist Marcel Mauss, Jousse studied the fundamental role of gesture in human knowledge, expression and memory. Published posthumously in 1969, *L'Anthropologie du Geste*, which summarises several

71 See Scott McQuire, 'Eternity's Hostage: The Camera and the Archive', in *Visions of Modernity* (London: SAGE, 1998), p. 134.

72 Stephen Barber, *Projected Cities: Cinema and Urban Space* (London: Reaktion Books, 2002), p. 21.

73 Ibid., p. 27.

74 Ibid., p. 61.

decades of research, examines the gestural process that causes human beings to interact with the world and its physical reality and how this constant interplay (*jeu*) structures and shapes memory. According to Jousse, human beings unconsciously assimilate the interactional gestures (*Gestes interactionnels*) that mould their sense of the real.[75] Individuals replay the gestures that they have assimilated in their body by expressing them unconsciously. This process of replay (*rejeu*) shapes human memory.[76] Becoming aware of the interactional gestures that they have unconsciously expressed, humans exert their will and agency to perform them in an intentional way. Finally, habit gives a new autonomy to gestures, which are then automatically performed.[77]

In *Un homme qui dort*, the character wishes to leave what Jousse calls the *Cosmos* by cutting himself off from others and refusing all interactional gestures. In his attempt to neutralise the social significance of his gestures, he tries to destroy the possibility of memory. A human being, who would live completely alone, outside the world, would have no memory at all, according to Janet. In *L'Evolution de la mémoire et de la notion du temps* (1927–8), the latter explains that memory is essentially a social phenomenon. In order to illustrate his thesis, he uses the example of Robinson Crusoe who writes his journal because he hopes to return to society.[78] From a similar perspective, philosopher Henri Bergson also uses the example of Crusoe in order to demonstrate that individuals are never totally cut off from society:

> Vainly do we try to imagine an individual cut off from all social life. Even materially, Robinson Crusoe on his island remains in contact with other men, for the manufactured objects he saved from the wreck, and without which he could not get along, keep him within the bounds of civilization, and consequently within those of society.[79]

75 Marcel Jousse, *L'Anthropologie du geste* (Paris: Resma, 1969), p. 60.

76 Ibid., p. 34.

77 Ibid., p. 72.

78 See Stéphane Laurens and Toshiaki Kozakaï, 'Pierre Janet et la mémoire sociale', *Connexions*, 80 (2003), 59–75 (p. 59).

79 Henri Bergson, *The Two Sources of Morality and Religion*, trans. by R. Ashley Audra and Cloudesley Brereton (London: MacMillan and Co, 1935), p. 7.

The character invented by Perec always wanders in society, among people. Even his room, described as a desert island, is permeated with the noises of the street and of his neighbour. Although the character wants to withdraw from society, he continues to keep minimum contacts with others, for instance with his concierge. He eats daily at the restaurant and mingles with the crowd. He observes the world that surrounds him. He turns around to look at people, such as a police officer or his neighbour. He goes to cafés and bars, social places such as movie theatres, and looks at people dancing at night. Despite his desire for neutrality, he interacts with others, at least by looking at their gestures. The processes of *jeu* and *rejeu* conceptualised by Jousse structure the mise-en-scène and the editing of the film.

According to Jousse, the media of moving images, such as cinema and television, are revolutionary anthropological tools, which make it possible to gain a cinematic understanding of human gesture.[80] He compares human memory to a film on which interactions with the real are recorded.[81] Such interactions are 'edited' in the human body throughout its life. Jousse further develops his metaphor by creating an analogy between the camera and the human being, both having the ability to 'record' gestures.[82] Thus, humans are endowed with three essential cinematic features: the film, the camera and the editing. Reciprocally, cinema, which is not considered here as a disembodied machine, is endowed with human qualities, especially regarding its ability to constitute a living memory of gestures, which are not only recorded, but also constantly replayed, in interaction with the spectator.

In *Un homme qui dort*, the film's body produces a gestural process of memory that contradicts the character's desire for amnesia. For instance, in the chapter 'L'Apprentissage', two children, who look like twin brothers, run in the street and overtake the character. They make noise by sliding their ruler on the bars of a metallic fence that separates the pavement from the

80 Interestingly Barbara Grespi draws a parallel between Jousse and Epstein's conceptions of gesture. See Grespi, 'Mimismologie. Le geste cosmologique: Marcel Jousse et Jean Epstein', in *Geste filmé, gestes filmiques*, ed. by Christa Blümlinger and Mathias Lavin ([Milan]: Mimésis, 2018), pp. 35–53.

81 Jousse, *L'Anthropologie du Geste*, p. 60.

82 Ibid., p. 67.

road. Two similar takes of the same scene are successively edited, creating a strange effect of repetition and resonance, amplified by the metallic sound effects. In the first take, the character seems surprised by the children and looks at them intermittently. In the second take, he follows them with his eyes, without looking away. The editing creates an impression of déjà-vu that illustrates the impact of interactional gestures on human memory (see Figures 1.14 and 1.15). When, in 'La Destruction', the character runs in the rubble of buildings being demolished, Perec and Queysanne repeat the same editing process (see Figures 1.16 and 1.17). Apart from the prologue, in which he hurries to catch his bus, the character runs for the first time in the last part of the film, in the ruins of these Parisian buildings. The editing creates an effect of resonance (or, in Jousse's terms, an effect of replay) between the children's and the main character's running. The latter spontaneously performs a gesture that the children have symbolically communicated to him.

His memory is constantly brought back to his childhood, which, in an abstract way, is represented by an empty house located outside Paris. Although the house is not explicitly referred to as his childhood home in the film, Perec confirmed this assumption in an interview.[83] When, in 'La Rupture', the character detaches himself from society, the house looks empty and lifeless. The slow movements of the camera give the impression that the character gradually deserts his memory. At the end of the film, after his long dreamlike run in Paris, the character is shown crossing the empty rooms of his childhood home. Similarly to the scene with the children, the editing repeats the same shot twice, creating the strange effect of an instantaneous flashback. Although the character quickly walks straight ahead as if he was trying to escape the house, the editing gives a sense that he moves backwards.

The repetition of similar, and sometimes identical shots gives a particular rhythm to the editing. The character's obsession with the game of solitaire is metaphorical of the editing process.[84] He spends hours shuffling

83 Perec, *Entretiens et conférences*, p. 159.

84 In his analysis of Perec's novel *Un homme qui dort*, Bertharion compares the game of solitaire to an Oulipian constraint. See Bertharion, *Poétique de Georges Perec. '… une trace, une marque ou quelques signes'*, p. 45.

the cards, spreading them, moving them and creating new configurations, before reshuffling them. Like the shots of the film, the same cards reappear, but never in the same order. The narrator implicitly compares the cards manipulated by the character with shots (*plans* in French): 'Selon leur

Figures 1.14–1.19. *Un homme qui dort*: Two children run in front of the character (top); the latter runs in the ruins of a crumbling building (middle) and plays cards (bottom).

place, selon l'instant, chaque carte acquiert une densité presque émouvante. Tu protèges, tu détruis, tu construis, tu combines, tu tires plan sur plan' [According to its position and the possibilities of the moment, each card takes an almost thrilling density. You protect, you destroy, you construct, you calculate, you draw plan after plan]. In this regard, the character's gestures seem to activate the editing and memory processes of the film. The card game can be viewed as a metaphor of the character's life, which takes the form of an editing of replayed gestures. For instance, in 'La Rupture', the character walks down the stairs of a movie theatre, and stubs out his cigarette; the exact same shot is reused in 'L'Inquiétude'. The effects of desynchronisation and repetition between the image and the voice-over also stimulate the audience's memory through their interaction with the character's gestures. While the character is shown playing cards in 'La Rupture', the narrator describes his fascination with solitaire at the end of the following chapter (see Figures 1.18 and 1.19). As a result, the process of replay invites the spectators to weave links between the text and the visual fragments of the film.

Gestural Shocks and the Archive

Memory is not only shaped by habit, but also by the gestural shocks of modern life. In the chapters 'L'Inquiétude', 'Les Monstres', and 'La Destruction', the rhythm of the film gradually speeds up. Textual and visual shocks disrupt the mechanics of the character's everyday gestures. Philosopher Walter Benjamin discusses the notion of shock in his essays on modernity, which, according to him, unsettles the nature of human experience and, by extension, of memory. He distinguishes between immediate, partial, fragmented and isolated experience, shaped by urban shocks (*Erlebnis*), and authentic and long experience, which roots human beings in an historical continuity (*Erfahrung*):

> The greater the shock factor in particular impressions, the more vigilant consciousness has to be in screening stimuli; the more efficiently it does so, the less the impressions

> enter long experience [*Erfahrung*] and the more they correspond to the concept of isolated experience [*Erlebnis*].[85]

The industrial age endangers *Erfarhung* in favour of *Erlebnis*. Consequently, '[t]he human organism increasingly becomes a surface. [...] What are lost in this process are memory traces and the full experience of the event [...],' Mary Ann Doane explains.[86]

According to Benjamin, people who experienced the movements of a metropolis for the first time were terrified.[87] In the wake of the industrial development of cities in the nineteenth century, urban masses were subjected to sensorial shocks which turned city life into a traumatic experience. The automation imposed upon human bodies by industrialism conditioned the behaviour of urban masses, making them capable of absorbing the violent stimuli resulting from the transformation of everyday life in modern society. As Doane writes, consciousness and the rationalisation of time are defence mechanisms that enable individuals to shield themselves from the pathological effects caused by shocks.[88] For instance, the masses of automatons in Edgar Poe's short story 'The Man of the Crowd' (1840) seem to be indifferent to shocks: 'His pedestrians act as if they had adapted themselves to machines and could express themselves only automatically. Their behaviour is a reaction to shocks,' Benjamin argues.[89] As already suggested in our study on automaton, the automation of gestures works like a protective shield which brings about memory loss: 'They live their lives as automatons and resemble Bergson's fictitious characters who have completely liquidated their memories.'[90] Unlike the Baudelairean *flâneur* who partakes the frightening and exhilarating experience of the

85 Walter Benjamin, 'On Some Motifs in Baudelaire', in *Walter Benjamin: Selected Writings. Vol. 4, 1938–1940*, ed. by Howard Eiland and Michael W. Jennings, trans. by Edmund Jephcott and others (Cambridge, MA: The Belknap Press of Harvard University Press, 2006), p. 319.

86 Mary Ann Doane, *The Emergence of Cinematic Time: Modernity, Contigency, the Archive* (Cambridge, MA: Harvard University Press, 2002), p. 13.

87 See Benjamin, 'On Some Motifs in Baudelaire', p. 327.

88 See Doane, *The Emergence of Cinematic Time*, p. 14.

89 Benjamin, 'On Some Motifs in Baudelaire', p. 329.

90 Ibid., p. 330.

city by observing the thousand tiny gestures of Parisians, but like in Poe's short story, the character of *Un homme qui dort* dreams of letting himself be dragged by the flow of an undifferentiated, out of focus and reassuring crowd (see Figure 1.20).[91] Until the chapter 'Les Monstres', the character believes that his neutrality can protect him from shocks.

For Benjamin, cinema is a medium that conditions the spectators to be stimulated by urban shocks, in the same way that machines accustom workers to respond to jolts, and that the traffic signals or escalators regulate the movements of the crowd:

> In a film, perception conditioned by shock [*chockförmige Wahrnehmung*] was established as a formal principle. What determines the rhythm of production on a conveyor belt is the same thing that underlies the rhythm of reception in the film.[92]

In Perec and Queysanne's film, the character is a city dweller who often goes to the cinema. Although he is conditioned to experience shocks, his indifference is not permanent, his gestures resist the mechanical monotony of his conditioning and his solitude makes him vulnerable to anguish. By rejecting others, wallowing in solitude and repeating the same gestures that nobody imposed on him, he weaves the threads of his misfortune and feeds his anxiety. Refusing to blame society, the narrator takes a critical look at the character's behaviour: 'Combien de fois as-tu refait les mêmes gestes mutilés, les mêmes trajets qui ne conduisent jamais nulle part?' [How many times have you repeated the same mangled gestures, the same itineraries that never lead you anywhere?]. In the last chapters, the rise of anxiety in the character's behaviour is rendered through visual, sound and textual effects. Evoking Baudelaire's poem 'Les Petites Vieilles', Perec's text in 'Les Monstres' highlights the character's anxious experience of the urban crowd that is full of 'monstres aux gestes mécaniques' [monsters with mechanical gestures]. Compared to monsters, people appear to

91 See Baudelaire's poem 'Les Petites Vieilles' which highlights the impact of urban shocks on the gestures of passers-by. The chapter 'Les Monstres' in which Perec and Queysanne film old ladies on several occasions evokes Baudelaire's poem as well as Agnès Varda's Parisian films such as *L'Opéra Mouffe* (*Diary of a Pregnant Woman*, 1958; see Figure 1.21).

92 Benjamin, 'On Some Motifs in Baudelaire', p. 328.

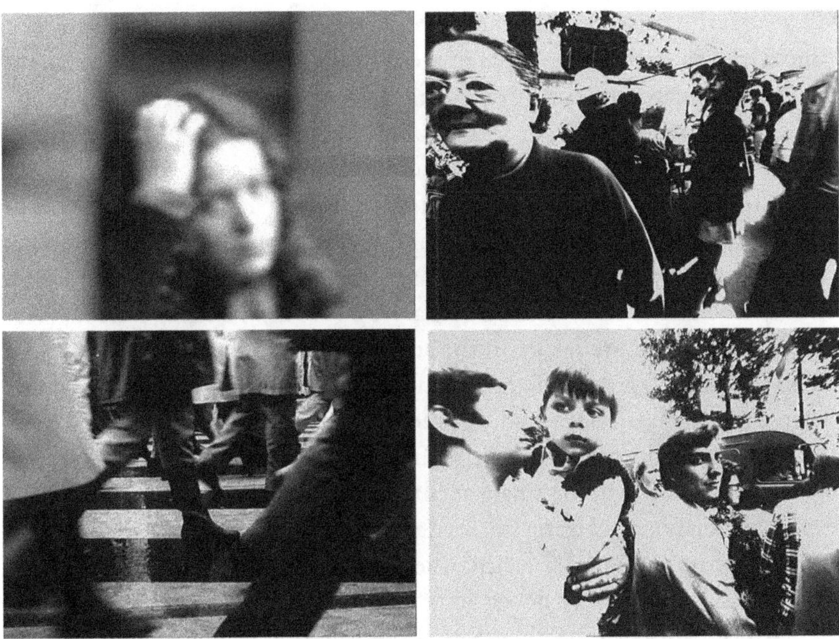

Figures 1.20–1.23. *Un homme qui dort*: Perec and Queysanne capture the movement of crowds in the streets of Paris.

have lost their humanity. Like in an expressionistic film, their representation is distorted through the character's subjectivity. Obliterating the upper parts of their bodies in order to emphasise the mechanical aspect of their gait (see Figure 1.22), the camera turns them into a mass of automatons. The experience of shock is amplified by the frenetic movements of the camera, the rhythm of the editing, the highly contrasted black-and-white photography, the expressive intonation of Ludmila Mikaël and the aggressive soundtrack, which artificially and artfully convey the character's anxiety.

However, if we pay attention to the documentary dimension of these images shot in the streets of Paris, people seem neither excluded nor monstrous; their gestures look neither weary ('gestes las de vaincus') nor mechanical ('gestes mécaniques'). Some of them walk alone, while others speak to each other or smile at the camera (see Figure 1.23). In the chapter 'Les

Monstres', the mise-en-scène itself produces shocks. In some shots, the camera movements force people to move, walk rapidly or recoil. The intrusive camera creates the reality of the film by causing and capturing people's spontaneous reactions in the streets. In his essay film *Level Five* (1996), Chris Marker suggests that the camera has the power to provoke actions. For instance, he speculates that, in 1912, inventor Franz Reichelt would have never dared to jump from the first level of the Eiffel Tower with his prototype of parachute, if a camera was not filming his prowess. The camera is compared to a hunter who targets a prey. As Susan Sontag puts it, '[...] there is something predatory in the act of taking a picture.'[93] Although, in *Un homme qui dort*, the camera does not cause tragic actions, its movement triggers reactions in the crowd. People start to become agitated, turn their heads and make gestures of surprise. In *La Vie filmée. 1930–1934* (1975),[94] a documentary made up of amateur films shot in the early 1930s, Perec observes the behaviour of anonymous people who did not know how to react in front of the camera. By feeling the necessity of moving, they perform gestures they would have never done if a camera was not staring at them.

Not only does the aesthetics of shock crack apart the character's routine in *Un homme qui dort*, it also impacts on the spectator's reception of the film. According to Deleuze, cinema – as a spiritual automaton – can produce thoughts in the spectator's mind through shocks: 'It is only when movement becomes automatic that the artistic essence of the image is realised: *producing a shock to thought, communicating vibrations to the cortex, touching the nervous and cerebral system directly.*'[95] During the silent era, Soviet filmmakers, especially Eisenstein, aimed to strike the spectator's mind through the shocks of the editing.[96] As Deleuze explains, the effects

93 Susan Sontag, *On Photography* (Harmondsworth: Penguin, 1979), p. 14.

94 *La Vie filmée: 1930–1934*, dir. by Claude Ventura and Michel Pamart, written by Georges Perec (France Régions 3, 1975). *La Vie filmée* is a series of documentaries which, by using footage of home movies, present the everyday life of French people from 1924 to 1954.

95 Deleuze, *Cinema 2. The Time-Image*, p. 156.

96 In the early 1960s, familiar with Eisenstein's theories, Perec wanted to create a journal, entitled *La Ligne Générale*, to pay tribute to the Soviet director. He also acknowledged Eisenstein's influence on *Un homme qui dort*'s non-linear editing. See Perec, *Entretiens et conférences*, p. 175.

of opposition in Eisenstein's films create a shock that enables the spectator to conceive the totality of the film by unifying its parts. Simultaneously, the emotional power of images stimulates the spectator's subconscious:

> The whole is no longer the logos which unifies the parts, but the drunkenness, the pathos which bathes them and spreads out in them. From this point of view images constitute a malleable mass, a descriptive material loaded with visual and sound features of expression, synchronised or not, zig-zags of forms, elements of action, gestures and profiles, syntactic sequences.[97]

All the expressive elements of the image shape a 'primitive language or thought'.[98] Gestures in particular generate and release the emotional power of a film.

The editing of *Un homme qui dort* is structured according to a formal principle of opposition, which consists in juxtaposing – sometimes in a contradictory way – visual, sound and textual elements. In 'La Destruction', Queysanne and Perec implicitly refer to the end of Eisenstein's *Strike* (1925), in which the violent suppression of a strike is cross-cut with the slaughter of a cow. The two directors inserted a brief shot showing the slaughter of a white horse, filmed by Georges Franju in his famous documentary *Le Sang des Bêtes* (*Blood of the Beasts*, 1949) – a short film that documents the tasks of slaughterers and butchers in the slaughterhouses of Vaugirard and La Villette (see Figure 1.24). A worker shoots down the horse with a captive bolt pistol. The animal abruptly collapses on the ground. The rapidity of the gesture amplifies the violence of the shock. Struck by 'the unfathomable shot of the calves' heads'[99] in *Le Sang des Bêtes*, Kracauer explains the extent to which dreadful images can remain engraved in one's memory: 'The mirror reflections of horror are an end in themselves. As such they beckon the spectator to take them in and thus incorporate into his memory the real face of things too dreadful to be beheld in reality.'[100] In his monograph on Franju, Raymond Durgnat writes that, despite the 'intense experience' provided by *Le Sang des Bêtes*, spectators usually remember the

97 Deleuze, *Cinema 2. The Time-Image*, p. 159.
98 Ibid.
99 Kracauer, *Theory of Film*, p. 305.
100 Ibid., p. 306.

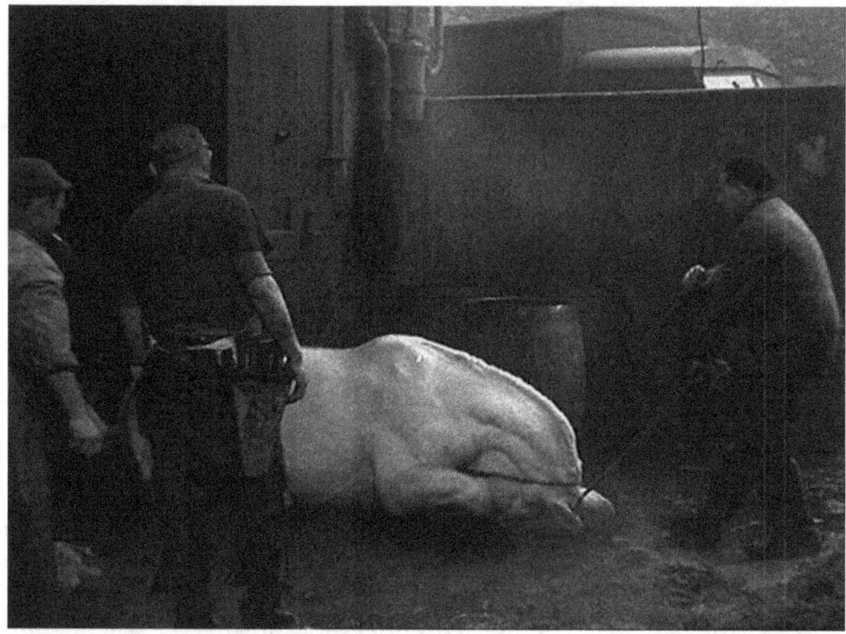

Figure 1.24. *Un homme qui dort; Le Sang des Bêtes*: A worker slaughters a white horse.

film 'in a very abstract way'.[101] They are unable to describe the film in detail, and often remember the death of the white horse, which is 'the film's first shock'.[102] Similarly, in *Histoire(s) du cinema* (1989–99), Godard suggests that if spectators usually forget the ins and outs of the narrative in Hitchcock's films,[103] they remember emblematic objects, such as the glass of milk in *Notorious* (1946) or the hairbrush in *The Wrong Man* (1956). Juxtaposing short clips of Hitchcock's films, Godard's editing highlights the dynamic relationship between object and gesture: a foot knocks over a key in a manhole, a hand grasps a hairbrush or Norman Bates's hand stabs Marion Crane's body. Gestural shocks impact on the spectator's memory

101 Durgnat, *Franju*, p. 34.

102 Ibid.

103 See *Histoire(s) du cinéma*, chapter 4(a) *Le Contrôle de l'univers*.

beyond the narrative context of the film. In this respect, gestures can be potentially decontextualised and interact with the images and gestures of other films, while preserving their emotional intensity.

In the documentary *La Vie filmée*, Perec is aware of the capacity of cinema to archive gestures. Before the invention of film, memory was mainly archived in the form of fossilised images, architectural relics and written documents. By archiving movement and gesture, cinema can amass a memory of ephemeral traces of life. Agamben gives the cinematic gesture the power of liberating the traditional image from its intrinsic immobility.[104] Similarly, in *La Vie filmée*, Perec considers gesture to be the key element that defines the specificity of cinema: the camera can record instants and motions that would have left no mark otherwise. However, Perec notices that the silent pictures are not rich in information. A man opens his mouth and articulates silent sounds, but what is he saying? Who are these anonymous characters moving in front of the camera? In which contexts do people perform their gestures? Information seems to be located somewhere around the image. Due to the lack of context, gestures imbue the silent pictures with indeterminate meanings. These fragile traces of an incomplete memory ceaselessly question the spectator.

Giving the gestures a dreamlike quality, the editing of *Un homme qui dort* juxtaposes fragments of decontextualised gestural sequences. Perec and Queysanne often seem to awaken 'the dream of a gesture', to borrow a phrase from Agamben.[105] In an enigmatic sequence of 'L'Apprentissage', the character, as well as two anonymous men get out of a black Citroën DS, driven by a chauffeur, in the courtyard of a prestigious building (that resembles the Elysée Palace).[106] In accordance with the editing process analysed in the previous section, the same shots are repeated several times, with slight variations. In two different shots, Spiesser's character reads the daily newspaper *Le Monde* and smokes a cigar, in an elegant black suit, before getting out of the car; a man with grey hair, who waves and smiles at the camera as if greeting journalists, and another man, who puts his

104 See Agamben, 'Notes on Gesture', pp. 54–5.

105 Ibid., p. 55.

106 The scene was filmed in the courtyard of the CNRS (Centre national de la recherche scientifique), in Gif-sur-Yvette. See Perec, *Entretiens et conférences*, p. 159.

hat on without looking at the camera, also get out of the black car. The same gesture of opening the car is shown six times, with three different characters. To whom are their gestures addressed? Are these images the last fragments of a memory on the verge of vanishing? Or do they represent a fantasy? The lack of narrative context highlights the indeterminacy of their gestures. As Agamben suggests, gestures can communicate with the spectator beyond their narrative purpose,[107] by expressing emotions, sensations, fantasies, pathologies or taboos. In *Un homme qui dort*, the spectator wonders about the potential meaning of gestures, and, like the first spectators of early silent films, is filled with wonder, confronted with images that escape all preconceived significations and permeate his or her memory.

The indeterminate quality of the silent images is amplified by the directors' refusal to delineate their meaning by the text. Similarly, through the neutral, rational and technical commentary that describes the slaughterers' activities in *Le Sang des bêtes*, Franju refuses to put the emotional shock of gestures into words.[108] According to Agamben, '[…] the gesture is essentially always a gesture of not being able to figure out something in language.'[109] In *Le Sang des bêtes*, gestures communicate something unsaid that cannot be determined by words. Critics often compared Franju's short film with Resnais's *Nuit et Brouillard* (*Night and Fog*, 1956).[110] In the post-war context, the systematic slaughter of animals could evoke – in the collective memory – the mass killings that took place in the concentration camps during the Second World War. Without considering these two realities equivalently, the spectator, with his or her historical knowledge, can reshape the reality depicted in Franju's documentary through his or her imagination, memory and emotions.[111] Kracauer significantly collects the horror of *Le Sang des bêtes* and the Holocaust in the same sentence:

107 Agamben, 'Notes on Gesture', p. 57.

108 See Nina Perivolaropoulou, 'Le Travail de la mémoire: dans *Theory of Film* de Siegfried Kracauer', *Protée*, 32.1 (2004), 39–48 (p. 46).

109 Agamben, 'Notes on Gesture', p. 58.

110 Durgnat, *Franju*, p. 43.

111 See Perivolaropoulou, 'Le Travail de la mémoire', p. 47.

> In experiencing the rows of calves' heads or the litter of tortured human bodies in the films made of the Nazi concentration camps, we redeem horror from its invisibility behind the veils of panic and imagination. And this experience is liberating in as much as it removes a most powerful taboo.[112]

More than a tribute to Eisenstein and Franju, the gesture of *Le Sang des Bêtes* provokes a memory shock that resounds in the last sequences of *Un homme qui dort*. The character's gestures obliquely communicate a taboo that can be approached in the light of Perec's autobiography.

In the Footsteps of Perec's Childhood: The Archives of the City

Written in 1965, *Un homme qui dort* is directly inspired by the depression that Perec experienced in 1956.[113] The slow and difficult emergence of his autobiographical project followed many byways until the mid-1970s. In the film, the writer left traces of his personal and literary life in the character's room, including the reproduction of the painting *Le Condottière* (*Portrait of a Man, called Condottière*, 1475) by Antonello de Messine, which is a very significant leitmotiv, not to say a signature, in Perec's writing.[114] In many respects, the film takes on a new dimension when gestures are considered in the light of the writer's autobiographical work, which he intensely developed in the first half of the 1970s, with, on the one hand, the unfinished project entitled *Lieux*, and, on the other hand, the publication of *W ou le souvenir d'enfance* (*W or the Memory of Childhood*) in 1975. According to Philippe Lejeune, *Lieux* is the basis of

112 Kracauer, *Theory of Film*, p. 306.

113 See Bellos, *Georges Perec: A Life in Words*, p. 149.

114 In *W ou le souvenir d'enfance*, Perec explains his fascination with the Renaissance portrait which he identifies himself with; like the Condottière (and by coincidence like Jacques Spiesser), the writer has a scar above his upper lip. (See Georges Perec, *W or the Memory of Childhood*, trans. by David Bellos (London: Vintage, 2011), pp. 108–9.) Warren Motte analyses the scar as 'a site of mourning' in Perec's work. (See Warren Motte, 'The Work of Mourning', *Yale French Studies*, 105 (2004), 56–71 (pp. 63–5).)

all the autobiographical work that Perec wrote between 1969 and 1975.[115] The writer planned to write – over the course of twelve years – a book describing twelve Parisian places which had a personal resonance in his life, including the rue Vilin, where he spent the first years of his childhood. Describing a different place each month, he kept his notes in a sealed envelope, sometimes with other documents such as photographs.

The writer's interest in the archive, time, memory and urban change permeates the adaptation of *Un homme qui dort*. Even though Perec had to suspend his work on *Lieux* during the shooting of the film in 1973, all the places were supposed to appear in the film.[116] Cinema is a medium that archives gestures, things and places as they are at the moment of their recording. Considering *Un homme qui dort* as a cinematic appendix of *Lieux* makes it possible to reflect on one of the most elusive aspects of the film: the relationship between gesture and memory. The character wants to forget something that is never explicitly mentioned, but only metaphorically suggested by the representation of his childhood home. Although the character's intention is to condition himself to forget, the reiteration of everyday gestures becomes the driving force of a memory process that highlights Perec's interest in archive images. In the film, gestures embody a living and moving memory of places.

One year after the release of *Un homme qui dort*, Perec published *W ou le souvenir d'enfance* in which he attempts to recollect his childhood memories.[117] His parents, who were both Jewish, got married in 1934. Perec was born in 1936 and grew up at 24 rue Vilin, in the neighbourhood of Ménilmontant, in the twentieth arrondissement. Enlisted in the French army, his father died from a wound incurred in combat in 1940. Deported to Auschwitz in 1943, his mother was murdered in the camps.[118] As Perec

115 Philippe Lejeune, *La Mémoire et l'oblique: Georges Perec autobiographe* (Paris: POL, 1991), p. 146.

116 For instance, Perec and Queysanne shot a picture of the character's hand punching his bus ticket in Place d'Italie. See Perec, *Entretiens et conférences*, p. 161.

117 According to Bellos, '[i]t was during their work on the film of *A Man Asleep* that Perec told Queysanne about his next book, which would be called *W*.' See Bellos, *Georges Perec: A Life in Words*, p. 538.

118 See ibid.

tells in *W ou le souvenir d'enfance*, the Second World War disrupted his life and memory:

> 'I have no childhood memories': I made this assertion with confidence, with almost a kind of defiance. It was nobody's business to press me on this question. It was not a set topic on my syllabus. I was excused: a different history, History with a capital H, had answered the question in my stead: the war, the camps.[119]

From 1969, Perec started to investigate his childhood. Every year, he returned to the street where he grew up in order to meticulously describe it.[120] In Perec's mind, the street remains strongly associated with the Second World War and the deportation of his mother.[121] The street was gradually destroyed in the 1970s and 1980s, creating, for Perec, a necessity to record the memory of the place before its total disappearance. In the final shot of *Un homme qui dort*, the character walks along the rue Vilin. Perec felt the need to create an effect of resonance with his own childhood.[122] In *W ou le souvenir d'enfance*, Perec mentions the shooting of *Un homme qui dort*:

> Rue Vilin
>
> We lived in Paris, in the xxth *arrondissement*, in Rue Vilin. It's a shortish, roughly S-shaped street that leads uphill from Rue des Couronnes to some steep steps giving on to Rue du Transvaal and Rue Olivier Metra (this intersection is one of the last street-level points from which you still have a view over the whole of Paris, and it is where Bernard Queysanne and I filmed the closing shot of *Un Homme qui dort* in July 1973). Today, Rue Vilin has been three-quarters demolished. More than half the houses have been razed, leaving waste ground, pilling up with rubbish, with old cookers and wrecked cars; most of the houses still standing are boarded up.[123]

Perec's memory resurfaces in the ruins of the street. The shots that show the character running in the rubble of demolished buildings were probably

119 Perec, *W or the Memory of Childhood*, p. 6.

120 In the documentary *En remontant la rue Vilin* (1992), Robert Bober tells the relationship between Perec and the rue Vilin.

121 See Perec, *L'Infra-ordinaire* (Paris: Seuil, La Librairie du XXe siècle), pp. 20–1.

122 See Perec, *Entretiens et conférences*, p. 161.

123 Perec, *W or the Memory of Childhood*, p. 47.

filmed in Belleville, close to Ménilmontant. These images could evoke post-war Italian neorealist films, such as Roberto Rossellini's *Germany, Year Zero* (1948), in which the characters live in the ruins of Berlin, performing the most mundane gestures of everyday life in this disaster zone. Ruins can threaten human memory with destruction and cause the loss of the self.[124] In *Un homme qui dort*, the ruins are the abstract expression of the character's memory and, by extension, of Perec's own memory. Overexposed, the ghostly presence of the character disappears in a bright white light that annihilates his gestures and identity. He has to run away from the ruins in order to have a chance to remember and find his sense of self, his humanity, again.

Although such ruins were not caused by war, the trauma of the Second World War is projected onto the ruins of Perec's childhood neighbourhood, where he lived with his parents from 1936 to 1942. In *La Vie filmée*, Perec comments on several pictures shot in 1931 in Ménilmontant, in the streets where he grew up. These images show children playing in the streets and looking into the camera. Describing the capacity of images to awaken buried memories and sensations, Perec imagines that he could have been one of those children. Other images represent large crowds in the boulevard de Ménilmontant. Perec suggests that, perhaps, his father, mother and grandparents are walking among these gesturing crowds. Michel de Certeau argues that places are 'like the presences of diverse absences' since they are haunted by people's gestures and spirit.[125] By capturing the trace of gestures, film can make the memory of a place at a precise moment of its history visible. For Certeau and Luce Giard, '[g]estures are the true archives of the city.'[126] Every day, people make gestures that shape the experience of the city, as well as the history of places. By filming those gestures, the camera records their trace, which would otherwise remain invisible.

124 See Aumont, 'La Traversée des ruines', in *L'Invention de la figure humaine*, ed. by Aumont, pp. 30–1.

125 Certeau, *The Practice of Everyday Life*, trans. by Steven Rendall (Berkeley: University of California Press, 1988), p. 108.

126 Michel de Certeau and Luce Giard, 'Ghosts in the City', in *The Practice of Everyday Life. Volume 2: Living and Cooking*, trans. by Timothy J. Tomasik (Minneapolis: University of Minnesota Press, 1998), p. 141.

The rue Vilin, especially the upper part of the street, became an iconic place in the history of French cinema. This picturesque street of the old Paris was accessible by two famous stairs, the first one between the rue Vilin and the crossroads of the rue Piat, the rue de Transvaal and the rue des Envierges,[127] and the second one between the rue Vilin and the passage Julien-Lacroix. These two stairs appear in numerous films, such as René Guissart's *Ménilmontant* (1936), Jean Cocteau's *Orphée* (*Orpheus*, 1950), Albert Lamorisse's *Le Ballon rouge* (*The Red Balloon*, 1956) or Gene Kelly's *Gigot* (1962). The end of *Un homme qui dort* consists in a long panoramic sequence shot at 540 degrees, which starts at the junction of the rue de Transvaal and the rue Piat, at the top of the stairs (that are not visible on screen). The camera makes a first slow movement at 360 degrees, and films the facades of the rue de Transvaal, the rue des Envierges and the rue Piat, as well as the heights of the rue Vilin. After the completion of the first lap, the camera performs the same circular movement again, and stops when the character crosses the rue Vilin and goes down the stairs leading to the passage Julien-Lacroix. If the first part of the panoramic shot is luminous and enlivened by the silhouettes of a few passers-by and inhabitants, the rue Vilin is conversely reduced to a dark street corner. The shot lasts eight minutes; it was supposed to last at least four more minutes but the laboratory partially destroyed the film.[128] Two long fade-outs made it possible to preserve the fluidity of the panoramic shot,[129] although a part of the film representing the rue Vilin disappeared in the accident, which, in a symbolic way, anticipated the total destruction of the street. Perec and Queysanne film a place, the memory of which is in the process of disappearing.[130] By

127 Coincidentally Queysanne first had the idea to shoot the final shot of *Un homme qui dort* at the junction of the rue Piat and the rue de Transvaal, without knowing that Perec had spent his childhood in this place. (See Bellos, *Georges Perec: A Life in Words*, pp. 528–9.) In 1976, in the television programme *Chemins*, Perec goes down the stairs and walks in the rue Vilin. (See Georges Perec and Viviane Forrester, 'Le Belleville de Georges Perec', *Chemins*, Antenne 2, 22 March 1976.)

128 See Perec, *Entretiens et conférences*, p. 161.

129 Ibid.

130 Bellos recounts that, during the take, a five-year old child suddenly went out of 24 rue Vilin, where Perec had grown up, and ran in the street. Such a scene is not visible, probably because of the partial destruction of the film. See Bellos, *Georges Perec: A Life in Words*, p. 529.

contrast, Lamorisse, in *Le Ballon rouge*, provided a vivid and bustling representation of the neighbourhood, inhabited by the gestures of numerous children. In the final minute of *Un homme qui dort*, life reappears in the background, at the intersection between the passage Julien-Lacroix and the rue des Couronnes, enlivened by the gestures of people in the distance: the character seems to return to the world of the living.

The filmic adaptation of *Un homme qui dort* enabled Perec to archive the fleeting trace of gestures in a changing city. Cities do not change only through the demolition of old buildings and the construction of new neighbourhoods. People also transform the memory of cities, as well as their own memory, through their everyday practices, changes of life and gestures. *Un homme qui dort* is integral part of Perec's autobiographical journey. The character's wanderings mirror Perec's life and personal history. In 1978, Perec continued to reflect on the relationship between places, memory, archive and autobiography in the film *Les Lieux d'une fugue*, which he directed with the cinematographer of *Un homme qui dort*, Bernard Zitzermann. *Les Lieux d'une fugue*, which is a film without any actor, tells the story of the eleven-year-old Perec who ran away from his aunt's home in Paris. Rather than recreating the Paris of the 1940s, Perec filmed the places as they were in the 1970s, by trying to apply the Oulipian constraint of the sestina again. Just like *Un homme qui dort*, the film highlights the difficulty of recollecting, as well as the absent presence of the past. Memory is embodied, and indirectly reenacted by the gestures of passers-by and city-dwellers (including Perec himself) who walk by chance in front of the camera.

Conclusion

First, *Un homme qui dort* explores the relationship between human gestures and the film's body. Everyday gestures mirror the mechanical and automatic features of the cinematic machine. On the one hand, by analogy with the camera, the character turns into an ambulatory automaton who wanders in Paris and simulates gestures of everyday life. On the other hand, by analogy with human consciousness, the film integrates the character's gestures into a memory process. To follow Väliaho's argument, the moving image 'becomes a sort of gesture itself', with its own means of expression: 'The moving image does not simply re-present bodily gestures, poses and movements but, instead, harnesses gestures into its technological positivity by becoming immanent to them in terms of dynamically modulating the body.'[131] As a result, gestures, in their interaction with the various components of the cinematic medium, prove fundamentally intermedial (see Chapter 3).

Secondly, *Un homme qui dort* forms an archive of bodily traces, which are at once fleeting and reiterable. Through the ghostly presence of the character who wanders in the changing urban spaces of Paris, *Un homme qui dort* conveys a spectral memory ('mémoire spectrale'), to borrow Derrida's expression.[132] The film forms an archive of bodily traces, which are at once fleeting and reiterable. The relationship between the archive and gesture in film is paradoxical. The cinematic medium is at once 'an effective way of "preserving" the past' and 'a most efficient way of liquidating traditional forms of memory',[133] as we have seen through Benjamin's analysis of shocks in urban modern life. This paradox is mirrored in the character's trajectory throughout the film. On the one hand, by mimicking the mechanical and automatic features of the cinematic machine, the character conditions his most ordinary gestures in the hope of suppressing his memory. On the other hand, as explained above, the character's gestures are incorporated into a memory process that is activated by the expressive means of cinema.

Discussing 'how gestures can serve as vital indicators of traumatic experience'[134] in Claude Lanzmann's film *Shoah* (1985), Nicholas Chare argues that '[g]esture permits the past to be felt in the present'.[135] As will be

131 Väliaho, *Mapping the Moving Image*, p. 31.

132 Cited in Adolfo Vera, 'Le Cinéma ou l'art de laisser revenir les fantômes: une approche à partir de J. Derrida', *Appareil*, 14 (2014) <https://journals.openedition.org/appareil/2115> [accessed 17 August 2018] (para. 4 of 14).

133 McQuire, *Visions of Modernity*, p. 150.

134 Nicholas Chare, 'Gesture in *Shoah*', in *Gesture and Film*, ed. by Chare and Watkins (London: Routledge, 2017), p. 46 (first publ. in *Journal for Cultural Research*, 19.1 (2015), 30–42).

135 Ibid., p. 49.

explored further in the following chapter that focuses on crucial aspects of performance and film acting, such an understanding of gesture profoundly characterises the aesthetics of Chantal Akerman, who shares with Perec similar preoccupations with memory, Jewishness and everyday gesture.

CHAPTER 2

Gestural Styles and Acting Styles in Chantal Akerman's Domestic Territory

In the context of a reassessment of *la politique des auteurs* by the *Cahiers du cinéma* in the mid-1960s, writer and film critic Claude Ollier argued that the notions of authorship and style cannot be reduced to the repetition of personal themes and obsessions, but rather raise the question of the invention of original forms and/or of the renewal of traditional forms on every level of cinematic creation (image, sound, narration, performance, etc.).[1] Focusing on the example of Jerry Lewis's slapstick comedies, Ollier suggested analysing the extent to which the American actor and director succeeded in the 1950s and 1960s in reinventing the aesthetics of gag popularised in the 1910s and 1920s by filmmakers and actors such as Charlie Chaplin and Buster Keaton. From this perspective, stylistic analysis requires identifying the singularity of an author in relation to the history of forms in which s/he inscribes her/himself. As Meyer Shapiro argues, style involves the creation of forms expressing not only the artist's individuality, but also the common traits of a group, as well as the ideology of a specific period of time:

> Style is, above all, a system of forms with a quality and a meaningful expression through which the personality of the artist and the broad outlook of a group are visible. It is also a vehicle of expression within the group, communicating and fixing

1 Jean-André Fieschi, Jean-Louis Comolli, Michel Mardore, André Téchiné, Gérard Guégan and Claude Ollier, 'Vingt ans après. Le cinéma américain, ses auteurs et notre politique en question', in *La Politique des auteurs: Les textes*, ed. by Antoine de Baecque (Paris: Cahiers du cinéma, 2001), pp. 141–2.

> certain values of religious, social, and moral life through the emotional suggestiveness of forms.[2]

This chapter will examine the extent to which the notions of quality, expression, communication and sociocultural values can be used to describe and analyse the correlation between style and gesture in Chantal Akerma's cinema.

First, gestural styles can be defined as the expression of lifestyles (*styles de vie*). Drawing on numerous thinkers of the nineteenth and twentieth centuries such as Simmel, Mauss, Agamben, or Bourdieu, Marielle Macé discusses the notion of 'stylistique de l'existence' [stylistics of existence] by stressing the relationship between life and style.[3] While the sociological concept of lifestyle has become one of the slogans of consumer society since the 1950s,[4] Macé attempts to re-conceptualise the idea of *style de vie* in a philosophical and interdisciplinary manner. She defines a style as the singular way that shapes a form of life in a collective process of sociocultural and political exchanges.[5] In this sense, a *style de vie* can be regarded as the individual's singular manner of living within society. His or her behaviours, postures, rhythms and gestures are at once collectively shaped and markers of individuation.[6] Even though gestures are socially and culturally shaped, they also bring nuances that singularise the individual.[7]

In the mise-en-scène of a film, the relationship between the character's body and its environment determines the way the actors perform in the space delineated by the director. Individuals have their specific ways of moving and gesturing to comprehend their environments. When actors create their characters, they need to take the coordination between their body image and body schema into consideration. Shaun Gallagher insists on the difference between the body image and the body schema, that is,

2 Meyer Shapiro, *Theory and Philosophy of Art: Style, Artist, and Society* (New York: Georges Brazillier, 1994), p. 51.

3 Macé, *Styles*, p. 25.

4 Ibid, p. 46.

5 Ibid., p. 23.

6 Ibid., p. 255.

7 See Citton, *Gestes d'humanités*, p. 36.

'between a conscious awareness of one's own body and a non-conscious performance of the body'.[8] On the one hand, the awareness of one's body image is at once 'perceptual, cognitive, and emotional'.[9] First, one's body is partially perceived in immediate consciousness; second, it is conceptually constructed through consciousness and intellect; and third, it is affectively and emotionally felt. On the other hand, the body schema supposes a 'non-conscious [and operative] performance of the body', in which '[...] the body acquires a certain organisation or style in its relations with environment':[10] the postures and movements are non-consciously activated – often by habit – by the sensori-motor apparatus. Gallagher insists on the idea that the body schema is the 'style' that gives a shape to the body within a specific environment. In film acting, actors need to construct their character's body image first in order to let their body schema move in the environment of the film.

In Chapter 1, I examined the relation between the character's gestures and the modern environment of Parisian urban spaces through the notions of automation, conditioning, everyday gesture, wandering and memory. This second chapter will explore the concept of gestural style by focusing on three films by Akerman in which the physical and dynamic relationship between the body and domestic spaces structures her mise-en-scène. When the Belgian director performs as an actor in her films, she uses the stylistic features of her body schema and body image in order to mould her characters. In her first short film *Saute ma ville* (*Blow Up My Town*, 1968), the 18-year-old director plays the role of a solitary young woman who blows up her mother's kitchen and herself. In *L'Homme à la valise* (*The Man with the Suitcase*, 1983), Akerman, who 'plays a caricatured version of her own persona rather than her real self',[11] explores issues of gender, borders and isolation. Although they were made sixteen years apart, both films, which

8 Shaun Gallagher, 'Body Image and Body Schema: A Conceptual Clarification', *The Journal of Mind and Behavior*, 7.4 (1986), 541–54 (p. 544).

9 Ibid., p. 546.

10 Ibid., p. 548.

11 Marion Schmid, *Chantal Akerman* (Manchester: Manchester University Press, 2010), p. 74.

are reminiscent of slapstick comedy, present strong similitudes in terms of gestural style.

I will compare Akerman's expressive and slapstick acting style with Delphine Seyrig's iconic performance in *Jeanne Dielman, 23, quai du commerce, 1080 Bruxelles* (1975). This pivotal long feature film in Akerman's career on the daily life of a housewife in Brussels 'epitomise[s] an era with its pressing questions about class, identity, gender and social oppression', Marion Schmid explains.[12] Although both Akerman in *Saute ma ville* and *L'Homme à la valise* and Seyrig in *Jeanne Dielman* act in a similar domestic environment – that is, a flat located in a metropolis – they coordinate their body images and body schemas in opposite ways and develop different acting styles. Whilst Akerman exaggerates the clumsiness of her characters' gestures, Seyrig reiterates routine gestures with a metronomic precision. The difference of acting styles, between the slapstick expressivity and the austere stylisation of gestures, is determined by the characters' reactions to framing and space.

In Akerman's cinema, the environment is always perfectly framed by the camera. The characters move in a rigid grid that conditions their behaviours and gestural styles.[13] When Deleuze analyses Akerman's cinema of the 1970s, he insists on the rigorous stylisation of her actors' bodily movements: 'It is this gest which reacts on the body giving it a hieratism like an austere theatricalization, or rather a "stylization".'[14] In this context, the term stylisation seems to refer to a non-naturalistic style of performance, which simplifies the forms, removes the unnecessary details and sticks to the main traits. Deleuze views Akerman's mise-en-scène as a slow ceremony of theatricalised gestures. Influenced by American experimental cinema and minimalist art in the early 1970s,[15] Akerman directs the actors' movements without letting them make unnecessary or spontaneous gestures. The hieratic style of acting described by Deleuze is particularly visible in Aurore

12 Ibid., p. 32.

13 See Youssef Ishaghpour, 'Le Flux et le cadre: Chantal Akerman', in *Cinéma contemporain: de ce côté du miroir* (Paris : Ed. de la Différence, 1986), pp. 260–1.

14 Deleuze, *Cinema 2. The Time-Image*, p. 196.

15 See Ivone Margulies, *Nothing Happens: Chantal Akerman's Hyperrealist Everyday* (Durham, NC: Duke University Press, 1996), pp. 48–53.

Clément's slow, controlled and steady gestures in *Les Rendez-vous d'Anna* (*The Meetings of Anna*, 1978) and Seyrig's performance in *Jeanne Dielman.*

Drawing on an interview between Akerman and Alain Philippon, Deleuze discusses the limits of the 'the excess of stylization', which results from the mastery of Akerman's framing that tends to dominate the style of acting.[16] Thanks to slapstick, Akerman introduces disorder and chaos in a space and frame that usually structure and regulate the female rhythms and behaviours. As Margulies notes, the slapstick influence helps Akerman subvert her relation to framing: 'Akerman has said that she breaks down her own structural mastery as a filmmaker by the use of different acting styles and personas. These different rhythms (including her own as a performer) counterpoint her dry, minimalist sobriety.'[17] The comic exaggeration enables Akerman to counterbalance the excess of gravity. In *L'Homme à la valise*, Akerman's body image and Charlie Chaplin-like gait, emphasised by the choice of specific clothes, especially the heels and trousers, underlines the slapstick quality of her acting style. At the same time, the tone of the film – close to the tragicomic spirit of *Saute ma ville* – also conveys a strong feeling of uneasiness, oddness and anxiety.

I will first examine the 'making-of' *Autour de 'Jeanne Dielman'* (1975–2004), filmed by Sami Frey during the rehearsals of the shooting of *Jeanne Dielman*, to consider the extent to which the interconnection between *style de vie* and performance in the film reveals the social and ethical construction of gesture. Second, I will analyse Akerman's slapstick acting style in *Saute ma ville* and *L'Homme à la valise*. On the one hand, Akerman's acting style mirrors her characters' rebellions against gender norms. Playing with the stereotype of female hysteria, the actor-filmmaker reflects on the social construction of the female body as well as the performativity of gender. On the other hand, she stages tragic gags that betray her characters' inability to use verbal language and that, ultimately, convey their anxieties and traumas in a way that recalls Perec's oblique approach to autobiography in *Un homme qui dort*. Entering Akerman's room or kitchen makes it possible to trace the genesis of gestures in their relation to sound and image, and

16 Deleuze, *Cinema 2. The Time-Image*, p. 196; see footnote 10, pp. 315–16.

17 Margulies, *Nothing Happens*, p. 166.

to analyse the formal, autobiographical and political strategies that result from their performance.

In Jeanne Dielman's Kitchen: Acting, Directing and the Reason of Gestures

The Creation of Jeanne Dielman: The Housewife and the Star

Made in the context of the feminist movements of the 1970s, *Jeanne Dielman* records the daily life of a housewife in Brussels with meticulousness. Akerman emphasises domestic gestures that have been long underrepresented in film history.[18] The character repeats the same rituals, gestures and tasks every day, such as cooking, cleaning or shopping. While *Jeanne Dielman* – a key film in modern European cinema – has already been extensively analysed, especially by Margulies[19] and Schmid,[20] the 'making-of' *Autour de 'Jeanne Dielman'* has received less critical attention. The 'making-of' provides valuable information on Akerman's creative process as well as on the context of filmmaking.

First, the film crew has the distinctive feature of being composed almost exclusively of women, except for the set designers and one of the assistant directors. From Seyrig's point of view – a leading actor in European auteur cinema as well as a feminist activist – the fact that women hold the key posts – director, cinematographer, sound engineers and assistant directors – changes the practice of filmmaking itself and modifies the relations of power and authority between the filmmaker, the actors and the technicians. The 'making-of' ends with an argument between Seyrig and the other female members of the crew about the working conditions of women in the film industry. The lack of male domination influences the

18 See Schmid, *Chantal Akerman*, p. 37.

19 See *Nothing Happens.*

20 Schmid, *Chantal Akerman*, pp. 32–50.

crew's ways of working, behaving and speaking, and disrupts the conventional hierarchy of traditional shootings.[21]

In the 'making-of', Seyrig is asked by a journalist to elaborate on her feminist views. She believes in the potential of women filmmakers to represent femininity and female stereotypes differently than male filmmakers do. Akerman shares the same conviction, arguing that the form of the films directed by women depends on their ability to express their own language and rhythms.[22] Influenced by Simone de Beauvoir, Seyrig fights against the idea of the predestination of women in patriarchal society and the fabrication of female gender identity from birth. Through the embodiment of Jeanne Dielman, a female character with multiple identities (housewife, mother, widow, prostitute and murderer), the actor reveals her desire to explore the representation of women differently. In her previous films, she performed more stereotypical types of female characters. In a way, Jeanne Dielman appears to be the concentrated image of Seyrig's previous mythical roles, from the widow in Alain Resnais's *Muriel ou le temps d'un retour* (*Muriel, or the Time of Return*, 1963) or the prostitute in Luis Buñuel*'s La Voie Lactée* (*The Milky Way*, 1969) to the fairy in Jacques Demy's *Peau d'Âne* (*Donkey Skin*, 1970) – the perfect housewife being stereotypically known as *une fée du logis* (a home fairy). Quoting Akerman, Margulies notes that '[the director] deliberately chose Seyrig "because she brought with her all the roles of mythical woman that she played until now. The woman in *Marienbad*, the woman in *India Song* …"'[23] Regarded as 'an independent aesthetic object in herself' as well as a star by Susan Sontag,[24] Seyrig was used by Akeman to 'subvert not only naturalism, with its categorical essences

21 Two years after the shooting of *Jeanne Dielman*, Seyrig directed the documentary *Sois belle et tais toi* (*Be Pretty and Shut Up*, 1976–81) which discusses the issue of sexism in the film industry. She interviewed twenty-three actors from different countries.

22 Chantal Akerman, Danièle Dubroux, Thérèse Giraud and Louis Skorecki, 'Entretien avec Chantal Akerman', *Cahiers du cinéma*, July 1977, p. 36.

23 Margulies, *Nothing Happens*, p. 145.

24 See Susan Sontag, 'Muriel ou le temps d'un retour', *Film Quarterly*, 17.2 (1963–4), 23–7 (p. 27).

(The Mother, The Housewife), but also the realist notion of type (individual traits epitomizing some collective configuration)'.[25]

As a result, Seyrig's performance in *Jeanne Dielman* is anti-naturalist. The 'making-of' shows her difficulty of embodying this character devoid of psychology and envisioned by Akerman as a pure moving image. *Jeanne Dielman*'s shooting highlights the decisive question of incarnation in cinema. Embodying 'an existence reduced to pure functioning'[26] is alienating for the character as much as for the actor herself. Akerman's interest in alienation, automation, anxiety, everyday gestures and self-control recalls Perec and Queysanne's *Un Homme qui dort*. Like Seyrig, the actor Jacques Spiesser felt alienated during the shooting, unsettled and exasperated by the lack of invention. However, Seyrig creatively contributes to the performance by reflecting on the reason of her gestures, not so much in their psychological dimension, than in terms of logic, practice, technique, habitus and ethos. The performance of a housewife's everyday gestures involves a level of cultural knowledge, experience, savoir-faire and technical mastery. This constructed image of the housewife raises the question of the construction of gender identity in the performance of gesture, by highlighting how social codes are embedded on the surface of the body.

Decoding Gesture: The Use of Kinesics in the Art of Directing

Filmmakers are the active spectators of their actors' performances. As directors, they have to observe, assess and direct their gestures and movements according to the meaning of the scene. The empirical practice of kinesics, that is, the study of bodily motions in space and in social interaction, is a prerequisite for directing as well as for acting. Filmmakers and actors have to be able to understand the expressive qualities and the cultural codes of gestures. As Warren Buckland explains, '[f]or kinesics, gestures and posture are not simply anatomical movements, but are ideological, because each society prescribes certain expected forms

25 Margulies, *Nothing Happens*, p. 145.
26 Schmid, *Chantal Akerman*, p. 38.

of behaviour over others yet presents that behaviour as natural, to be taken for granted.'[27] This semiotics of gestures is particularly visible in gender differences. Drawing on Ray L. Birdswhistell's works in kinesics, Buckland underlines the significance of the social construction of gender and shows how it is reflected in the way individuals move, behave and dress. The corporeal style, which is singular in its expressive qualities, is rooted in sociocultural patterns.

Maxine Sheets-Johnston insists on the 'intimate connection between style and quality'[28] in relation to bodily movement: '[...] *style* is originarily a matter of the qualitative structures of movement.'[29] She adds: 'Each behaviour is distinctively what it is precisely in virtue of its temporal – spatial and energic – quality.'[30] The terms amplitude, magnitude, effort, flux, dynamic variations, straight or curved lines, regularly used by Sheets-Johnston, make it possible to describe the qualities of gestures, not only in arts such as dance or cinema, but also in everyday life. During the rehearsals, Akerman pays close attention to the speed, amplitude and effort of Seyrig's gestures. The quality of her movements shapes the spectator's perception of the character and scene. When Seyrig does not know how to act, Akerman performs the gesture in front of her to indicate the degree of expressiveness she desires. The actor perceives the filmmaker's gesture, assesses it and decodes it. The director and the actor use their bodies to create the character. Following Guillemette Bolens's study on kinesic style, it seems here necessary to distinguish kinesis – which refers to the visio-motor perception of gestures in all their expressive components (amplitude, extension, coordination or speed) – from kinesthesis, which is the sensation of one's own movements.[31] The kinesic style encompasses all the movements that a person

27 Warren Buckland, 'Bodies in Filmic Space: The *Mise en Scène* of "Courtship Readiness" in *The Big Sleep*', *Senses of Cinema*, 66 (2013). <http://sensesofcinema.com/2013/feature-articles/bodies-in-filmic-space-the-mise-en-scene-of-courtship-readiness-in-the-big-sleep/> [accessed 10 May 2017].

28 Maxine Sheets-Johnstone, *The Primacy of Movement* (Amsterdam: J. Benjamins, 2011), p. 137.

29 Ibid., p. 138.

30 Ibid.

31 Bolens, *Le Style des gestes*, pp. 1–2.

A makes in actions that produce meaning both for A and for the person B who observes the gestures. Gestures are a source of perceptions, sensations and thoughts for B, and a way of being, expressing and communicating for A. The notions of kinesis and kinesthesis are useful to analyse the interaction between Akerman and Seyrig during the film rehearsals. They both simulate the character's gestures thanks to the perceptions and sensations they have experienced in their everyday life.

Furthermore, during the rehearsals, Seyrig attempts to communicate feelings in the gestures she has to perform. Whilst Akerman refuses to psychologise Jeanne Dielman's gestures, Seyrig wants to understand the character's interiority. This contradiction often leads to a lack of understanding between the actor and the filmmaker. Seyrig asks questions about Jeanne Dielman's inner life: what does she think when she cooks? What are her secrets? Akerman is often unable to answer these questions. As Schmid writes, she opted for a 'resolutely anti-psychological approach to character construction'.[32] Yet, as James Naremore explains, the actors' urge to express their characters' thoughts is essential in cinema, because the expression of everyday actions differs in film and reality: 'It is wrong to assume that expression in films is equivalent to behaviour in daily life. For one thing, most film actors are acutely sensitive to the purely rhetorical need to make their "thought" visible to the camera.'[33] Even in naturalist cinema, there is 'a degree of ostensiveness that marks it off from quotidian behaviour.'[34] For that reason, Seyrig, who was trained by Tania Balachova as well as by the Actors Studio in New York in the tradition of Stanislavski's acting method,[35] often asks questions about Jeanne Dielman's intentions. From Seyrig's viewpoint, the quality of a gesture is the expression of an intention or feeling.

For instance, the character, before going to bed, does her hair (see Figure 2.1). Akerman asks Seyrig to make slow, regular and long gestures

32 Schmid, *Chantal Akerman*, p. 36.

33 Naremore, *Acting in the Cinema*, pp. 71–2.

34 Ibid., p. 17.

35 See Carmen Fernandez, 'Seyrig, Delphine', in *Le Dictionnaire universel des créatrices*, ed. by Béatrice Didier, Antoinette Fouque and Mireille Calle-Gruber (Paris: Des femmes, A. Fouque, 2013). Ebook.

Figure 2.1. *Jeanne Dielman:* The character combs her hair.

when she combs her hair, rather than the irregular, jerky and hasty ones she made during the rehearsal. The actor asks Akerman to explain the reason of Dielman's gesture: why such pace and rhythm? Instead of explaining, Akerman performs the gesture in front of Seyrig. While the latter attempts to pinpoint the psychological intention of the gesture, Akerman is only interested in the visual quality of expression, that is, in the difference between an abrupt and a slow movement. Unconvinced, Seyrig insists on characterising Dielman's feeling. The director ends up suggesting that the gesture corresponds to a break in the character's day ('un moment de repos'). This indication helps Seyrig qualify the character's thought and inner life: 'Tu veux qu'elle soit plus rêveuse' [You want her to be dreamier], 'elle prend plaisir à ça' [she enjoys it]. In a way, the words *rêveuse* (dreamy) and *plaisir* (pleasure) psychologise Dielman's behaviour and reveal Seyrig's need to understand the character's inner life in order to perform the gesture of combing her hair. Even though Seyrig remains frustrated in her wish to build the character's interiority, she succeeds in influencing Akerman's mise-en-scène by focusing on the technical precision of gestures, rather than on their psychological components.

Ethnic Style, Lost Rituals and Technical Precision

The bodily interactions and verbal exchange between Akerman and Seyrig raise the question of transmission, especially in the domestic framework of the film. The kitchen is traditionally a space in which cultural codes, rites, traditions, cooking practices and specific gestures are taught to women through education and repetition. Cooking is an art of living that requires the learning of techniques and recipes, often transmitted from one generation to another. For example, in *Jeanne Dielman*, Seyrig follows the recipe of Akerman's aunt to prepare Wiener Schnitzel, a traditional Austrian dish made of breaded thin slices of veal or poultry, popular in European Jewish culture.[36] Being 'the first child of Jewish Polish immigrants who settled in Belgium in the late 1930s', Akerman grew up in a Jewish community.[37] As Schmid explains, '[Akerman] has revealed her continuing attachment to Jewish ritual despite the fact that, as she states, she is not a religious person.' She adds that

> [h]er marginal status as a Jew in a predominantly Christian society and her belonging to a minority group of immigrants with distinct cultural customs and traditions fostered in her, from an early age, a sense of alterity and non-belonging, which has crystallised as a major theme in her work.[38]

In *Jeanne Dielman*, Akerman reiterates certain family rituals and cooking traditions, which tended to disappear after the death of her grandfather.[39] As Akerman admitted, her film is imbued with a nostalgia for lost rituals,[40] which she reenacts in collaboration with Seyrig.

In *Gesture and Speech*, Leroi-Gourhan studies the aesthetic dimension of gestures in everyday life, especially the 'aesthetic behaviour'[41] and

36 See Akerman, *Chantal Akerman: Autoportrait en cinéaste* (Paris: Cahiers du cinéma, Centre Pompidou, 2004), p. 23.
37 Schmid, *Chantal Akerman*, p. 2.
38 Ibid., p. 3.
39 Akerman, *Chantal Akerman: Autoportrait en cinéaste*, p. 23.
40 Ibid., p. 24.
41 Leroi-Gourhan, *Gesture and Speech*, p. 271.

'ethnic style'[42] of human beings. The concept of ethnic style highlights the significance of transmission in everyday life: 'The ethnic "tonalities" of certain attitudes, certain gestures of politeness or communication, walking rhythms, dietary and hygienic customs, are transmitted from one generation to the next.'[43] The example of cooking is particularly enlightening. Giard notes that

> [...] the everyday work of cooking seems, in the private sphere, entirely doomed to repetition, a repetition of an archaic structure, a knowledge linked to very ancient social codes, stabilized in old forms of equilibrium, that is, in an obscure and hardly rational medley of preferences, necessities, and received customs.[44]

Yet she observes the revolution of cooking practices in contemporary Western societies on account of the accelerated changes of *styles de vie*. With the development of electrical appliances, some technical gestures sank into oblivion:

> Already, many gestures and processes that were commonplace for my grandmothers' generation, ways of operating that were part of a young girl's normal apprenticeship and of her (average) savoir faire capital, have been erased from common consciousness and no longer subsist except in the childhood memories of certain people [...].[45]

It is no coincidence that Giard starts her chapter on cooking practices by quoting Seyrig sharing her experience in *Jeanne Dielman*. According to the latter, Akerman loved the domestic gestures she was performing, such as 'washing the bathtub, knitting, doing the dishes' because they belonged to 'the world of her childhood'.[46] The filmmaker stands in the position of the 'little girl observing her own mother's gestures, intently and from a certain distance', Margulies writes.[47]

42 Ibid., p. 278.
43 Ibid., p. 277.
44 Giard, 'Gesture Sequences', in *The Practice of Everyday Life. Volume 2: Living & Cooking*, p. 201.
45 Ibid., p. 202.
46 Ibid., p. 199.
47 Margulies, *Nothing Happens*, p. 90.

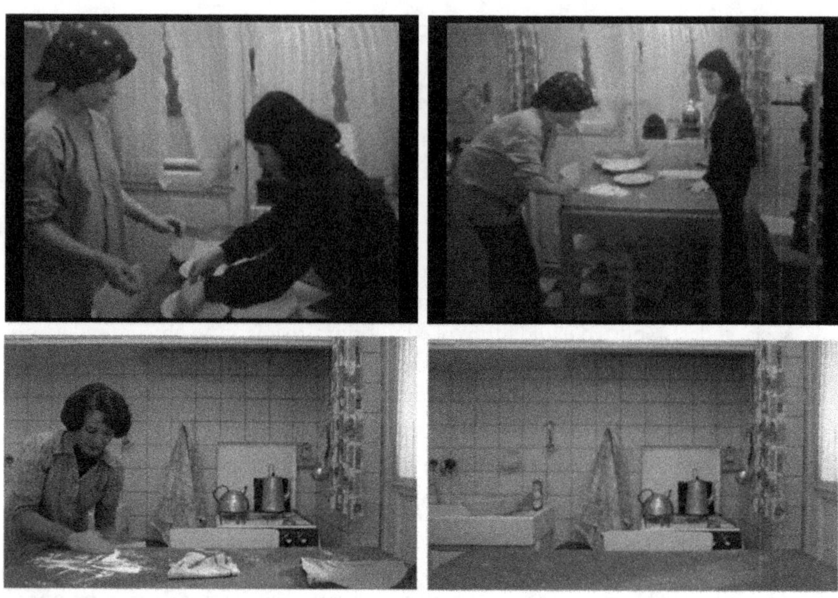

Figures 2.2–2.5. *Autour de 'Jeanne Dielman'*; *Jeanne Dielman*: Akerman shows Seyrig how to prepare the recipe of Wiener Schnitzel (top); the character keeps the leftover of flour and cleans the kitchen table (bottom)

In the 'making-of', the actor and the filmmaker are rehearsing the scene in which Jeanne Dielman prepares Wiener Schnitzel (see Figures 2.2 and 2.3). Seyrig and Akerman discuss every step of the recipe that the director punctiliously wrote in the screenplay, based on the observation of her mother's and aunts' gestures.[48] Akerman describes and slightly mimes her mother's way of cooking. Drawing on her own experience and memories, Seyrig, even if she follows Akerman's instructions, does not hesitate to contradict the young director. Their exchange makes it possible to consider the difference between the performance of everyday gestures in life and in cinema, as well as the nuance between the technical accuracy and the expressiveness of gestures. Giard explains, '[t]he technical gesture, to

48 See *I Don't Belong Anywhere: The Cinema of Chantal Akerman*, dir. by Marianne Lambert (2015).

be distinguished from the expressive gesture that translates a feeling or a reaction, is first defined by its utilitarian aim, its operating intention.'[49] Cinema blurs the distinction between the technical and the expressive gesture. Akerman pays more attention to the manner of doing and to the stylistic qualities of the gesture than to the actual efficacy of the movement. She wants to emphasise the sensual (not the psychological) expressivity of the movement. At the same time, Seyrig is concerned about the technical coherence of her performance. When Seyrig spreads the escalope in the flour, she holds the meat with her fingertips, whilst Akerman incites her to take the escalope in her hand firmly, to feel the sensation of the meat in her hand. Seyrig argues that the technical gesture is not correct: if she uses her fingertips, it is because she needs to cover all the surface of the escalope with flour. The filmmaker and the actor have to negotiate the tension between the technical precision of the gesture and its visual perception, its accuracy and its sensuality. They also express different ways of doing, practising and cooking, because of their own personal experiences and memories that impact deeply on the style of the performance. Interestingly, they often ask the make-up artist Eliane Marcus for advice on the way of cooking and performing in the kitchen, using her experience to strengthen the precision of gestures.

In her essay on film acting, Jacqueline Nacache notes the ambiguity of technical gestures that have become more and more precise in modern cinema, by contrast with the excess of expressiveness in silent cinema. If their exactitude produces an effect of truth, especially when they are filmed in long shots (and thus do not seem to be feigned by the actors), they can consequently reduce film acting to the execution of a repertoire of gestures.[50] Although Seyrig is preoccupied with the technical precision of Jeanne Dielman's gestures, she also attempts to understand the reason of her character's gestures, in accordance with her habitus and ethos as a housewife, in order to avoid performing them in an impersonal way.

49 Giard, 'Gesture Sequences', in *The Practice of Everyday Life*, p. 202.

50 Nacache, *L'Acteur de cinéma*, pp. 58–9.

The Habitus and Ethos of the Housewife

Cinema can reproduce and convey the bodily techniques of a specific cultural and social milieu, which in *Jeanne Dielman* is the Brussels petit bourgeois domestic space. In his famous essay 'Techniques of the Body', Mauss considers the impact of cinema on the construction of female behaviours. He observes that French young women walk in the same way as New York nurses. According to the anthropologist, the only rational explanation of such a phenomenon has to be found in cinema. 'In fact, American walking fashions had begun to arrive over here, thanks to the cinema.'[51] This preliminary observation is the starting point of Mauss's demonstration. He adds: 'This was an idea I could generalise. The positions of the arms and hands while walking form a social idiosyncrasy, they are not simply a product of some purely individual, almost completely psychical arrangements and mechanisms.'[52] With the notion of habitus, he analyses how our bodily techniques are imparted by social practices. Habitus is the corporeal expression of the sociocultural norms, structures and values that shape the way of being of an individual.[53] The social construction of human postures and gestures proves particularly visible in terms of gender differences.

According to Macé, the notion of habitus in Mauss's theory is 'modal', in the sense that it invites anthropologists to study corporeal forms and capacities as well as gestural modes and styles.[54] When Bourdieu develops the concept of habitus in the 1970s, he rather insists on class differences. According to him, habitus is a system that generates 'pratiques classables'[55] [classifiable practices] and makes it possible to classify and differentiate these practices. In Bourdieu's thought, the social indicators (such as rich and poor) and the differences in taste resulting from class differences need to be taken into account in the analysis of those practices. Habitus produces

51 Mauss, 'Techniques of the Body', trans. by Ben Brewster, *Economy and Society*, 2.1 (1973), p. 72.

52 Ibid.

53 Ibid., p. 73.

54 Macé, *Styles*, p. 76.

55 Bourdieu, *La Distinction*, p. 169.

lifestyles, that is, a system of sociologically qualified signs – which can be gendered for instance – visible in the bodily expression of individuals.[56]

During the rehearsals, Seyrig tries to characterise Jeanne Dielman's habitus, both in the modal and sociological sense of the term, and to decode the signs that are embedded in the character's actions, behaviours and gestures.[57] In doing so, she makes suggestions to Akerman, adds new gestures and slightly influences the mise-en-scène. The rehearsal during which Seyrig prepares the Wiener Schnitzel is particularly instructive for two reasons. First, Seyrig concludes that Jeanne Dielman is not a very good cook, since she prepares food in advance. After preparing the breaded escalopes, the character puts them in the fridge, rather than cooking them or serving them immediately, which impacts on the quality of the food. Second, Seyrig pinpoints the character's habit of wasting nothing. When she starts throwing the flour out, she realises that her character, due to her social milieu, would not waste so much flour (see Figure 2.3). Her gesture itself – she tries to put the flour in her hand before throwing it away – reveals to her that what she is doing is irrelevant. Seyrig's attempt to characterise Dielman's habitus enables her to construct the rest of the scene. Indeed, she suggests pouring the egg in a cup to keep it in the fridge, rather than wasting it, and ending the shot on the immaculate kitchen table (see Figures 2.4 and 2.5). Seyrig's suggestions were partially followed by Akerman. The 'making-of' does not show the next steps of the rehearsal, such as the precise timing of the scene. Some gestures certainly changed during that process, as the film in its final version demonstrates.

During the rehearsals, Seyrig, who refuses to be a passive performer, influences the micro (and not the macro) aspects of the mise-en-scène. She does not aim to take control of Akerman's mise-en-scène, but to construct and inhabit her character. Thanks to a good understanding of the housewife's habitus and ethos, she can appropriate her character's gestures and incorporate her personal experience in order to embody Jeanne Dielman. Unlike habitus, ethos refers to a person's moral attitude within a

56 Ibid., p. 170.

57 Regarding the issue of class, it is notable that the actor and the director come from different social backgrounds – whereas Akerman was raised in a lower middle class family, Seyrig grew up in an intellectual milieu.

social group, which can be seen through their way of being and behaving. According to Agamben, gesture in cinema 'opens the sphere of *ethos* as the more proper sphere of that which is human'.[58] Overstepping the binary distinction between gesture as a means to an end and gesture as an end in itself – like dance for instance – Agamben suggests that gesture shows a means without end. In this sense, gesture must not be confused with action and must not be reduced to the finality of an act of production. Gesture reveals itself in its corporeal qualities (such as effort, endurance, dexterity, clumsiness or amplitude) that reflect an individual's moral attitude and ethical relationship with the world and others. I will further discuss the notion of ethos in my analysis of Akerman's slapstick films.

In the Stanislavksi method of acting, actors need to understand and analyse the operative, psychological, moral and social purpose of their characters' actions in order to construct their inner life and give their gestures their true quality. The understanding of the finality of the act (in relation to the broader meaning of the narrative and of the character's trajectory) determines the style of their gestures. In *Jeanne Dielman*, one can observe the reverse. It is the austere, hieratic and rigorous quality of Jeanne Dielman's gestures, imposed by Akerman from the beginning, which enables Seyrig to progressively understand Jeanne Dielman's behaviour and actions and to consequently change specific gestures (such as avoiding wasting food). For Akerman, the style of gestures appears to matter much more than the profound meaning of the action. Deprived of the possibility to internalise Jeanne Dielman's psychology, Seyrig learns how to construct her role gesture after gesture, assimilating her character's habitus and ethos gradually. Strikingly, in *Saute ma ville* and *L'Homme à la valise* Akerman's acting style and her characters' ethos contrast with Seyrig's and Dielman's.

58 Agamben, 'Notes on Gesture', p. 56.

Slapstick Gestures and Tragic Gags

While, during the first two days of the filmic diegesis, Jeanne Dielman reiterates her domestic rituals with the same regularity and exactitude, during the third and last day her routine is gradually disturbed and shows signs of disorder. These mishaps in the character's metronomic routine evoke the aesthetics of Akerman's slapstick films such as *Saute ma ville* and *L'Homme à la valise*. Slapstick is a type of physical comedy that stages the malfunction of the mechanics of gesture, expressing suffering through certain behavioural pathologies. Bergson considers gestures in physical comedy as essentially automatic, mechanical and involuntary. He argues that the body can make people laugh, in a social context, due to its stiffness and marionette-like appearance.[59] By contrast, the intensity of slapstick gestures is seen by Macé as the sign of a corporeal resistance against the pressure of labour and behavioural conditioning.[60]

Stressing the idea of resistance in her study of Akerman's cinema, Jenny Chamarette analyses the performance of carnivalesque and *burlesque* gestures in Akerman's comedy *Demain on déménage* (*Tomorrow We Move*, 2004). Chamarette defines the *burlesque* as an 'intermedial mode',[61] which developed in Vaudeville theatre in Europe and the United States in the nineteenth century, and later in French cinema with Max Linder and in Hollywood with Buster Keaton's, Roscoe 'Fatty' Arbuckle's and Charlie Chaplin's slapstick comedies. The French term *cinéma burlesque*, which is used to describe Jacques Tati's and Pierre Etaix's as well as Chaplin's and Jerry Lewis's comedies, has 'generic relations to slapstick, physical comedy and screwball comedy'.[62]

59 Bergson, *Laughter: An Essay on the Meaning of the Comic*, trans. by Cloudesley Brereton and Fred Rothwell (New York: The Macmillan Company, 1914), pp. 8–9.

60 See Macé, *Styles*, pp. 256–7.

61 Jenny Chamarette, 'Burlesque Gestures and Bodily Attention: Phenomenologies of the Ephemeral in Chantal Akerman', in *Phenomenology and the Future of Film: Rethinking Subjectivity beyond French Cinema* (Basingstoke: Palgrave Macmillan, 2012), p. 156.

62 Ibid., p. 155.

Inspired by Chaplin,[63] Akerman's use of slapstick, which is not necessarily comical, can express an anxious feeling of uneasiness. In her self-portrait *Autoportrait en cinéaste*, Akerman often gives tragic connotations to the term *burlesque* or uses it as a counterpoint to the lexical field of sadness.[64] She also portrays herself as a sad clown.[65] In her discussion of Akerman's *Histoires d'Amérique* (*American Stories: Food, Family and Philosophy*, 1989), Schmid argues that the intersection of 'tragic and comic registers' and the 'juxtaposition of traumatic tale and burlesque performance' are bound to Akerman's Jewishness: 'As Akerman explains in *Autoportrait*, sadness and laughter are inseparably linked in Jewish culture and Jewish humour – that oft evoked quintessentially Jewish trait – is directly born out of the horrors of History.'[66]

With the aim of defining the essential features of Akerman's slapstick acting style in *Saute ma ville* and *L'Homme à la valise*, I will first analyse the revival of slapstick in the context of the post-New Wave. The notions of self-representation, tragic gags and crisis of authorship are crucial to understand Akerman's slapstick films, as well as other post-New Wave films.

The Revival of Slapstick in Post-New Wave Cinema

In *The Time-Image*, Deleuze analyses the New Wave and post-New Wave cinema in terms of body representation. He contextualises the New Wave in the framework of 'the cinema of bodies'[67] which emerged in the late 1950s and 1960s with John Cassavetes, Michelangelo Antonioni and Andy Warhol. The New Wave filmmakers explore the intense relationship between the characters' bodies and their environment by theatricalising their everyday gestures, attitudes and postures. The characters are

63 See Chantal Akerman and Elisabeth Lebovici, 'Losing Everything that Made You a Slave', in *Chantal Akerman: Too Far, Too Close*, ed. by Dieter Roelstraete and Anders Kreuger (Antwerpen: Ludion and M HKA, 2012), p. 98.

64 See Akerman, *Chantal Akerman: Autoportrait en cinéaste*, pp. 76–9.

65 Ibid., p. 29.

66 Schmid, *Chantal Akerman*, p. 91.

67 Deleuze, *Cinema 2. The Time-Image*, p. 196.

constantly moving in spaces that modulate their gestural styles. They are running, falling, bumping into each other and closely interacting with all the tangible elements of the setting. Hence the parallel that Deleuze draws between the New Wave and slapstick cinema.[68] This preoccupation with space and gesture was already at the centre of Eric Rohmer's first major article, 'Le Cinéma, art de l'espace', published in the late 1940s in *La Revue du cinéma*, which examines the specificity of gesture in cinema and, more particularly, the spatial language of slapstick comedy. In the space and frame of a film, the expressive lines of the body shape what Rohmer calls 'a "cineplastic" of gesture'.[69] He considers the relationship between body and space as the driving force of cinematic expression, and slapstick comedy as the paradigm of such a relation.

The confrontation between the character's body and the world lies at the heart of the New Wave filmmakers' cinematic research, influenced by American behaviourism, Keaton's cinema and Rossellini's neorealism. As Douchet explains very well, the New Wave directors organise the stylistic and narrative principles of their mise-en-scène from the characters' roaming in space. The finality of their actions matters less than the expression of their moral attitude.[70] The street becomes the New Wave's most emblematic space. The physical relationship between the character and the world is mostly expressed in urban environments open to encounters, chance, accidents and surprises.

Emerging from the mid-1960s, the post-New Wave, in line with the New Wave, focuses on the ritualisation of gestures and the violent coordination of attitudes and postures. According to Deleuze,

> [t]he post-new wave will continually work and invent in these directions: the attitudes and postures of the body, the valorizing of what happens on the ground or in bed, the speed and violence of co-ordination, the ceremony or theatre of cinema which is revealed […][71]

68 Ibid., p. 315.

69 Rohmer, *The Taste for Beauty*, trans. by Carol Volk (Cambridge: Cambridge University Press, 1989), p. 20.

70 Douchet, *Nouvelle Vague*, p. 153.

71 Deleuze, *Cinema 2. The Time-Image*, p. 195.

Deleuze is aware of the limits of the 'cinema of bodies', which, in some cases, highlights the everyday life of marginal characters to the point of wallowing in blandness, unjustified physical violence or pathological behaviours.[72] Some post-New Wave filmmakers critically examine these pitfalls and stereotypes. In Perec and Queysanne's *Un Homme qui dort*, the character's excessive quest for solitude, as we have seen in Chapter 1, is undermined by the critical distance emerging from the interconnection between the voice-over and the image. Thanks to the editing and the post-synchronisation of the soundtrack, the actor's bodily movements are incorporated into a network of signs that highlight the polysemy of his gestures. In the last part of the film, through camerawork, editing and sound effects, Perec and Queysanne develop an aesthetic of shock which produces metaphors on conditioning, alienation, self-destruction and memory. Other directors choose to embody their critical discourse in the actor's body itself. Drawing on the codes of slapstick comedy, Akerman, Godard, Moullet, Cavalier and Tanner give prominence to bodily expressivity in order to negotiate the notions of marginality, violent gestures and/or pathological behaviours.

Etymologically, the term slapstick (which originates from the clapper (*battacio*), a percussive instrument used in *commedia dell' arte*) refers to two wooden slats used to create a loud noise and exaggerate comically the physical violence of the actors' gestures. In this genre of comedy, laughter is profoundly associated with pain, suffering and even death as the idiom 'dying laughing' (*mourir de rire*) indicates. Muriel Andrin, who analyses 'the darker side of an apparent joyful genre,' insists on the 'extreme violence' of the tradition of slapstick which, in Hollywood, emphasises the mechanics of gestures in the context of American industrialised society.[73] Hyperbolic, emphatic, excessive and destructive, the comedians' gestures evoke the behaviours of hysterical patients. Andrin explains that '[...] the burlesque character, soiled, disfigured, deprived of its physical and moral integrity, embodies the disintegration of the self'.[74] Such a description relevantly

72 Ibid., p. 196.

73 Muriel Andrin, 'Back to the "Slap". Slapstick's Hyperbolic Gesture and the Rhetoric of Violence', in *Slapstick Comedy*, ed. by Tom Paulus and Rob King (New York: Routledge, 2010), p. 227.

74 Ibid., p. 230.

characterises the slapstick aesthetics in post-New Wave cinema – although the slapstick is often much more discreet than in classical Hollywood cinema and sometimes appears in a few scenes of a film only.[75] Post-New Wave filmmakers do not necessarily aim to pay tribute to classical Hollywood slapstick comedy. They refashion some essential features of the genre in a personal and/or political way.

Samuel Beckett and Alan Schneider's short experimental film entitled *Film* (1965), starring Buster Keaton, is emblematic of the renewal of the slapstick tradition. The old man played by Keaton hides his face, turns his back to the camera, walks along the walls, avoids the look of others and cloisters himself in a room. His body is less a body that provokes laughter than a body that suffers. The actor's physical presence in the cinematic space reveals his problematic relationship to the world and others. Likewise, the issues of marginalisation and solitude, as well as the tension between interior and exterior spaces are often central in post-New Wave films.

In traditional slapstick comedies, actor-directors such as Keaton and Chaplin usually represent their characters' bodies in difficult positions. Their bodies are tested in their ability to withstand shocks and to get back on their feet. Their relation to power, but also their authority, is put to the test. Similarly, when Akerman, Godard, Moullet and Cavalier play themselves in front of the camera in films that intertwine social and political considerations with autofictional or autobiographical preoccupations, their suffering bodies occupy a central position. For example, in *Anatomie d'un rapport* (*Anatomy of a Relationship*, 1976), Moullet and his partner Antonietta Pizzorno reflect on the sexuality of a heterosexual couple. In a very humorous way, Moullet performs the crisis of the post-New Wave male author, at a time when feminist discourses developed in post-May 1968 society thanks to the Mouvement de Libération des Femmes (Women's Liberation Movement) and challenged gender stereotypes in cinema. Moullet's manner of considering women, sexuality and cinema

75 Bergala considers Tati's and Godard's slapstick style as being 'erratique' [erratic] and 'discret' [discreet], two adjectives which can more broadly qualify the revival of slapstick in post-New Wave cinema. See Alain Bergala, *Godard-Tati, un burlesque erratique et discret*, online video recording, Cinémathèque française, 30 April 2009, <http://www.cinematheque.fr/video/132.html> [accessed 16 April 2017].

is directly called into question. His character's sexual frustration gives the film its slapstick tonality.

The slapstick influence becomes symptomatic of the crisis of authorship that emerged in the late 1960s. In Jacques Tati's *Playtime* (1967), Monsieur Hulot roams and disappears within the anonymity of the crowd. Several extras wear his clothes, move and gesture in the same way as he does. His perfectly identifiable style loses its singularity in the modern world of consumer society and mass tourism. In this capitalist and technocratic environment, the author's identity and originality appear to be vulnerable and, even worse, are threatened with dissolution. One year later, the most emblematic author of the New Wave decided to disappear of his own free will and to occupy a marginalised position in the film industry in order to reflect on the politics of image and sound: 'In 1968, after a decade of influential and prolific filmmaking, Jean-Luc Godard disappeared from view,' as Colin McCabe writes, adding that '[h]e disappeared by refusing to make films as he had done before'.[76] Breaking with his image of New Wave author, Godard started to shoot militant films with Jean-Pierre Gorin and the Dziga Vertov Group. The act of shooting becomes the framework for a sociopolitical deconstruction. In *Vladimir et Rosa* (*Vladimir and Rosa*, 1970), the political discourse and the cinematographic language are deconstructed and disrupted by the irruption of slapstick comedy, evoking the Marx Brothers, the Three Stooges and the Keystone Cops.[77] In the opening sequence, the filmmakers associate slapstick with political protests: three cops violently beat some demonstrators with exaggeratedly large wooden sticks. Godard performs the role of an 'idiot', a character he will embody again in the particular context of the 1980s (Chapter 3 will discuss more extensively Godard's crisis of authorship in *Prénom Carmen*).

Finally, in *Ce Répondeur ne prend pas de message* (*This Answering Service Takes No Messages*, 1979), Cavalier grieves the death of his wife and attempts to exorcise his pain. He covers his head with bandages, like a badly burned

76 MacCabe, *Godard: Images, Sounds, Politics*, p. 18.

77 See Federico Rossin, 'Marx au grand magasin. L'idiotie et le burlesque dans les films du groupe Dziga Vertov', trans. by Jean-Pierre Cometti and Andrea Paganini, *Vertigo*, 40 (2011), 73–9.

person or a casualty of war.[78] Despite its desperate and self-destructive tone, the film is not devoid of dark humour. The filmmaker's relation to objects and to the space of the building in which he cloisters himself is a source of tragic gags. For instance, Cavalier tries to melt soap on the hotplate of his kitchen (in an explicit reference to the Holocaust),[79] rings the doorbell of his absent neighbours, breaks down the door of a *chambre de bonne* or paints the windowpanes of his flat in black. Jean Cocteau coined the notion of tragic gag to characterise Buñuel's surrealistic inventions in *L'Âge d'or* (*The Golden Age*, 1930).[80] In Cavalier's film, the tragic gags produce metaphors about his difficulty in communicating his traumatic experience of mourning. Gesture becomes a means to overcome the loss of meaning of words and images.

According to Agamben, gesture is a gag in the sense that it expresses the impossibility of communicating something through verbal language. The gag 'indicates first of all something put in someone's mouth to keep him from speaking and, then, the actor's improvisation to make up for an impossibility of speaking'.[81] This obstruction of language leads the actors to use their body as a medium of expression. The paralysis of language is central in Akerman's cinema. In *Saute ma ville* and *L'Homme à la valise*, she films the painful (and sometimes playful) interaction of the character's body with the domestic space, as well as with the opposite sex.

78 Alain Cavalier and Jean-Louis Jeannelle, 'Alain Cavalier: le filmeur, la caméra et le spectateur', *Itinéraires*, 4 (2009), 175–91. <https://journals.openedition.org/itineraires/1282> [accessed 17 August 2018].

79 Ibid.

80 See Pierre Kast, 'Une fonction de constat. Notes sur l'œuvre de Buñuel', *Cahiers du cinéma*, December 1951, p. 11.

81 Giorgio Agamben, 'Kommerell, or On Gesture', in *Potentialities: Collected Essays in Philosophy*, ed. and trans. by Daniel Heller-Roazen (Stanford: Stanford University Press, 1999), p. 78.

Subverting the Domestic Space in Akerman's Slapstick Cinema: Ethos and Acting Style

The resurgence of slapstick in modern cinema is rooted in the political and sociocultural evolutions of post-war Western society. Instead of simply paying tribute to the genre, Tati – and, to a lesser extent, Godard – refashions it to scrutinise the mutation of behaviours in modern society.[82] As for Akerman, she delineates a specific territory: the kitchen, and more broadly the domestic space. In *Saute ma ville*, made in her mother's kitchen in November 1968, Akerman pictures herself as a clumsy young woman resisting and subverting the conventional rhythms assimilated by women in patriarchal society. Her character disrupts the tasks that are conventionally associated with women, such as cooking or cleaning.

When Akerman describes herself as 'a female Charlie Chaplin',[83] she does not intend to pastiche Chaplin, but to construct a sense of slapstick based on feminine rhythms, gestures and postures. Her reference to Chaplin seems to reveal a lack of great slapstick female actors in the history of film. Slapstick comedy is a genre that is unquestionably dominated by male stars. The great authors like Chaplin, Keaton or Tati are also the leading actors and main characters of their films. Known for his expertise on slapstick, Peter Král argues that women are essentially incompatible with this genre of comedy: in short, he explains that women, especially when they are beautiful, are simply not funny.[84] His essentialist and misogynist view that mostly focuses on beauty standards does not offer a convincing study of the role of women in slapstick comedy, especially as he omits to mention the first major female slapstick Hollywood star Mabel Normand. In early film history, Alice Guy-Blaché also made *burlesque* films that show the (often-under exploited) comic potential of women, such as *Madame a des envies* (*Madam's Cravings*, 1906) that focuses on the subjective experience of a pregnant woman.

82 See Bergala, *Godard-Tati, un burlesque erratique et discret.*

83 Akerman and Lebovici, 'Losing Everything that Made You a Slave', p. 98.

84 Peter Král, *Le Burlesque ou morale de la tarte à la crème* (Paris: Stock, 1984), p. 321.

Significantly, the French New Wave revitalised the representation of the female body, sometimes by drawing on the codes of slapstick comedy, for instance, in Godard's films starring Anna Karina. Michel Marie, who underlines the 'fantasy and spontaneity' of Karina's acting style, notes: 'Godard returned to a certain Hollywood tradition, a close partnership between director and actress. They renewed the model established between Mack Sennett and Mabel Normand, Charlie Chaplin and Paulette Godard.'[85] Akerman's singularity consists in refashioning certain features of slapstick as a filmmaker and as an actor. Her position of author enables her to film her body according to her own desires, rhythms and preoccupations.

Akerman considers *Saute ma ville*, in which she invades her mother's kitchen and subverts all the domestic tasks that are supposed to be done by women, as 'the opposite of *Jeanne Dielman*: the story of a girl who talks back to her mother, who explodes the norms that confine women to womanly tasks, who breaks everything in the kitchen and does everything in a crooked way.'[86] Her style of acting is highly expressive. Her exaggerated gestures, gait, attitudes and postures convey 'the mocking, chaotic and self-annihilating subjectivity of a young woman'[87] as well as expressing the character's inner impulses on the surface of the body. When she frenetically polishes her shoes with very large and imprecise gestures to the point

Figures 2.6–2.7. *Jeanne Dielman; Saute ma ville*: Jeanne Dielman and Akerman's character perform the same action in contrasting ways.

85 Marie, *The French New Wave*, pp. 122–4.

86 Akerman and Lebovici, 'Losing Everything that Made You a Slave', pp. 97–8.

87 Chamarette, *Phenomenology and the Future of Film*, p. 143.

of blackening her legs, she certainly aims to disrupt the bodily techniques her parents imparted to her, and that Seyrig reenacts in *Jeanne Dielman*. When Jeanne Dielman polishes her son's shoes, she stands straight and makes only necessary gestures in a rigorous manner. Although their actions are similar, the visual perception of the characters' ethos is fundamentally contrasted. While Jeanne Dielman's gestures manifest an excessive need for control and exactitude, Akerman's bodily movements are clumsy and self-aggressive (see Figures 2.6 and 2.7). In *L'Homme à la valise*, Akerman still makes hasty and large gestures that prove inadequate to the tasks she has to do; for example, she drops the lid of the tea jar by trying to open it with a spoon. She voluntarily insists on her lack of bodily coordination in order to create visual gags.

In interviews, Akerman has often highlighted the clumsiness and the lack of efficiency of her gestures. Her clumsiness is the mark of her nonconventional *style de vie* that conveys class and gender tensions in normative society, therefore contradicting the two requirements theorised by Mauss: tradition and efficiency. There is indeed a correlation between Akerman's gestural style in life and her acting style:

> My body is very important in a movie, it says something by itself; it has the weight of the Real. I can't have actresses playing my clumsiness. It seems impossible for me to be in a restaurant without knocking something over – my gestures are too large, or I'm pursuing my thoughts and get startled. You're out of convention with your own body, with your own way of moving. When I was a child, and being raised in such a conventional bourgeois high school, I thought it was a question of class, I attributed my non-conformity to the fact that I was a Jew. I didn't attribute it to gender then, but I realised later that the other girls were already built to fit what a young woman was raised to become, in conformity with their future as women in a normative society.[88]

The filmmaker became aware of the weight of conventions and norms in the patriarchal educational system, and of their impact on the habitus of young girls. Akerman considers clumsiness as the bodily expression of her resistance against the heteronormative behaviours that are imparted to women. The quality of her gestures mirrors a moral attitude, which is indeed subversive. '[…] [F]aire des spaghettis, ça, c'est ni bien ni mal, mais

88 Akerman and Lebovici, 'Losing Everything that Made You a Slave', p. 98.

les manger salement, ça c'est pas très bien' [Cooking spaghetti is neither good nor bad, but being a messy eater is not very good], Akerman writes about her character's behaviour in *Saute ma ville*. She distinguishes the neutrality of the action – her character cooks spaghetti – and her manner of eating – she is a messy eater – insisting, similarly to Agamben, on the intimate interrelation between the style of gesture and the character's ethos.[89]

The Visual and Sound Interplay of Gestures: The Ethics of Gag

Sixteen years after her first short film *Saute ma ville*, Akerman explores the ethical relation to the other in the domestic space of *L'Homme à la valise*, a medium-length film produced by Institut National de l'Audiovisuel (INA) for the French television anthology series 'Télévision de chambre', which includes eleven episodes directed by post-New Wave filmmakers such as Pierre Zucca, Jean-Claude Brisseau, Benoît Jacquot and André Téchiné. In the film, Akerman's character, who is a filmmaker, goes through a personal crisis. After two months of absence, she returns to her flat where Henri (Jeffrey Kime), an acquaintance, has moved in, and to her utter despair, does not intend to move out. As she becomes obsessed with the man's presence, the writing of her new screenplay becomes impossible: she loses the mastery of her language. She tries to avoid him as much as possible and progressively shuts herself away in her bedroom. At the end, her only link with the outside world is a television set connected to a video camera that is filming the street. Structured as a *huis clos*, the film raises the question of the relationship between language and gesture. The character is unable to express her desires through words. She does not succeed in asking the man to move out. Rather than using verbal language in order to communicate with him, she is paralysed and cannot articulate an audible sentence, hence the performance of gags. Recalling *The Great Dictator* (1940), in which Chaplin plays the role of a persecuted Jewish barber living in a country equivalent to Nazi Germany, Akerman

89 See Akerman, *Chantal Akerman: Autoportrait en cinéaste*, pp. 76–7.

questions the relationship between the mute vulnerability of the slapstick gesture and the power of verbal language.

Symbolically, the neurosis strikingly develops in relation to the bathroom (which adjoins the female character's bedroom), a place where sexual differences are expressed in a very intimate way and where the presence of the man loudly resounds. Every day, the noise of the electric razor or his early morning singing and whistling performances disturb her. In the morning of her first day of cohabitation with Henri, she enters the bathroom and sees him standing fully naked near the bathtub. The appearance of male nudity reveals the 'colonisation of the woman's space'[90] by the man's body image. In his sociological analysis of the body image, Paul Schilder has demonstrated how the social and emotional distance between individuals is visible through the interplay between their postural models:

> It is clear that social distance is partly concerned with the question of how near to ourselves we want to have the body of the other person concerned, and that the whole conception of social distance gets its real meaning only when we consider the postural model of the body in its relations to the postural model of the bodies of others.[91]

From the beginning of *L'Homme à la valise*, Akerman's character tries to create a distance between her own body image and the man's body image, which are diametrically opposite to one another.

Akerman has voluntarily underlined the visual contrast between the two characters, in terms of gender, height, behaviour, clothing or manner. Such strong oppositions appear to create irreconcilable differences. The man's efforts to interact or communicate are systematically denied by the woman's behaviour and postures. She avoids eye contact, turns her back on him and answers to his questions by briefly saying 'non'. At the beginning of the film, the configuration of the flat and, by extension, the female character's relation to her own territory symbolically changes when she realises she will have to share her flat with Henri. She decides to move the desk

90 Schmid, *Chantal Akerman*, p. 76.

91 Paul Schilder, *The Image and Appearance of the Human Body: Studies in the Constructive Energies of the Psyche* (New York: International Universities Press, 1950), pp. 242–3.

from the living room (where the man sleeps) to her bedroom. He makes slight movements towards her, showing his intention to help her, which she ignores. Their bodies are desynchronised in terms of tempo and rhythm. He strides, but moves slowly; she walks fast, but takes small steps. They get in each other's way and their bodies bump into one another. When the man stops following her and stands in the corridor, the frame cuts his head and gives a truncated image of his body, partly obliterated by the woman's refusal to look at him or, at least, to acknowledge his presence. As Maurice Merleau-Ponty writes, gestures, in order to make any form of communication possible between individuals, need to be intentionally reciprocal:

> The communication or comprehension of gestures comes about through the reciprocity of my intentions and the gestures of others, of my gestures and intentions discernible in the conduct of other people. It is as if the other person's intention inhabited my body and mine his. The gesture which I witness outlines an intentional object.[92]

In *L'Homme à la valise*, the two characters' gestures clearly lack reciprocity. Although she rejects the man's intentions, those intentions nevertheless inhabit her body. Indeed, she moves, behaves and gestures in reaction to his presence, and also to his movements. For example, she speeds up in the corridor when the man tries to catch her up. Their two postural schemas are in discord, but respond to each other.

The female character's 'paranoid sensibility'[93] structures her problematic relation with the other. Rather than considering Henri as someone to discover, she attempts to reduce him to a surface, a predictable routine and a familiar stereotype, to the point of constructing a reversed image of herself. Drawing on her experience of screenwriting, Akerman's character notes all the steps of Henri's daily routine on a big sheet of paper. She unsuccessfully attempts to predict his actions from the sounds his gestures make (at what time he wakes up, goes to the bathroom or leaves the flat). The sounds disrupt the perception of Henri's monolithic image. While she tries to control Henri's life, her own daily routine becomes structured by

92 Maurice Merleau-Ponty, *Phenomenology of Perception*, trans. by Colin Smith (New York: Routledge, 2005), p. 215.

93 Margulies, *Nothing Happens*, p. 164.

the man's presence or absence. All the sounds that he produces symbolically modulate her postures and impact on her rhythms. She often stands in a posture of listening, orienting her body towards the source of the noises. As Roland Barthes explains in his essay entitled 'Listening', noises crucially shape our perception of space. Barthes focuses on the domestic space which, similar to an animal territory, is saturated with familiar sounds ('differentiated slamming of doors, raised voices, kitchen noises', and so on).[94] Like animals on the lookout, human beings are sensitive to unfamiliar noises that invade their (domestic) territory. In *L'Homme à la valise*, the female character's body is tense when, keeping Henri under close surveillance, she listens to the noises he makes. If the man's body resounds through space and time, it also resounds within her. As a result, gestures need to be considered not only in their visual but also aural qualities.

When analysing Tati's *Playtime*, Bolens notes how the audience is often encouraged to investigate the source of a sound irrupting in an image, at first non-identified. The complex relationship between the sound and the movement that produces it stimulates the spectators' kinesic intelligence[95] and can shape their perception of space. Spreading through time and space, sound transcends the boundaries of the visible and the invisible, and can draw the characters' as well as the spectators' attention towards the off-camera space.[96]

In cinema, the acoustics of gesture also structures the perception of time. In *L'Homme à la valise*, the division of the narrative in twenty-eight days highlights the weight of time in Akerman's mise-en-scène. This film belongs to the modernist tradition of 'ritualised cinema', defined by Michel Chion as a genre which, by limiting dialogue, 'frees the ear and allows to hear how sounds and movement organise time'.[97] Margulies compares the use of off-screen sound in *L'Homme à la valise* to Bresson's *Un condamné*

94 Roland Barthes, 'Listening', in *The Responsability of Forms: Critical Essays on Music, Art, and Representation*, trans. by Richard Howard (Berkeley: University of California Press, 1991), p. 246.

95 See Bolens, *Le Style des gestes*, pp. 131–2.

96 See Véronique Campan, *L'Ecoute filmique: Echo du son en image* (Saint-Denis: Presses universitaires de Vincennes, 1999), p. 74.

97 Chion, *Film, a Sound Art*, p. 111.

à mort s'est échappé (*A Man Escaped*, 1956), a cornerstone of ritualised cinema.[98] While attempting to dismantle his wooden cell door with a spoon, a prisoner, named Fontaine, carefully listens to the movements of the guards who are patrolling. Being on the watch for any suspicious noises, he performs slow, cautious and irregular gestures. The effort of the process, combined with the necessity to hear the slightest noise that resonates in the corridor, creates a tension between the on-screen and off-screen actions and between the prisoner's and the guards' gestures. 'There is a dynamic correlation between the body producing the sound and the body of someone listening to the sound,' Martine Huvenne notes about Bresson's film.[99] She adds: 'The more I listen to the details in the sound, the more I am able to experience and to replay his movements and gestures in my own body.'[100]

However, pinpointing the source of a sound can be a complex exercise. As Chion argues, there is often a certain degree of 'indeterminacy' and mystery in acousmatic sounds (i.e. the sounds one can hear without seeing their source).[101] For example, while Akerman's character starts brushing her teeth in the bathroom, she carefully listens to the noises her flatmate is making (see Figure 2.8). These sounds, which have a metallic and irritating resonance, are indeterminate and thus stimulate the character's '*acousmatic* imaginary',[102] which involves not only the inner simulation of the action but also a process of interpretation and speculation: the 'motor image'[103] generated by the sound does not necessarily correspond to the reality of the performed gesture. Because her attention is focused towards the off-camera space, her gestures are particularly slow. She delicately grabs the tube of toothpaste and puts it down without making the slightest noise. Then she slowly gets closer and leans her ear against the door (see Figure 2.9). When the man moves in the corridor, she shudders, quickly moves back

98 Margulies, *Nothing Happens*, p. 164.

99 Martine Huvenne, 'Sound in Film as an Inner Movement. Towards embodied Listening Strategies', in *Moving Imagination: Explorations of Gesture and Inner Movement*, ed. by Helena De Preester (Amsterdam: John Benjamins, 2013), p. 141.

100 Ibid., p. 142.

101 Chion, *Film, a Sound Art*, p. 39.

102 Ibid.

103 See Huvenne, 'Sound in Film as an Inner Movement', pp. 141–2.

Figures 2.8–2.9. *L'Homme à la valise*: The character brushes her teeth and leans her ear against the bathroom door.

to the washbasin, turns on the tap and very energetically brushes her teeth. By making a lot of noise, she wants to be heard by the man, and thus to appear normal. Disturbed by the silence in the off-camera space, she slows down her gesture as well as the flow of water. The man knocks on the door and offers to buy something for her at the bakery. She refuses and tries to hear his reaction. She moves closer to the door once more while the man is leaving the flat. In this quiet environment, the two characters' worlds are permeable, despite the spatial separation. The sounds circulate and resonate from one room to another. One can listen and be heard. Their sonic bodies co-exist in an anxious choreography that plays with the acousmatic imaginary of the characters and of the spectator. The resonance of the man's movements through space affects the woman's gestures, especially in terms of speed, rhythm and coordination. Jennifer M. Barker defines a sonic body, not as a body that makes sound, but as a body that 'resounds',[104] thus following Jean-Luc Nancy who writes: 'Resonance is at once that of a body that is sonorous for itself and resonance of sonority in a listening body that, itself, resounds as it listens.'[105] When the sound propagates in space, it resounds within and outside the body.

104 Jennifer M. Barker, 'Sonic Bodies. Listening as Acting', in *Theorizing Film Acting*, ed. by Aaron Taylor (New York: Routledge, 2013), p. 252.

105 Jean-Luc Nancy, *Listening*, trans. by Charlotte Mandell (New York: Fordham University Press, 2007), p. 56.

Slapstick Tragedy

Hysteria

In *L'Homme à la valise*, Akerman's slapstick style of acting appears in the way she acts 'the symptoms stereotypically associated with female hysteria',[106] such as nervous breakdown, bulimia or emotional dependence. These symptoms produce gestures and postures, which are stereotypically viewed as 'theatrical'. Rae Beth Gordon has demonstrated the strong relationship between pathologies, including hysteria, and slapstick performance. In her essay *Why the French Love Jerry Lewis*, she analyses the influence of hysteria on early French comedy, and more broadly on slapstick cinema. At the end of the nineteenth century, the hysterical gesture and gait, popularised in the press, were imitated by performers in cabaret and early films:

> Gestural exaggeration is an hysterical trait because the *expression* of desire is an absolute need for hysterics. At the same time, it earned them the label of 'theatrical'. Corporeal anomalies, along with automatic, repeated gestures, tics, grimaces, and contractures, characterise the pathologised body at the centre of performance style in cabaret and early film comedy.[107]

For example, the permeability between the hysterical behaviour, studied by the neurologist Jean-Martin Charcot at the Pitié-Salpétrière Hospital, and the slapstick performance is strikingly visible in the short film *Good Night, Nurse!* (1918) in which Roscoe 'Fatty' Arbuckle and Buster Keaton imitate the disordered gestures of a nymphomaniac female patient (see Figures 2.10 and 2.11). Hysteria deregulates bodily rhythms and thus provokes arrhythmia, which is, according to Lefebvre, symptomatic of a pathological trouble.[108] Arrhythmia is an essential stylistic feature of slapstick comedy – a genre that celebrates the catastrophe of gestures and exalts the fall of bodies. Naremore underlines the 'exaggerated forms

106 Schmid, *Chantal Akerman*, p. 78.

107 Rae Beth Gordon, *Why the French Love Jerry Lewis: From Cabaret to Early Cinema* (Stanford: Stanford University Press, 2001), p. 22.

108 Henri Lefebvre, *Eléments de rythmanalyse* (Paris: Syllepse, 1992), p. 62.

Figures 2.10–2.11. *Good Night, Nurse!*: Roscoe 'Fatty' Arbuckle, alongside Buster Keaton, imitates the gestures of a nymphomaniac female patient.

of *bodily* incoherence'[109] in comedy, while Didi-Huberman, drawing on Bergson, describes the comic gesture as a 'compulsive-arrhythmic' one ('geste compulsif-arythmique')[110] that is irregular and unpredictable. Král insists on the idea that the actors' slightest gestures reveal a malaise at the root of several pathologies, such as anxiety, bulimia or frenzy.[111] The nightmarish quality of slapstick comedy always feeds on reality, everydayness and ordinary objects. The irrationality results from the inner impulses expressed on the surface of the body itself.

As a filmmaker and actor, Akerman disrupts the everyday order through arrhythmic gestures. While obscurity grows in *L'Homme à la valise* until total darkness, she develops several gags, constructed on very ordinary situations, which reveal the character's impulsive temperament and the irrationality of her relationship with the man. For example, after realising she forgot her key, she decides to enter the flat by passing through the window of the kitchen, rather than ringing the bell and letting Henri open the door. Furthermore, the first and last breakfast she shares with him highlights the way the filmmaker plays on arrhythmic gestures. The female character's movements are weary, listless and weak in terms of amplitude,

109 Naremore, *Acting in the Cinema*, p. 76.

110 Georges Didi-Huberman, *Le Danseur des solitudes* (Paris: Minuit, 2006), p. 92.

111 Král, *Le Burlesque ou la morale de la tarte à la crème*, p. 119.

while the male character makes large and dynamic gestures, noisily grabbing all the objects on the table and eating with appetite. Disturbed in her routine, she becomes more and more withdrawn, and looks in the opposite direction, as if she wanted to turn her back on him. Finally, she suddenly leaves the dining room by knocking over the chair. The arrhythmic interaction between the man and the woman escalates in this impulsive and antagonistic gesture, which explicitly expresses her deep anxiety and her urge to exit the room.

In feminist theory, hysteria has been reconsidered as the symptom of the impossibility for women to access their own language. Therefore, they are condemned to imitate the masculine language. According to Luce Irigaray, the hysterical woman is imprisoned in her own body. She has two modes of expression: muteness and mimetism. Irigaray explains:

> Hysteria: it *speaks* in the mode of a paralysed gestural faculty, of an impossible and also a forbidden speech … It speaks as *symptoms* of an 'it can't speak to or about itself' … And the drama of hysteria is that it is inserted schizotically between that gestural system, that desire paralyzed and enclosed within its body, and a language that it has learned in the family, in school, in society, which is in no way continuous with – nor, certainly, a metaphor for – the 'movements' of its desire. Both mutism and mimicry are then left to hysteria. Hysteria is silent and at the same time it mimes.[112]

In *L'Homme à la valise*, hysteria generates gags. The character played by Akerman is unable to express her desires through words. Rather than communicating verbally with the man peer to peer, she is paralysed and cannot articulate an audible sentence. She attempts several times to talk to Henri by whispering through the bathroom door. When, for the first time, Akerman's character expresses her dissatisfaction, the noise of the electric razor symbolically covers her speech, which Henri therefore cannot hear. Facing the powerlessness of her words, she furiously kicks the man's shoes in the corridor, miming what she cannot say out loud.

112 Luce Irigaray, *This Sex Which Is Not One*, trans. by Catherine Porter (Ithaca, NY: Cornell University Press, 1985), pp. 136–7.

Gestures of Exile

The anxiety that is conveyed in Akerman's slapstick performance exceeds the question of gender differences. Akerman belongs to the second generation of Holocaust survivors. The taboo of her mother's deportation to Auschwitz, which was never mentioned during Akerman's childhood, deeply impacted her whole work.[113] In her last film *No Home Movie* (2015), she asks questions to her mother about the Second World War. Although Akerman's very close relationship to her mother, as well as the trauma of the Holocaust, have been frequently evoked in interviews, books, radio programmes or video installations,[114] *No Home Movie* conveys the matrix of her work for the first time in the form of a film. The central figure of the mother, the trauma of the Shoah and the meticulous exploration of the domestic space converge like a self-evident fact. Until *No Home Movie*, she kept these recurrent issues at a distance through fiction or by implicitly expressing them through the muteness of gestures. Although, at first glance, nothing in *L'Homme à la valise* appears to be reminiscent of the Second World War, Schmid interprets the character's isolation in such a perspective: 'Her room resembles a watch-tower or a prison cell, the character's self-imposed confinement evoking the concentrationary universe which is present in so many of Akerman's films independent of their tone and style.'[115] Akerman insists on the thematic relationship between borders and the concentration camps in her films:

> My obsession with borders comes from the camps. When you touch on that limit – and I touched it very closely through my mother, who was in the camps but was never able to talk through her anxiety – this border becomes the source of anxiety, it becomes an 'anxious Abject'. [116]

113 Schmid, *Chantal Akerman*, p. 2.

114 See Chantal Akerman, *Marcher à côté de ses lacets dans un frigidaire vide*, installation (*Walking Next to One's Shoelaces in an Empty Fridge*, 2004); Chantal Akerman, Philippe Langlois and Franck Smith, 'Marcher à côté de ses lacets dans un frigidaire vide', *Atelier de Création Radiophonique*, France Culture, 9 March 2008.

115 Schmid, *Chantal Akerman*, p. 77.

116 Akerman and Lebovici, 'Losing Everything that Made You a Slave', p. 96.

> If I put myself into a kind of a prisoner situation, it is because my mother passed that along to me.[117]

A border can be geopolitical, as in *De l'autre côté* (*From the Other Side*, 2002) – a documentary examining the physical frontier between the United States and Mexico – or domestic, as in *L'Homme à la valise* wherein the dividing walls of the flat can be viewed as borders separating the woman's territory from the man's. The anxiety generated by the traumatic experience of the camps is passed down from the first to the second generation[118] and conveyed in Akerman's film through a double conflict: on the one hand, the character has difficulty writing and, on the other, interacting with the opposite sex. Although the mother figure is absent from the film, Akerman's inability to cut the umbilical cord could be considered, from a psychoanalytical perspective, through the gender conflict that opposes the female character to Henri. As Irigaray suggests,

> [a] woman, if she cannot in one way or another recuperate her first object, i.e. the possibility of keeping her earliest libidinal attachments by displacing them, is always exiled from herself. Yet, it is very difficult for her to find in her relationship with men the means for overcoming that loss of the first relationship with the mother's body.[119]

The rejection of the man's presence, which is felt as a source of invasion, conflict and oppression, could be interpreted in relation to Akerman's refusal to distance herself from the primary attachment with her mother, hence the filmmaker's self-portrait as a woman in exile and a prisoner reenacting the experience of the 'anxious Abject', that is, Auschwitz. Akerman admits herself: 'The only person I didn't succeed in making that split with was my mother, because she was a camp survivor, and I was born when she was older, in 1950. I still think of myself as an old child …'[120]

117 Ibid., p. 103.

118 The process of transmission of traumatic experiences from one generation to another has been analysed by Marianne Hirsch in her seminal article on postmemory. See Hirsch, 'The Generation of Postmemory', *Poetics Today*, 29.1 (2008), 103–28.

119 Luce Irigaray, 'Women's Exile', trans. by Couze Venn, *Ideology and Consciousness*, 1 (1977), 62–76 (p. 76).

120 Akerman and Lebovici, 'Losing Everything that Made You a Slave', p. 98.

Similarly, Ishaghpour highlights the significance of Akerman's Jewish identity to explain the very strong relationship with her mother, as well as the nomadic imprisonment of the filmmaker Anna – Akerman's fictive double in *Les Rendez-vous d'Anna*.[121] The notion of exile, at the core of Akerman's filmography, is conveyed through the compulsive repetition of similar rituals, actions, postures and gestures from one film to another, such as eating, writing or waiting. The motifs are repeated, ruminated or more exactly *ressassés*. In 2004, in the self-portrait she published on the occasion of the Centre Georges Pompidou retrospective, Akerman describes herself as a 'ressasseuse', and considers her life and work as a long 'ressassement'.[122] The word refers to the idea of obsessively brooding over the same words, stories, ideas or potentially traumatic memories. The theme of *ressassement* has been analysed by Schmid who aims 'to capture the dynamics of *ressassement*'[123] in Akerman's work, and Hannah Mowat who also analyses the processes of repetition in her films.[124] In order to expand the reflection on the notion, it can be argued that Akerman's *ressassement* in her films is also gestural.

In the essay 'Le Geste ressassant', Bernard Vouilloux analyses the meaning of *ressassement* in the literary work of Maurice Blanchot. In 1983, by reworking the Freudian concept of repetition compulsion, the writer revisited some of his texts published before the Second World War, to retrospectively reconsider them in the light of the 'absolute' event – Auschwitz and the concentrations camps – which haunts post-war society.[125] Similarly, Akerman's work cannot escape the absolute event – an event that preceded her birth, but that she diffusely broods over in a creative process of postmemory. Vouilloux attempts to develop the notion of *ressassement* in the visual arts, as well as in music, and wonders whether it

121 Ishaghpour, *Cinéma contemporain*, p. 264.

122 Akerman, *Chantal Akerman: Autoportrait en cinéaste*, p. 9.

123 Schmid, *Chantal Akerman*, p. 13.

124 Hannah Mowat, 'Gesture and the *cinéaste*: Akerman/Agamben, Varda/Warburg' (unpublished doctoral thesis, University of Cambridge, Trinity Hall, 2015), pp. 56–68.

125 See Bernard Vouilloux, 'Le Geste ressassant', in *Le Geste, suivi de Le Geste ressassant* (Brussels: Lettre volée, 2001), pp. 48–9.

is possible to *ressasser* – a word which essentially relates to verbal repetition – through gestures. Painting being a spatial art, the temporal dimension of the *ressassement* is visible in the creative process of production that reveals the repetitive and obsessive nature of the artist's gesture, for example, through the numerous sketches that culminate in the painting. The idea of *ressassement* is especially visible in the lines and strokes that the artist continuously applies to the surface. The artwork that results from the *geste ressassant* records the different layers of the creative process, sometimes to the point of becoming confused.

In the light of Vouilloux's essay, the *geste ressassant* appears to be fundamental in Akerman's work, especially in *L'Homme à la valise.* The act of rumination does not only develop itself by the everyday repetition of the same gestures, but especially in relation to her previous works such as *Saute ma ville, Je, tu, il, elle* (*I You He She*, 1974), *Jeanne Dielman* or *Les Rendez-vous d'Anna*, and even to her future ones, like *Golden Eighties* (1986).[126] Akerman's gestures in *L'Homme à la valise* are rooted in the temporal continuity of her filmography. Gesture in cinema incorporates time – past and future – into the actor's body. As Deleuze explains, the body in cinema does not exist in present time, but integrates what comes before and after each phase of movement; the embodiment of time is particularly visible in the everyday attitudes of fatigue and waiting:

> The daily attitude is what puts the before and after into the body, time into the body, the body as a revealer of the deadline. [...] Perhaps tiredness is the first and last attitude, because it simultaneously contains the before and the after [...][127]

As a source of impatience, stress, impulsivity and self-awareness, time puts pressure on the body and generates gestures. The pressure of time on the body is forceful in situations of boredom. At the end of *L'Homme à la valise*, while Akerman is waiting for Henri after he left the flat, she is disconcerted, does not know what to do and cannot work. Waiting leads to boredom and fatigue. She paces up and down the corridor with her

126 Schmid analyses the references to *Les Années 80* (*The Eighties*, 1983) and *Golden Eighties* (1986), in *Chantal Akerman*, p. 75.

127 Deleuze, *Cinema 2. The Time-Image*, p. 189.

right hand in her pocket, smokes and sometimes leans against the wall and looks at her feet. She seems to be drawn by the ground and the walls, as if the weight of time makes her body heavier to the point of changing its relation to gravity. The weariness of her body makes all the transitional movements – 'the before' and 'the after' – perceptible.

Through *ressassement*, the character's gestures link the past and the future of Akerman's cinema. As Margulies points out, Akerman's tics in *L'Homme à la valise* 'replicate, in a comic register, the ideas that inform her films in general'[128] through the agency of the filmmaker's body. The character's compulsive gestures are often related to the act of eating, as exemplified by the scene when she voraciously eats Henri's ratatouille in secret. Interestingly, Mowat draws a parallel between *ressassement* and mastication.[129] As Margulies explains, food and the act of writing reveal the paradox of Akerman's domestic exile:

> The issues here, as in *Meetings with Anna*, are those of nomadism and celibacy. Discussing Franz Kafka, Gilles Deleuze and Félix Guattari explore nomadism in terms of a complex articulation of relations to food and to writing. By this scheme, food is linked to a fixed place, that of planting and harvest, and territorialisation connotes an attachment to family and to conservative values. Conversely, writing – the use of language, and the creative act – results in exile, a deterritorialisation from social conventions (though not all writing is necessarily deterritorialised).[130]

Food, as a marker of territorialisation, is often associated with patriarchal values in Akerman's cinema. For instance, in a scene of *Les Rendez-vous d'Anna*, the main protagonist (Aurore Clément), who travels across Europe and stays in hotels, sees a food tray and male black shoes on the ground, near one of the hotel room doors. She bends over, squats and slowly manipulates the shoes which, like in *Jeanne Dielman*, are symbolical of the patriarchal order, before compulsively eating the peas in the plate (see Figure 2.13). With uprooting arises the anxious feeling of the loss of the self. Food appears to reveal the need to survive and the urge to regain, through gestures, the lost rites that structure the affective and

128 Margulies, *Nothing Happens*, p. 165.

129 Mowat, 'Gesture and the *cinéaste*', p. 67.

130 Margulies, *Nothing Happens*, p. 164.

nostalgic relation to home. There is a close relationship in Akerman's cinema between the act of feeding and the practice of filmmaking; or, in other words, a tension between her characters' biological and affective needs and the mechanical and technological process of filmmaking which can potentially be dehumanising. When Akerman voraciously eats spaghetti in *Saute ma ville* (see Figure 2.12) or the pack of sugar in *Je, tu, il, elle* (see Figure 2.14), her gestures are regressive: she bends over her plate or eats on her bed, in an impulse of retreat from the outside world.

In the last part of *L'Homme à la valise*, before cloistering herself inside her room, she orders food, as if she was preparing for survival, including ten bags of frozen spinach, two green salads, four cans of green peas and a gas camping stove. A few shots show her in the dark, as though in a cave, eating on her bed (see Figure 2.15), next to the television set, which she has connected to her video camera in order to watch the street and keep an eye on Henri going back and forth. The high-angle shot highlights the grid pattern of the street as a place of surveillance. Paradoxically, the television set, like a window, opens the room onto the outside world, but it is a mediated and framed world without any horizon, which reflects the

Figures 2.12–2.15. *Saute ma ville; Les Rendez-vous d'Anna; Je, tu, il, elle; L'Homme à la valise*: The repetition of the act of eating in Akerman's films.

filmmaker's own entrapment and marginality as she essentially remains in the liminal border of the frame. Akerman has placed a stack of film reels on the television set, thus highlighting the metacinematic meaning of the scene. Indeed, the shot thematises Akerman's complex relationship with cinema. The picture within the picture – and frame within the frame – shows the sociocultural and historical divide between the interior space, which confines women to domestic tasks, and the public sphere of the street, which is a territory traditionally occupied by men. When she touches the screen, tracking Henri as he crosses the street, Akerman seems to reflect on her practice of filmmaking and conditioning as a woman filmmaker, showing how her aesthetics is rooted in her personal history as well as in her phenomenological and sociocultural experience of the world. Strikingly, *L'Homme à la valise* anticipates her essay film entitled *Là-bas* (*Down There*, 2004), shot in Israel, where the same tension between inside and outside, food and filmmaking can be observed, and where Akerman broods over her 'condition as an exile and a Jew'.[131]

Conclusion

The concept of gestural style shows the proximity and difference between the aesthetics of gesture in life and in film. This is best exemplified in the female characters' clumsy gestures in *Saute ma ville* and *L'Homme à la valise* that evoke and exaggerate Akerman's clumsiness in her daily life. Throughout her filmography, the Belgian director develops acting styles that are stylised or exaggeratedly expressive rather than naturalistic. In cinema, even a 'natural' manner of acting amplifies certain stylistic features of the body schema and body image. Imbued with specific sociocultural markers, the 'natural' gestural style of an actor is shaped by specific acting techniques.

That being said, the difference between gestural styles in life and in film often proves to be a matter of nuances or degrees, as the discussion

131 Schmid, *Chantal Akerman*, p. 123.

about the technical accuracy and the expressiveness of gestures in *Jeanne Dielman* shows. Beyond their differences, acting styles and *styles de vie* both entail the subject's performance, either in the context of a film or in the framework of domestic life for instance. The notions of ethnic style, aesthetic behaviour, habitus, gender identity and ethos are useful to analyse gestural styles in terms of performance, corporeal modalities and social distinction. As will be discussed in Chapter 5, the inscription of gesture in a specific territory, which is mostly domestic in the films examined in this chapter, highlights the tension between collective and individual modes of performance. In the social, cultural, political and ideological grid of the domestic territory, Jeanne Dielman and the characters played by Akerman do not behave, react and gesture in the same manner.

Just as in Perec and Queysanne's *Un homme qui dort*, the analysis of Akerman's films reveals a crisis of the everyday. The characters' needs for daily rituals and predictable gestures convey their anxiety. The aesthetics of violence and (self)destruction result from a gestural *ressassement*, which imbues daily routine with psychotic repetition, obsessive constraints and disruption. The mechanical performance of everyday gestures eventually goes wrong to the point of announcing a catastrophe in the making. The ruins of Paris in *Un homme qui dort* echo the final scene of *Saute ma ville*, in which the character commits suicide by turning on the gas stove: the explosion of the kitchen is rendered through sound effects evoking war. In Akerman's cinema, slapstick amplifies the catastrophe of gestures through gags, extreme behaviours and bodily disorders. The frame of daily routine is threatened with imbalance and destruction. In Perec's and Akerman's works, the themes of repetition and *ressassement*, gesture and automatism, rituals and obsessive behaviours are reminiscent of the historical disaster and family tragedies of the Second World War.

Finally, gestural styles develop and produce cinematic forms. The aural and visual qualities of gesture must be considered in relation to the style of mise-en-scène, especially in terms of framing, sound and editing. Focusing on Godard's *Prénom Carmen*, the next chapter examines the correlation between gesture and film aesthetics further. Similarly to Akerman in *L'Homme à la valise*, Godard portrays himself as a filmmaker in crisis. He identifies himself not only with Chaplin but also with Buster Keaton, another major master of slapstick comedy.[132] Unlike the paternalistic director embodied by François Truffaut in *La Nuit américaine* (*Day for Night*, 1973), Godard goes through a crisis of authority. Far from showing himself in a position of strength, he performs a vulnerable character. Self-representation becomes a strategy to critically reflect on his own practice of filmmaking. Reaffirming the primacy of gestures in cinema, Godard draws on silent cinema, Beethoven and Rodin to reflect on the gestural ontology of the audiovisual image and reveal the intermedial potential of gestures in cinema.

132 In the film, the character played by Godard holds Robert Benayoun's book *Le Regard de Buster Keaton* (1982).

CHAPTER 3

Gesture, Image and Intermediality in Jean-Luc Godard's *Prénom Carmen* (*First Name: Carmen*, 1983)

After a decade of militancy and exploring the possibilities of video, Jean-Luc Godard returned to cinema in the late 1970s. According to Colin McCabe, Godard started with *Sauve qui peut (la vie)* (*Every Man for Himself*, 1980) 'a postmodern survival course', working with small crews and focusing on 'the questions of art, sexuality, and politics'.[1] Jean-Louis Leutrat adds, '[t]he work of the 1980s can only be evaluated in the light of everything that preceded it.'[2] This period in Godard's cinema is often considered a return to the great masters of art history, myths and, to a certain extent, the New Wave. Like Leutrat,[3] Laura Mulvey sees a strong connection between *Prénom Carmen* (1983), a free adaptation into contemporary France of Prosper Mérimée's tragic short story *Carmen* (1845), and *Pierrot le fou* (1965), which 'was already a version of the Carmen story'.[4] Yet the rewriting of the Carmen story emphasises the gap that separates the New Wave and Godard's post-New Wave long feature films. The commonalities between his 1960s and 1980s films paradoxically highlight the discrepancies between the two periods. In

1 Colin McCabe, 'Jean-Luc Godard. A Life in Seven Episodes (to Date)', in *Jean-Luc Godard: Son + Image, 1974–1991*, ed. by Raymond Bellour and Mary Lea Bandy (New York: The Museum of Modern Art, 1992), pp. 20–1.

2 Jean-Louis Leutrat, 'The Declension', in *Jean-Luc Godard: Son + Image, 1974–1991*, ed. by Bellour and Bandy, p. 23.

3 See ibid.

4 Laura Mulvey, 'The Hole and the Zero. The Janus Face of the Feminine in Godard', in *Jean-Luc Godard: Son + Image, 1974–1991*, ed. by Bellour and Bandy, p. 84.

this sense, Guy Scarpetta is right to note the difference of tone between *Pierrot le fou* and *Prénom Carmen*. The horizon of Carmen and Joseph's story is no longer utopia and dream, but manipulation, ratios of power, domination, lies and ploys.[5]

While robbing a bank with her gang, Carmen (Maruschka Detmers) falls in love with the watchman Joseph (Jacques Bonnaffé). Manipulating Uncle Jean (also named Monsieur Godard and performed by Godard himself), a retired filmmaker living in an asylum, she plans to use the shooting of a film as a ploy to kidnap a rich industrialist. Godard parodies himself as an author in crisis, interned like Jean-Pierre Mocky, another director of his generation. Godard stylises his own body image by insisting on a few recognisable traits – the slightly bent silhouette, a persona lost in his thoughts with a somewhat unkempt appearance – and on iconic objects – his black coat, the black-rimmed glasses, the woolly hat, the cigars, the typewriter and the books.[6] In the meantime, Joseph's fiancée Claire (Myriem Roussel) rehearses Beethoven's string quartets with the Prat Quartet.

When *Prénom Carmen* was released in 1983, Godard predicted that '[...] the cinema and [himself might] die at the same time'.[7] In the film, the director portrays himself as a powerless author waiting for the end of film history and the survivor of a civilisation of cinema that seems to be on the verge of vanishing.[8] Godard's binding of film history to his own life

5 Guy Scarpetta, 'Docteur, est-ce que l'âme a un corps ?', *Artpress*, January 1985, p. 45.

6 Like Chaplin and his bowler hat, cane and worn clothes or Hitchcock's cameos, the filmmaker creates a perfectly identifiable persona, which in *Prénom Carmen* parodies the authorial image that he constructed in the media. Through specific props, gestures and clothes, he gives an easily identifiable shape, quality and ethos to his body image. Interestingly Cecilia Sayad also compares the 'similar silhouette[s]' of Godard and Woody Allen who met in Godard's *Meetin' WA* (1986). See Cecilia Sayad, *Performing Authorship: Self-inscription and Corporeality in the Cinema* (New York: I.B. Tauris, 2013), p. 111.

7 Jean-Luc Godard and Gideon Bachmann, 'The Carrots are Cooked: A Conversation with Jean-Luc Godard', *Film Quarterly*, 37.3 (1984), 13–19 (p. 19).

8 See Antoine de Baecque, 'Jean-Luc Godard et la critique des temps de l'histoire', *Vingtième Siècle*, 117 (2013), 149–64 <https://www.cairn.info/revue-vingtieme-siecle-revue-d-histoire-2013-1-page-149.htm> [accessed August 2018] (para. 27 and 29 of 51).

cannot be reduced to a merely narcissistic and egocentric posture. The idea of the death of cinema, which proves particularly persistent in Godard's films from the 1980s onwards, alludes to the director's mortality as a human being, the twilight of an historical era defined by capitalism and the end of the cinematic art as it was invented in the nineteenth century.[9] In the 1980s, Godard condemned the power of television, which, according to him, threatens the essence of the cinematic image, by failing to address the spectators as active subjects. The filmmaker, who explored the potential of video and made films for French television in the 1970s and 1980s (see the analysis of *France/tour/détour/deux/enfants* (1977) in Chapter 5),[10] criticises less the medium itself than its use by the audiovisual industry.

Similarly, Ishaghpour denounces the effects of television, which, by eliminating the distance between the image and the audience, do not simulate the latter's faculties of listening, seeing and imagining.[11] Unlike the cinematic screen, which is a surface of projection, video offers a flat surface that is devoid of the imaginary, Ishaghpour argues,[12] while pointing to contemporary cinema's struggle to exist as a distinctive medium.[13] Godard defines cinema as a medium 'which deals in human gestures and actions (unlike painting or music and dance) in their reproduction'.[14] Similarly to Agamben, he considers gesture as the key element that characterises the essence of cinema. However, television, which also reproduces the movement of the human body and exhibits the corporeal qualities of gestures, challenges the medium specificity of cinema. Given that both media share their respective techniques, what is it that fundamentally distinguishes the televised moving image from the cinematic image? Ishaghpour explains that television – especially from the 1980s onwards when the multiplication of channels encouraged the practice of channel hopping – broadcasts

9 Ibid. (para. 32 of 51).

10 Throughout the 1980s, he never stopped experimenting with video and making films for television, including *Soft and Hard* (1985) and *Grandeur et décadence d'un petit commerce de cinéma* (*Rise and Fall of A Small Film Company*, 1986).

11 Ishaghpour, 'La Télévision', in *Cinéma contemporain: De ce côté du miroir*, p. 19.

12 Ibid., p. 24.

13 Ibid., p. 35.

14 Godard and Bachmann, p. 19.

a continuous flow of impersonal and interchangeable images without any aura.[15] By contrast, as I will demonstrate in this chapter, the cinematic image for Godard is not the disembodied product of the technique of mechanical reproduction, but is essentially shaped by the filmmaker's gestures. Ever since the Lumière brothers and Méliès, the filmmakers' hands have formed the history of cinema. The productive relationship between the filmed gestures and the gestures of creation gives birth to the cinematic image. As explained by Marie-José Mondzain, the New Wave contributed to the emancipation of gestures, both in the practice of filmmaking and film acting, changing the spectators' relation to the real and the image, as well as stimulating their imagination.[16]

In *Prénom Carmen*, the gestures of filmmaking are conceived of as an act of resistance. The film reflects on the crucial role of gesture in the creation of cinematic images. The disenchanted criticism of television and, more broadly of the pressure of capitalism in society,[17] is counterbalanced by the filmmaker's attention to the gestures of creation. In this respect, the concept of the death of cinema becomes a productive idea that enables Godard to reaffirm his 'love of the cinema'.[18] While criticising the rising power of television and video which threatens the nature of the image as well as the spectator's imagination, Godard develops intermedial strategies to revitalise the cinematic image. He creates what Deleuze names a 'pluri-dimensional, pictorial and musical gest',[19] weaving a complex network of gestures in order to 'compose' the film, from the rehearsals of the string quartet to the visual and sonic bodily attitudes of the lovers, inspired by Rodin's sculptures. In a fictional world that is at once violent and chaotic, the interplay between Rodin's sculptures and Beethoven's music becomes a source of gestural exchanges that interconnect the scattered fragments of the film while shaping the spectator's perception of the sound and image.

15 Ishaghpour, *Cinéma contemporain*, p. 26.

16 Marie-José Mondzain, *Homo spectator* (Paris: Bayard, 2007), p. 262.

17 The film insistently refers to Godard's militant work of the late 1960s and early 1970s. More than fifteen years after *La Chinoise* (1967), Godard shows himself dwelling on similar political ideas.

18 Godard and Bachmann, p. 15.

19 Deleuze, *Cinema 2. The Time-Image*, p. 195.

As Albertine Fox argues, '*Prénom Carmen* continues the work undertaken in *Sauve qui peut (la vie)* and *Passion* (1982) in its efforts to re-conceptualise notions of the "visible", and the process of "making visible", through the organisation of sound and the activity of listening.'[20] In Godard's cinema, '[s]ound and image are presented as the two autonomous but inseparable "images" of cinema [...].'[21] Indeed, *Prénom Carmen* highlights the relationship between sound and image, between the gestures of music-making and the gestures of filmmaking, and between the act of listening and the act of seeing. As Fox, who refers here to Adorno, suggests, this relationship manifests itself in the choice of Beethoven's late string quartets: 'Whilst Beethoven suffered from drastic hearing loss during the composition of the late quartets, his music possesses "the gift of sight".'[22] Inspired by the relationship between music and image in silent cinema, Godard seeks to restore the capacity of the image to communicate with the spectator through 'non-verbal forms of communication',[23] such as gesture, listening, gaze, rhythm and music. Finally, by developing an analogy between the gestures of performing music, of carving and of filmmaking, Godard invites us to rethink the concept of intermediality from a gestural perspective.

Rethinking the Ontology of Cinema: Gesture, Image, Sound and Music

The philosophers Mondzain and Agamben both see in gesture the essential feature that defines the ontology of cinema, but in different ways. On the one hand, according to Agamben, gesture is the element that forges the medium specificity of cinema. Unlike the traditional arts

20 Albertine Fox, *Godard and Sound: Acoustic Innovation in the Late Films of Jean-Luc Godard* (London: I.B. Tauris, 2018), p. 67.

21 Ibid., p. 57.

22 Ibid., p. 72.

23 Ibid., p. 68.

like painting, the camera mechanically reproduces gesture and releases it from the paralysis of the image. It is in this sense that Agamben argues that, fundamentally, '[t]he element of cinema is gesture and not image.'[24] On the other hand, in contrast to Agamben, Mondzain, who focuses on the gestures of filmmaking rather than only on the filmed gestures, suggests that the notions of gesture and image are closely related. She argues that, similarly to the traditional still image, the cinematic image is crafted by human hands, and not only by the technology of mechanical reproduction.[25]

In the essay *Homo Spectator*, Mondzain emphasises the gestural dimension of the image in a way that is relevant to the understanding of Godard's cinema of the 1980s. She conceptualises the image by analysing the paintings of the Chauvet Cave in the Ardèche, inhabited during the Upper Palaeolithic period. By focusing on the role of gestures in their creation, she attempts to problematise the relationship between the artist, the image and the spectator. First, she postulates that the birth of the image requires a certain distance between the artist's body and the wall: the human hand guides the eye on the rocky surface, and the arm maintains a distance between the body and the image to come.[26] Second, the body and the wall are united when the artist places the pigments on the surface by using his or her hands or mouth.[27] Third, the body moves away. The gesture of separation and linkage ('geste d'écart et de lien') structures the human relation to the image.[28] After having merged with the image, the hand must withdraw.[29] It is through this fundamental gesture of separation that the image is thus able to reach the spectator. The margin that separates the body from the image structures the act of seeing.

In his famous essay 'The Work of Art in the Age of Its Technological Reproducibility', Benjamin emphasises the significance of the work of the

24 Agamben, 'Notes on Gesture', p. 54.

25 Marie-José Mondzain, *Images (à suivre): de la poursuite au cinéma et ailleurs* (Paris: Bayard, 2011), p. 25.

26 See Mondzain, *Homo spectator*, p 28.

27 Ibid., p. 29.

28 Ibid., p. 28.

29 Ibid., p. 29.

hand in the production of the aura of images, which disappears with the techniques of mechanical and industrial reproduction: 'For the first time, photography freed the hand from the most important artistic tasks in the process of pictorial reproduction – tasks that now devolved upon the eye alone.'[30] By contrast, Mondzain argues that the artistic use of modern technologies such as photography and cinema requires the necessary gesture of separation ('l'exigence d'écart et de séparation') that characterises the non-mechanical forms of art.[31] Only the filmmaker's gesture is able to give birth to the image and to acknowledge the spectator as a subject. Through tactility ('la palpation du monde'),[32] the hand enables the image to communicate with the spectator.

Tactility and Rhythm

Mondzain's definition of the image, which emphasises the notions of gesture, tactility, trace, distance, margin and spectatorship, resonates with Godard's intentions in *Prénom Carmen*. The filmmaker insists on the role of human gesture in the fabrication of the cinematic image, which he considers to be a trace, like the traces left on the walls of the caves.[33] As Pethő points out, in *Histoire(s) du cinéma* Godard, like Agnès Varda in *Les Glaneurs et la Glaneuse* (*The Gleaners and I*, 2000), '[seems] to work on the reconstruction of a certain "aura" of the moving image' by foregrounding the role of the filmmaker's hand and tactile gestures in its production.[34]

> [...] [B]y these gestures of indexicality and touch that emphasise both the physical presence of reality before the apparatus, before the director's body and the palpable

30 Benjamin, 'The Work of Art in the Age of Its Technological Reproductibility', p. 102.

31 Mondzain, *Homo spectator*, p. 202.

32 Ibid., p. 203.

33 Jean-Luc Godard and Sylvie Steinebach, 'Les Signes du mal à vivre. Entretien avec Jean-Luc Godard', *L'Avant-scène cinéma*, March 1984, p. 8.

34 Pethő, *Cinema and Intermediality*, p. 351.

> experience of images they behold or handle, [Varda and Godard] at least manage to effectively mediate a kind of auratic experience.[35]

Referring to Leroi-Gourhan, Godard argues that the style of filmmaking depends on the relationship between the camera and the gesture.[36] In the 1980s, Godard experimented with new cameras in order to rethink the link between the artist's gesture and the image. In the summer of 1983, just before the release of *Prénom Carmen* in September, *Cahiers du cinéma* published a long interview with Godard and the engineer Jean-Pierre Beauviala about the Aaton 8–35, a new prototype of camera that the two men tried to design from the mid-1970s. Originally Godard had wanted a small and high-quality 35 mm camera that he could keep close at hand in order to be able to use it quickly in any situation of everyday life. For instance, in the first shot of *Passion*, the sky is filmed with the Aaton 35, a model that is slightly larger than the Aaton 8–35.

With this small camera, Godard intended to invent a new way of shooting a film, with a reduced crew and less movement around the camera. He aimed to avoid the constraints and norms of classical shootings that usually condition the gestures of creation.[37] During the first days of the shooting of *Prénom Carmen* Godard used the Aaton, but had to hire a focus puller because of technical problems with his camera. Godard considers the arrival of Isabelle Adjani, to whom he had originally given the role of Carmen, as the 'instant fatal'.[38] When she arrived with her make-up artists and assistants, the crew widened, and the gestures of filmmaking changed.[39] After Adjani left the shooting a few days later, due to feeling unprepared for Godard's demands, the filmmaker switched cameras, giving up the Aaton 35 (and its unresolved problems of focus) and choosing instead the Arriflex, a more conventional apparatus. As a consequence, the form and

35 Ibid.

36 Alain Bergala, Jean-Luc Godard and Jean-Pierre Beauviala, 'Genèse d'une caméra. Premier épisode', in *Jean-Luc Godard par Jean-Luc Godard*, ed. by Alain Bergala (Paris: Edition de l'étoile, 1985), p. 522.

37 Ibid., p. 520.

38 Ibid., p. 537.

39 Ibid., cited by Bergala, p. 536.

style of the film evolved. With the Aaton 35 Godard had sought a certain freedom as a filmmaker, thanks to the lightness of movement and the manoeuvrability of the camera. In the interview with Beauviala, the director describes the sensation of agility he experienced during the rehearsals of *Prénom Carmen*, highlighting the crucial relationship between the hand, the object and vision.[40] He explains that he has less time to see when he spends a lot of energy managing a large crew on a conventional film set.[41]

While with the camera Aaton 8–35, Godard had wished to develop the agility of the filmmaker's hand, he actually succeeds in conveying the sense of touch when performing in front of the camera. In *Prénom Carmen*, his performance remains very tactile. At the beginning of the film, Uncle Jean makes the objects of his hospital room resound. Like a blind man, he frantically and noisily touches the windowpanes, as well as the other objects, such as the bed, the typewriter and his own body (see Figures 3.1 and 3.2). As Deleuze writes on Godard's cinema, '[t]he body is sound as well as visible.'[42] Godard shows the filmmaker's ability to manipulate and design the sounds that have, in the sequence described above, a particular resonance and precision, as if the author had carefully selected, isolated and intensified them. Michel Chion analyses how filmmakers can emphasise the sounds of gestures and 'give noise to the body through sound effects' by recreating the sounds in real life and giving them a 'rendering' adapted to the cinema.[43] Although Godard uses direct sound,[44] he reveals the musicality of gestures by emphasising the rhythmicity of the human body. His urge to touch all the components of his environment reveals his wish to 'touch the image',[45] to create a trace within the film, and to be connected to the filmed world, framed by the camera, before becoming separated from it. He touches the surface, then pulls his hands back. As

40 Bergala et al., 'Genèse d'une caméra', p. 553.

41 Godard, *Jean-Luc Godard par Jean-Luc Godard*, p. 534.

42 Deleuze, *Cinema 2. The Time-Image*, p. 193.

43 Chion, *Film, a Sound Art*, p. 237.

44 Fox, *Godard and Sound*, p. 67.

45 Raymond Bellour, '(Not) Just an Other Filmmaker', *Jean-Luc Godard, Son + Image 1974–1991*, ed. by Bellour and Bandy, p. 226.

Figures 3.1–3.2. *Prénom Carmen*: Godard's character touches the windowpanes of his hospital room as well as his own body.

Leroi-Gourhan points out, rhythm and trace are two interrelated notions. He defines human rhythm as a dynamic image (*image dynamique*), shaped by gesture and voice, which can take the form of a graphic trace thanks to the work of the hand.[46] Rhythms generate forms and model the relation of an individual to space and time.[47] By highlighting the rhythmical nature of his gestures, Godard draws the spectator's attention to the sound quality of the image and, ultimately, emphasises the crucial role of the musicians' gestures in the creation of the forms of the film.

The Gestural Creation of Cinematic Images

Distances, Relations and Interplays

Drawing on silent cinema, Godard reflects on the audiovisual dimension of gesture and on the productive relationship between the soundtrack and the image. In the title *Prénom Carmen*, the word *prénom* (first name) points to what comes before the name, or, in other words, before language. And what comes before language, according to Lacan, is the

46 Leroi-Gourhan, *Le Geste et la parole II*, p. 144.

47 Ibid., p. 135.

Imaginary,[48] or, in cinematic terms, the image. Alternatively, however, it might be music, as Godard considers in the film synopsis.[49] Godard attempts to show things before they are named by returning to a form of cinema which precedes the advent of talking pictures: 'Les enfants vont jouer à Carmen; comme autrefois Chaplin. Car c'est vrai que c'est un film muet.' [Children are going to play Carmen; like Chaplin in the old days. Because it is true that it is a silent film.][50] From this perspective, the director develops the interplay between the visual, musical and gestural aspects of the cinematic image, which, in silent cinema, tend to stimulate the spectator's imagination: 'The silent reel was supported by sound ideograms of an indeterminate nature supplied by a musical accompaniment that maintained a distance between the individual and the image imposed from the outside,' Leroi-Gourhan explains.[51] By contrast, the perfection of representation in sound films and television tends to plunge the spectator's perception into a state of passivity that neutralises his or her effort to interpret and imagine:

> The margin for individual interpretation is drastically reduced because the symbol and its contents are almost completely merged into one and because the spectator has absolutely no possibility of intervening actively in the 'real' situation thus recreated.[52]

Although Leroi-Gourhan's assertion is debatable, as sound, for example, enables filmmakers to develop the off-camera space and explore the boundaries between the visible and the invisible, by stimulating the spectator's kinesic intelligence (as pointed out in Chapter 2), his argument indirectly evokes Godard's criticism of the 'terrorism of language' pervasive in television, due to the domination of the text over the image.[53]

48 See Powrie's Lacanian interpretation of *Prénom Carmen* in Phil Powrie, 'Godard's *Prénom Carmen* (1984), Masochism, and the Male Gaze', *Forum for Modern Languages Studies*, 31.1 (1995), 64–73 (pp. 67–8).

49 Cited in Raymond Lefèvre, 'Avant le nom (le langage) des enfants jouent à Carmen', in *Jean-Luc Godard* (Paris: Edilig, 1983), p. 115.

50 Ibid.

51 Leroi-Gourhan, *Gesture and Speech*, p. 213.

52 Ibid.

53 Godard and Bachmann, p. 14.

'There are no more images today. As Jean-Pierre Gorin used to say in the time we worked together: "Films are no longer seen, they are read"', Godard states.[54] Strikingly, his resistance to the dominant use of the audiovisual medium manifests itself in *Prénom Carmen* through the relationship between the image and the music and, more broadly, the soundtrack. The combination of heterogeneous forms, the hybridisation of the audiovisual medium, and the proliferation of analogies between music and film aim to foster the spectator's active reception.

Godard considers that the spectator's position is threatened by television, as the latter is an instrument of 'power in its pure state'.[55] The filmmaker denounces the dominating power of the medium of television, which is 'causing the decline of the images' and makes the spectator feel 'impotent'.[56] The relationship between the image and the spectator is annihilated: '"Video" means "I see", but what is happening is that with the complicity of the masses video becomes the medium of those who do not want to see.'[57] In *Prénom Carmen*, Godard associates video with violence, robbery and kidnapping. Before the hold-up, Joseph, armed with a rifle, scatters people who stand in front of the bank, while a voice-over repeats: 'Vidéo, vidéo, qui veut de la vidéo?' [Video, video, who wants video?]. According to Godard, the dominant use of television annihilates the distance necessary to constitute the subjectivity of the spectator who is hypnotised by the image, or rather by the semblance of image. Television fabricates oblivion rather than memory and blocks off the communication between the image and the spectator.[58] Godard denounces the perceptive alienation of the masses caused by the power of television.[59]

Criticising television for not taking the margins into consideration, Godard argues that his position as a filmmaker, which is 'in the margin',

54 Ibid., p. 18.
55 Ibid., p. 15.
56 Ibid., pp. 18 and 15.
57 Ibid., p. 18.
58 Godard and Steinebach, p. 8.
59 Scarpetta considers Godard to be a post-Brechtian author in the sense that the filmmaker manipulates the Brechtian distancing effects to denounce the alienation of perception itself. See Scarpetta, 'Docteur, est-ce que l'âme a un corps ?', p. 44.

is similar to the position of the spectator. 'I am in the place of the public, of the onlookers. In fact to be in the margin, that is the real position of the public.'[60] As considered above with reference to Mondzain, the image, which exists from the moment the artist's hand moves away, addresses the spectator's gaze in the margin that separates them. In the video essay *Scénario du film 'Passion'* (1982), in which the director discusses the creative process of *Passion*, Godard explains that the image, in order to be seen, needs first to be received by the artist and the spectator. He raises the palms of his hands in the direction of the white video screen in order to 'voir' [see], and then directs them towards his gaze in order to 'rece-voir' [receive, or re-see-ve] (see Figures 3.3 and 3.4). He argues that the filmmaker, like a spectator, faces the image, contrary to the television newscaster who sits with his or her back to it. As Raymond Bellour writes on Godard, '[the filmmaker] must maintain with respect to the image, and to the life from which it emanates, the distance necessary for it to exist as an image, in its dimension of belief and revelation.'[61] Godard aims to restore the spectator's gaze by showing the image as a trace left by the artist's gesture. By distancing himself from the image, the filmmaker enables the spectator to exist as an active subject.

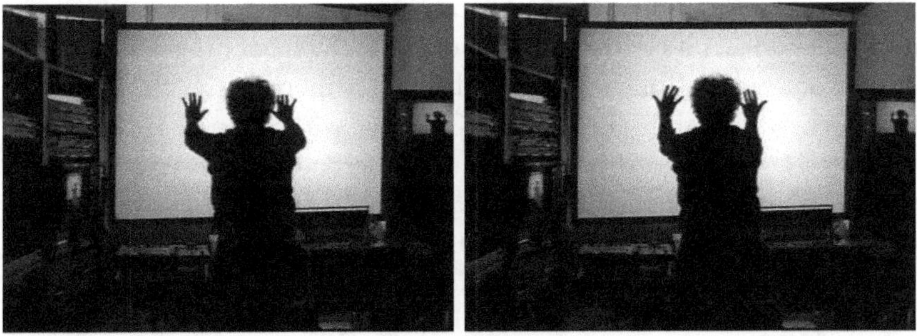

Figures 3.3–3.4. *Scénario du film 'Passion'*: Godard raises his hands in front of a white screen.

60 Godard and Bachmann, p. 17.

61 Bellour, '(Not) Just an Other Filmmaker', p. 226.

The necessary distance between the image and the spectator is problematised in a pivotal sequence of *Prénom Carmen*, in which the languorous song 'Ruby's Arms' (1980) by Tom Waits temporarily replaces Beethoven (before the end of the sequence when Godard interweaves Beethoven and the popular song). While waiting for Carmen in the hotel room, Joseph sensually strokes the television screen with his right hand. Due to problems of reception, the screen displays an absence of image. Like all the television screens of the hotel, the screen remains imperturbably the same, an object without image indifferent to Joseph's desperate urge for affectivity. The character, who cannot detach himself from the surface of the screen (see Figure 3.5), does not look at it and, consequently, does not exist as a spectator. His hand, which merges with the screen, becomes itself a semblance of a hand. Following this, a long shot shows Joseph lying over the television set, inert and weakened, before falling down on the ground (see Figure 3.6), while Carmen enters the room and opens the curtains. Joseph gets back onto his feet and kisses her (see Figure 3.7). The bluish and cold colour of the shot, which differs from the yellow and warm tones of the other scenes in the hotel, evokes the glazed paper-like quality of advertising images, as well as the bluish light of the television screen. The image, and more particularly the image of Carmen, filmed in close-up, is turned into a fetish, a product of male fantasy. However, unlike the inert and lifeless television screen, Carmen responds to Joseph's stroke and detaches herself from his gesture. In the next shots, closely followed by her lover, Carmen crosses the rooms of the suite, which all include a television set with a blurred screen (see Figure 3.8). Although the eroticisation of her naked body could remind us of the representation of Brigitte Bardot in *Le Mépris* (*Contempt*, 1963), Carmen resists Joseph's possessive and aggressive gestures. Against the fetishisation of her body, she affirms her subjectivity ('J'ai envie de dormir toute seule' [I want to sleep alone]), imposing a distance between herself and Joseph who is too frustrated to listen to her. Significantly, not only is she filmed in full shot rather than in close-up, but she also repeatedly leaves the frame of the camera when Joseph approaches her too closely. Her image is constructed, with difficulty, in the distance that separates her from the male gaze.

Figures 3.5–3.8. *Prénom Carmen*: Joseph strokes the TV screen of his hotel room, before touching Carmen's face; the latter leaves the room.

In *Prénom Carmen*, Godard seems to question his way of representing women during the New Wave. According to Geneviève Sellier, the female characters of the New Wave, rather than being constructed as subjects, are mostly subjected to the male gaze (with only a few exceptions such as Agnès Varda's *Cléo de 5 à 7* (*Cléo from 5 to 7*, 1962) or Alain Resnais's *Hiroshima mon amour* (*Hiroshima, My Love*, 1959)). She demonstrates how Anna Karina, a 'woman-child', is infantilised by Godard who represents her as the Pygmalion-like artist would his model.[62] Through Carmen's story, Godard reproduces the pattern of the femme fatale fetishised by the male gaze, which is emblematic of the New Wave, as Sellier explains: 'Female characters in these films are the male hero's fears and desires made concrete and

62 Sellier, *Masculine Singular*, pp. 153–64.

the viewer only has access to them through his gaze.'[63] However, Godard, who remains influenced by the feminist discourses of the late 1960s and 1970s, calls into question the powerful figure of the paternalistic author. According to Mulvey, the filmmaker's 'self-parodic' performance challenges the fetishist representation of the female body. In *Prénom Carmen*, the male gaze ultimately proves impotent:

> He depicts the film director's dilemma as hopelessly fetishistic, his obsession with cinema and the female body as helplessly dependent, masochistic, exploitative. Cinema and sexuality merge into a condensation that is unashamedly masculine while also being apologetically impotent.[64]

The incestuous relationship between Uncle Jean and Carmen ironically mirrors the ambiguously exploitative relationship between the misogynistic filmmaker, who Godard intentionally embodies, and the heroine. However, Carmen succeeds in manipulating the male gaze by at once attracting it and keeping it at a distance. A dialectical gesture of attraction and rejection, which is first initiated in the film by Uncle Jean, sets the rhythm of the love story between Carmen and Joseph throughout the film. When Carmen visits Uncle Jean at the hospital, the director, who appears out of focus while the heroine is filmed in a fetishist close-up, strokes her face (see Figure 3.9). She immediately rejects his possessive hand gesture. Uncle Jean disappears off-screen but tries to compensate his lack of physical presence through language, by making a regressive pun in a disillusioned tone: 'C'est fou les jeunes. Ils oublient tout et ils n'ont que de la mémoire. Ils sont dans le trou … noir.' ['Young people are crazy. They forget everything, but they only have memory. They're in a black … hole.'] Similarly, Joseph mentions the black hole when he says to Carmen: 'J'ai trouvé … la prison … pourquoi ça s'appelle le trou' [Now I know … jail … why it is called 'the hole'], negatively linking, as Scarpetta points out,[65] female sexuality to masculine entrapment. On the one hand, Godard's character influences both Joseph's language and

63 Ibid., p. 149.

64 Mulvey, 'The Hole and the Zero', p. 82.

65 Scarpetta, 'Docteur, est-ce que l'âme a un corps ?', p. 47.

Figure 3.9. *Prénom Carmen:* Godard's character strokes Carmen's face.

gestures, highlighting the sensitive process of bodily and verbal exchanges that structures the relationship between the filmmaker and his leading actor. On the other hand, Godard's physical engagement in the film crucially challenges his own authority as a filmmaker.

Transmissions

Analysing the situation of filmmakers acting in their own films, Mondzain observes that the authors' performance in front of the camera can lead to a critical questioning of their relationship to power. The philosopher distinguishes power, when it establishes itself to the detriment of freedom and human relationship, from authority, which involves recognition, transmission and trust.[66] From this perspective, the film author develops an active relationship with the spectator, which is not based on domination, but on exchange and communication. In *Prénom Carmen*, such a relationship emerges through the filmmaker's act of resistance against power and through his struggle to live and exist as an artist. Far from being in a position of strength, Godard shows his vulnerability

66 Marie-José Mondzain, 'L'Auteur au risque de l'autorité de l'acteur', *Cahiers du cinéma*, July–August 2005, p. 14.

and unhappiness – his 'mal à vivre', as he says in an interview.[67] In the film, Uncle Jean is shown lying in his hospital bed in semi-obscurity, repeating in a guttural voice 'être … être …' [to be … to be …]. According to Mondzain, the creation of images is a difficult and demanding process which emphasises the artist's weakness, and paradoxically constructs his or her authority and position as an author.[68]

In *Prénom Carmen*, as in *Soigne ta droite* (*Keep Your Right Up*, 1987) and *King Lear* (1987), Godard portrays himself as a powerless and marginal filmmaker, playing the role of the fool. By definition, the fool belongs to the margins of the narrative and mediates the author's perspective of the fictional world, as Cecilia Sayad demonstrates by drawing on Bakhtin: 'It is by the way as an outsider that the fool becomes the author's mask, representing the author's point of view and positioning this figure as marginal to the narrated world.'[69] Godard's marginalisation as a fool ultimately represents his 'increasing marginal position in the film market'.[70] Throughout the film, Godard, as a fictional character, shows himself being subjected to the professionals – 'On est des professionnels' [We are professionals], the leader of Carmen's gang affirms – who substitute the cinema for a kidnapping.

While performing the role of a fallen author manipulated by cynical gangsters, Godard symbolically transmits his authority as a fictional filmmaker to the musicians who lead the mise-en-scène thanks to the productive resonance of their gestures in the narrative. As Scarpetta notes, Godard distinguishes the self-proclaimed professionals, like the leader of Carmen's gang, from the real ones, such as the musicians.[71] In the final sequence, Uncle Jean, who is supposed to direct a scene in the dining room of the hotel, meets the Prat Quartet, which performs Beethoven's music,

67 Godard and Steinebach, p. 8.

68 Marie-José Mondzain and Pierre Lauret, 'Sans Image, il n'y a pas de *logos*. Entretien avec Marie-José Mondzain', *Cahiers philosophiques*, 113 (2008), 52–63 <https://www.cairn.info/revue-cahiers-philosophiques1-2008-1-page-52.htm> [accessed 18 August 2018] (para. 10 of 29).

69 Sayad, *Performing Authorship*, p. 112.

70 Ibid., p. 114.

71 See Scarpetta, 'Docteur, est-ce que l'âme a un corps ?', p. 44.

and shakes hands with the first violinist; through this symbolic gesture, he acknowledges the quartet's essential presence and creative role in the film. Then Uncle Jean, who uses a knife to make a wine glass and a plate tinkle, gives musical indications to the crew (Carmen's gang) behind him; he is always isolated in space, marginalised in the group; he stands still, holding a cassette player (his music-camera) in his arms, and then gradually retreats in a corner, near the quartet, saying to his assistant: 'Je ne travaille pas dans ces conditions' [I won't work under these conditions]. Manipulated as he is by Carmen, he is not the master of the film and has no hold on the equipment. In the second part of the sequence, which becomes much more chaotic and fragmented, the criminals shoot with their guns instead of using their camera, which leads to miscommunication, destruction and, ultimately, death.

Godard argues that unlike the gangsters' rifles, '[the camera] is not an instrument that sends out [...]':[72] the cinematic image exists first in the way it is received by the camera, thanks to the light. By comparing the camera, on the one hand, to a rifle,[73] and on the other, to a cassette player which plays music, Godard brings into opposition, in a metaphorical way, the act of shooting with a gun and the act of making a film with music. As a filmmaker-actor, Godard symbolically delegates the direction of the film to the quartet. By moving aside, he brings the musicians' gestures to the forefront. He uses Beethoven's music to 'compose' the film and gives the quartet the responsibility to 'direct' it. By exhibiting the craft of the musicians, Godard shows how their gestures produce the forms of the film and forge the spectator's reception of the image. Ultimately, the editing stimulates the spectator's active engagement by emphasising the link and the interval between the musicians' gestures and the moving image.

72 Godard and Bachmann, p. 18.

73 Sontag discusses the analogy between cameras and guns in her well-known essay 'Plato's Cave'. See Sontag, *On Photography*, pp. 14–15.

The Intermediality of Gestures: A Productive Dialogue between Film, Music and Sculpture

In *Prénom Carmen*, gesture not only causes subjects to interact, but also interconnects various media and arts, in spite of their differences. By stressing the relational and intersubjective qualities of gestures, Godard emphasises their crucial role as a medium of in-betweenness and invites us to rethink the concept of intermediality in cinema. According to Pethő, intermediality forges an 'in-between' space where arts and media circulate and interact:

> Cinema seems to consciously position itself 'in-between' media and arts, employing techniques that tap into the multimedial complexity of cinema, exploiting the possibilities offered by the distinctive characteristics of the media components involved in the cinematic process of signification, and bringing into play the tensions generated by media differences.[74]

By drawing on this definition, I aim to demonstrate the extent to which gesture in *Prénom Carmen* interconnects different media, subjects, art forms and heterogeneous modes of expression. As Jenny Chamarette explains, '[g]esture, in all its philosophical and embodied complexity, offers a means of thinking about intermediality and intersubjectivity, as a migratory, transitory process of meaning-making.'[75] She adds, '[g]esture is [...] what transmits expression, but also the modality through which expression is made perceivable.'[76] Making a film involves not only the interaction of different media, but also of different modes of expression which enter into dialogue and exchange their gestural properties.

Godard establishes intermedial equivalences between the script and the musical score, between the musical rehearsal and the shooting of the

74 Pethő, *Cinema and Intermediality*, p. 2.

75 Jenny Chamarette, 'Between Women: Gesture, Intermediality and Intersubjectivity in the Installations of Agnès Varda and Chantal Akerman', *Studies in European Cinema*, 10.1 (2013), 45–57 (p. 46).

76 Ibid., p. 48.

film, between the rhythm of the musical phrase and the rhythm of the editing, and between the musical instruments and the actors' bodies. The filmmaker interconnects the musicians' gestures with the lovers' gestures, which echo Rodin's sculptures and the movement of the waves. Gesture is the element that incorporates, develops and sets in motion the features of the other arts, not only by creating an in-between space that forges links between media, but also notably by exhibiting the creative process itself. The relation between the performing, musical and visual arts is made visible in the exhibition of the corporeal effort of making (whether it be making music, film or love) which tends to open the boundaries separating the different arts. The aural and visual qualities of gestures communicate between one another, generating rhythms and forms that circulate in the continuous flow of moving images. By fostering the analogy between the gesture of carving, of performing music and of making film, Godard highlights what unites the arts in cinema, while productively playing on their differences.

Beethoven, a Film Composer: Musical Dialogue and Gestus

At first sight, the use of Beethoven's music in *Prénom Carmen*, which replaces Bizet's original score, appears to underline Godard's return to the New Wave aesthetics. In *Le Nouveau monde* (*The New World*, 1962), *Une femme mariée* (*A Married Woman*, 1964) and *Deux ou trois choses que je sais d'elle* (*Two or Three Things I know About Her*, 1966), Godard makes use of numerous fragments from Beethoven's late string quartets. Although Godard reweaves an old leitmotif of his filmography, his reappropriation of Beethoven's music is revealing of a stylistic evolution between the New Wave and the post-New Wave. Godard's passion for the quartets is foregrounded in Rohmer's *Le Signe du Lion* (*The Sign of Leo*, 1959) in which a solitary character, played by Godard himself, repeatedly listens to the second movement of the fifteenth quartet during a party. He obsessively listens to the same fragment by replacing the stylus of the phonograph on the same groove. According to Aumont, Godard's gesture of interruption and repetition is similar to an act of editing. Due to being fragmented and repeated, the music has no decorative function here, but becomes a 'figure'.[77] In *Une femme mariée*, fragments of the quartets, limited to a few bars, are edited in relation to the other visual and aural elements of the film, such as the sound effects, the dialogue, the advertising posters and the actors' fragmented gestures.[78]

Although the quartets are still interrupted in *Prénom Carmen*, they are played in chronological order (the quartets 9, 10, 14, 15 and 16) and developed in the continuity of the sequences. The music is performed in relation to the cinematographic and narrative meaning of the film. The editing makes the continuity between Beethoven's music and the script visible and audible. The ideas, actions and gestures stem from the music. As Godard admits, '[…] the attack on the bank came to be after I heard a certain part of the 10th Quartet.'[79] Inspired by the collaboration between Eisenstein and Prokofiev in *Alexander Nevsky* (1938),[80] the filmmaker described each sequence in the script by referring to the tone, tempo and musical intentions of the quartets. The music enabled Godard to envision the actors' gestures. For instance, in sequence 14, he establishes a parallel between Joseph's gestures to Carmen and the musical accents, both described as 'profonds' [deep].[81] The intimate relationship between the music and the gestures alters the aesthetics of heterogeneity that usually defines Godard's style. Contrary to Akerman's theatricalisation of the body, which has been compared to Ozu's and Bresson's 'aesthetics of homogeneity',[82] Godard constantly plays with formal contrasts and variations of tempo. In *Prénom Carmen*, the filmmaker uses the jump cut to juxtapose the gestures

77 Jacques Aumont, *A quoi pensent les films* (Paris: Séguier, 1996), p. 265.

78 Ibid.

Moreover, Godard's interest in Maillol's sculptures in *Une femme mariée*, combined with Beethoven's music, anticipates the double influence of music and sculpture in *Prénom Carmen*. See Suzanne Liandrat-Guigues, *Cinéma et sculpture: un aspect de la modernité des années soixante* (Paris: L'Harmattan, 2002), p. 83.

79 Godard and Bachmann, p. 16.

80 For a detailed analysis of Eisenstein's influence on *Prénom Carmen*, see Fox, *Godard and Sound*, pp. 75–81.

81 See Godard, '*Prénom Carmen*: scénario', in *Jean-Luc Godard par Jean-Luc Godard*, p. 565.

82 Margulies, *Nothing Happens*, p. 56.

of the string quartet with Joseph and Carmen's bodily movements, thus dilating the time-space of the film.

Furthermore, as Phil Powrie notes, the film is a patchwork of genres, subverting the codes of family melodrama, thriller, love story and trial film, and mixing different acting styles: 'The love story is on the one hand made of elliptical gestures and violent clashes, and on the other intimate moments which combine the poetic with the vulgar.'[83] Yet, instead of emphasising the effects of 'dislocation' as Powrie suggests,[84] the film, especially its editing, creates a productive and unifying dialogue between the heterogeneous components which constitute it, such as the shots of the sea, the musical rehearsals and Carmen and Joseph's love story. According to Jacques Rancière, Godard, in *Prénom Carmen*, highlights the mysterious co-presence of the heterogeneous elements which usually compose the world, including music.[85] Rather than highlighting their antagonism, he connects them in 'the fusion music of images which unite, in one and the same breath, the noises of strings, of waves and of bodies'.[86] Although 'fusion' is not the most adequate term to qualify Godard's editing and gestural research given that he also emphasises the distance between these heterogeneous elements, the interrelation between the musicians' and actors' gestures generates shared motifs and rhythms.

Godard uses the editing to create a complex musical gestus, and the quartet's performance to compose the film musically and visually. The lovers' gestures can be in tune (*accordé*) and out of tune (*désaccordé*). In addition to *accords* and *désaccords*, the technique of gestural *raccords* (match cuts) aims to give its coherence and harmony to the film by connecting the shots of a scene like the pieces of a puzzle. For instance, during the bank attack, Godard creates a subtle match cut between the movement of Joseph's rifle,

83 Powrie, 'Godard's *Prénom Carmen* (1984), Masochism, and the Male Gaze', p. 66.

84 Ibid., p. 64.

85 According to Rohmer, music in Godard's cinema does not aim to accompany the image, but is filmed as being part of the world. See Eric Rohmer, *De Mozart en Beethoven: Essai sur la notion de profondeur en musique* (Arles: Actes Sud, 1998), p. 234.

86 Jacques Rancière, *Aesthetics and Its Discontents*, trans. by Steven Corcoran (Cambridge: Polity Press, 2009), p. 58.

which is waved in all directions, and the bow, which attacks the strings of the violin. The filmmaker connects the musical rehearsal to the act of shooting (in both senses of the word). The musical gestures are both gestures of linkage (*gestes de lien*), because they accompany the ongoing action of the bank robbery, and gestures of separation (*gestes d'écart*), because they are performed from a distance, in a separated time-space.

During the rehearsals, the musicians stop playing, comment upon their performance, and try to improve it by reworking some parts of the piece: 'Là ça deviant beaucoup plus dramatique' [There it becomes much more dramatic]; 'Il faut que ce soit plus violent' [It must be more violent.] Such recommendations, with which they annotate their score, determine the colour, mood, energy and rhythmic sensitivity of the musical phrase. The musicians adapt their gestures to the musical intention they want to achieve. Similarly, during the shooting of a film, filmmakers closely work with their actors in order to direct their performance. They ask them to make specific gestures appropriate to the meaning and/or form they want them to convey. After having recorded several takes of the same shot, they then select the best take to be included in the editing. During the sequence of the bank robbery, Godard shows such a process by successively editing two takes of the same shot. Joseph strides across the corridor, chasing the gangsters among the victims and the remaining clients, and bumps into a table in a slapstick way. The second take is much longer and developed than the first one, but Joseph's choreography looks almost identical, and gestural differences are barely perceptible. The actor Jacques Bonnaffé shows great precision and technical dexterity. His exaggerated gestures, somewhat reminiscent of Chaplin's *Burlesque on Carmen* (1915), leave no room for improvisation. Using his body as a musical instrument, the actor closely follows the director's indications and the annotations of the screenplay, as if following a musical score.

Godard's method of editing seems to evoke the Brechtian intention 'to make gestures quotable',[87] as Walter Benjamin writes. The process of interruption and repetition in *Prénom Carmen* would appear nonetheless to differ from the Brechtian gestus that Devin Fore compares with Eisenstein's

87 Benjamin, *Understanding Brecht*, p. 11.

technique of transitionless acting. This acting style, based on discontinuity, incorporates the 'devices of montage and mechanical assembly [...] into the body of the actor': 'Like the *gestus*, Eisenstein's montage dramaturgy works by producing collisions between discontinuous emotional states, resulting in a performance that is disjointed and full of counterpoints. Hence the designation "transitionless".'[88] By contrast, in *Prénom Carmen* Godard seems to restore a certain sense of continuity, despite the lack of linearity of action, by making visible the relations between the heterogeneous parts of the film as well as the transitions in the actors' performance. In the scene with Joseph described above, Godard edits the missing images preceding and following the first occurrence of the shot, reestablishing its cohesion and unity, rather than creating an effect of disjunction, as if the shot was 'torn' and Godard intended to 'mend' it.[89] The rehearsals of the Prat Quartet lend the film the shape of a work in progress, made up of interruptions and resumptions. Analysing the dialectics of disorder and order, discontinuity and continuity, disorganising and organising flux in Godard's films of the 1980s, including *Prénom Carmen*, Didier Coureau admits that although Godard's films look at first broken-up on the surface, they remain cohesive.[90] What is it that makes the pieces hold together if not the dialogue of gestures or, to use Petra Löffler's expression, 'the linkage of gestures'?[91]

88 Devin Fore, 'Gestus Facit Saltus: Bertolt Brecht's Fear and Misery of the Third Reich', in *Realism after Modernism: The Rehumanization of Art and Literature* (Cambridge, MA: The MIT Press, 2012), pp. 172–3.

89 The gesture of mending significantly appears in a sequence of the film. The filmmaker has torn his coat on exiting the underground: the contact with the world outside the psychiatric hospital has provoked a tear. While he is ruminating on capitalistic economy, his assistant (and nurse) mends the torn sleeve while listening to him. The gestures of mending and listening, like operations of editing, reintroduce cohesion and continuity.

90 Didier Coureau, 'Jean-Luc Godard. Ouverture de l'ère de la complexité esthétique. 1979–1985', in *Jean-Luc Godard 2, au-delà de l'image*, ed. by Marc Cerisuelo (Paris: Lettres modernes, 1993), p. 29.

91 Petra Löffler, 'Gesturing the Image. The Chain-Linking of Gestures in Jean-Luc Godard's *Passion*', in *Gestures of Seeing in Film, Video and Drawing*, ed. by Asbjørn Grønstad, Henrik Gustafsson and Øyvind Vågnes (New York: Routledge, 2017), p. 34.

From this perspective, the concept of gestus, as defined by Deleuze in *The Time-Image*, remains helpful when analysing Godard's gestural process of filmmaking. Drawing on Brecht, Deleuze does not consider the gestus as a discontinuous, disjointed and transitionless form of acting, but rather defines the notion in terms of gestural interconnection and coordination of bodily attitudes:

> What we call gest in general is the link or knot of attitudes between themselves, their co-ordination with each other, in so far as they do not depend on a previous story, a pre-existing plot or an action-image.[92]

Deleuze notes the pluridimensionality of Godard's audiovisual gestus in *Prénom Carmen*.[93] His definition of gestus echoes the concept of hypergesture theorised by Guerino Mazzola in free jazz and developed more broadly by Yves Citton.[94] Hypergesture refers to the connection of disparate gestures that enter into dialogue with one another despite their physiological dissimilarities. For example, although the gesture of a drummer could not be more different from the gesture of a saxophonist, they are united in a collaborative process of creation which produces shared rhythms, shapes and sounds. When Godard films the rehearsals of the Prat Quartet, he shows, in the foreground, the movement of the violinist's elbow in dialogue with the cellist's arms and hands. Their posture and gestural techniques adapt to the shape of their respective instruments. 'Le niveau *hypergestuel* résulte [...] des résonances subjectives perçues par les humains entre des gestes physiologiquement différents' ['Hypergesture results [...] from the subjective resonances that humans perceive between physiologically different gestures'], Citton explains.[95] The concept of hypergesture makes it possible to consider the intersubjective dimension of gestures which, rather than being isolated, achieve a

92 Deleuze, *Cinema 2. The Time-Image*, p. 192.

93 Ibid., p. 253–4.

94 See Guerino B. Mazzola, 'Geometry of Gestures', in *Flow, Gesture, and Spaces in Free Jazz: Towards a Theory of Collaboration*, ed. by Guerino B. Mazzola and Paul B. Charlin (Berlin: Springer-Verlag, 2009), pp. 79–87; Citton, *Gestes d'humanités*, pp. 52–6.

95 Citton, *Gestes d'humanités*, p. 55.

common object, through interpersonal relations, exchanges, resonances, dialogue, affective linkage and collaboration.

The aesthetics of *Prénom Carmen* is hypergestural on two levels. On the first level, within a single shot or scene, Godard highlights the hypergestural interaction between the musicians as they play, or between the characters as they make gestures. On the second level, Godard constructs hypergestural sequences by connecting the musicians' with the characters' gestures. The editing highlights the interplay between Beethoven's music and the narrative. For example, Godard creates a hypergestural choreography which simultaneously shapes the visual and aural perception of both the quartet's performance and the action taking place in the bank. Creative and destructive gestures are in dialogue with one another in a ballet of waving arms; the noise of the gunshots, typical of B movies – Godard made the film 'in memoriam small movies' – contrasts with the elevated style of Beethoven, while the indications of the first violinist, insisting on the violence of the musical phrase, heighten the energy of the shooting scene. The music and the image communicate remotely due to the parallel editing, but do not merge. By showing the subtle interaction between the musicians and the actors, who work to different rhythms, as well as in different places and times, Godard draws the viewer's attention to the craft of filmmaking which is a hypergestural form of art involving the close collaboration of multiple artists and performers, and the coordination of a plurality of technical and artistic gestures, from the writing, the preparation and the shooting to the editing and the mixing of the film.

Furthermore, the musical gestus coordinates the couple's attitudes. In Uncle Jean's flat, Carmen says to Joseph 'tirez-vous, attirez-moi' [get out, catch me] rejecting Joseph (*re-pousser*), and then attracting him (*at-tirer*), similarly to the musicians who up bow (*pousser*) and down bow (*tirer*). In French, when a violinist pushes the bow up or pulls the bow down, he or she *pousse* or *tire* the bow. In that sense, the dialectical movement of attraction and rejection that animates the couple's gestures is directly connected to the musicians' gestures of bowing. When Joseph approaches Carmen, she rejects him; when Joseph remains at a distance, she attracts him. Godard's film emphasises the relational and affective nature of gesture ('geste relationnel' [relational gesture] and 'geste affectif' [affective gesture], according to the terminology established by Citton).[96] For instance, the editing causes the curve of the violinist's arm to resonate with the movement of the lovers' bodies when they embrace or caress each other. As Deleuze points out,

> [...] in *First Name Carmen*, the attitudes of body continually refer to a musical gest which co-ordinates them independently of the plot; which takes them up and subjects to them to a higher linkage, but also frees all their potentialities; the rehearsals of the quartet are not limited to developing and directing the sound qualities of the image, but also the visual qualities, in the sense that the curve of the violinist's arm modifies the movement of the bodies which are embracing.[97]

The formal continuity between Myriem Roussel's and Maruschka Detmers's curved movements had been envisioned by Godard when he wrote the screenplay. As the script shows, Godard intended to create an effect of resonance between the curved movements of Claire's arm when she bows up and down in sequence 10, and the gesture of Carmen's arm when she embraces Joseph in sequence 11.[98]

Similarly to the musicians' gestures, the loving caress and embrace are forms of gestural exchange, through which the respective rhythms of Carmen and Joseph resonate in harmony, temporarily uniting them. As Irigaray explains in several essays, the caress, as the fertile basis of community life and intersubjectivity, is the 'most elementary gesture' of 'the fecundity of a love':[99]

> The caress is an awakening to intersubjectivity, to a touching between us which is neither passive nor active; it is an awakening of gestures, of perceptions which are at the same time acts, intentions, emotions. This does not mean that they are ambiguous but, rather, that they are attentive to the one who touches and the one who is touched, to the two subjects who touch each other.[100]

96 Citton, *Gestes d'humanité*, pp. 94–5.

97 Deleuze, *Cinema 2. The Time-Image*, p. 195.

98 Godard, *Jean-Luc Godard par Jean-Luc Godard*, p. 565.

99 Luce Irigaray, *An Ethics of Sexual Difference*, trans. by Carolyn Burke and Gillian C. Gill (London: The Athlone Press, 1993), p. 186.

100 Irigaray, 'The Wedding Between the Body and Language', in *Key Writings*, ed. by Luce Irigaray (London: Continuum, 2004), p. 20.

In the kitchen of Uncle Jean's flat, Joseph strokes Carmen's naked thighs, and she responds to the caress by taking his hands and guiding his gesture. Here, the caress echoes Irigaray's words: 'The caress is an awakening to a life different from the arduous everyday. It is a call to a return to you, to me, to us: as living bodies, as two, different and co-creators.'[101] Unlike Joseph's stroking of the television screen, the reciprocation and cocreativity of the caress, which does not imply the fusion of the bodies but on the contrary emerges from their differences, raises this gesture to the hypergestural level.

Yet the caress does not always lead to the unison of the bodies. The couple's relationship is also disrupted by the conflicting rhythms of their gestures which become more and more arrhythmic, especially in the final part of the film as Joseph's solitude grows. In the hotel room, Joseph strokes Carmen's yellow dressing gown and says: 'On caresse des projets et je te caresse' [We caress projects and I caress you.] Here, Joseph tends to objectify Carmen: the caress becomes a gesture of possession. Carmen, who stops combing her hair, calls out to Joseph and grabs hold of him, quoting Preminger's *Carmen Jones* (1954): 'If I love you, that's the end of you.' The discordance of their gestures, which progressively leads to unsettled and violent behaviour, is at its height when Joseph assaults Carmen in the shower, and frantically tries to have an erection. The violence and tension of their bodies, which Jean Narboni compares to Rodin's sculptures and Bacon's paintings,[102] are amplified by the stridence of Beethoven's music and the nervous strokes of the musicians' bows. As noted by Miriam Sheer, who analyses the extent to which Beethoven's music resonates with the actors' gestures in the film, '[Joseph's] frantic motions as he tries to rape Carmen in the shower mimic the motion of the agitated Scherzo of Op. 135.'[103] The diversity of rhythms, tempo and moods in Beethoven's quartets generates contrasting bodily rhythms and influences the gestural repertoire of the film.

101 Ibid.

102 See Phillippe Cassard, Marc Chevrie and Jean Narboni, 'Jean-Luc Godard et Beethoven', *Le Matin des musiciens*, France Musique, 28 May 2014.

103 Miriam Sheer, 'The Godard/Beethoven Connection: On the Use of Beethoven's Quartets in Godard's Films', *The Journal of Musicology*, 18.1 (2001), 170–88 (p. 185).

Capturing and Perceiving Gestures: The Cinematic Resonance of Rodin's Sculptures

Understanding the creative process of *Prénom Carmen* requires taking into consideration Rodin's influence on the actors' performances, as well as on Godard's mise-en-scène and editing, which are permeated with the sculptor's techniques of gestural repetition, transitional gesture and bodily fragmentation. In the preparation documents of *Prénom Carmen*, Godard juxtaposed some reproductions of Rodin's sculptures with Beethoven's quotes from his *Tagebuch*.[104] Godard asked the cinematographer Raoul Coutard, as well as the actors, to view Rodin's work. Faced with their lack of interest, as he repeated in several interviews, he gave up the idea of imitating his sculptures:

> Take Rodin, the sculptor. In the planning stage of *Prénom Carmen*, we had love scenes, which in the end did not become real love scenes in the film, and we wanted to make them like certain Rodin sculptures. In the end the actors didn't like the idea and we didn't do it like that, but we continued to call the love scenes 'the Rodin scenes'.[105]

Nevertheless, while editing and mixing the sound, Godard continued with his idea of giving the film a sculptural aspect. 'The sculptor works with two hands against a surface, he carves space, and since musicians are always speaking of audible space I think that the thing I'd like to lead them to do is to carve this audible space,' he explains.[106] By superimposing the sounds of the sea and the lovers' bodies, the filmmaker carves the spectator's perception of gestures through editing. Furthermore, even if they do not – strictly speaking – copy Rodin's sculptures, Godard, the actors and Coutard, who emphasises the bodies' volumes and angles through lighting, remain inspired by the sculptor's manner of capturing gestures.

104 See Godard, *Jean-Luc Godard par Jean-Luc Godard*, pp. 557–73.

105 Godard and Bachmann, p. 17.

106 Ibid.

Hybridity, Cohesion and Transition

Analysed by Leo Steinberg in his well-known essay on the artist, the tension between hybridity and cohesion that characterises Rodin's sculptures evokes Godard's heterogeneous but cohesive aesthetics. This tension in Rodin's figures which 'imply that all cohesion is hybrid'[107] breaks with classical anatomy and reveals the 'loss of wholeness'[108] in the representation of the body, which is guided by imagination. Steinberg notes that many of Rodin's sculptures which are 'precariously balanced or hoisted' seem to lose their equilibrium. 'Many have to do with falling,' he adds.[109] In *Prénom Carmen*, Godard repeatedly films the fall of the bodies to the ground. When Carmen and Joseph fight in the bank, they *fall* to the floor and suddenly *fall* in love. In Uncle Jean's flat, their bodies are spontaneously attracted by the walls or the ground, as if they could lose balance at any moment. Joseph leans on the wall to untie his shoes, and has to move when Carmen hits him by opening the door. A few minutes later, Joseph voluntarily slams the window on Carmen's body. Subsequently, the young woman repeats the same gesture to reject Joseph. Such repetitions echo Rodin's technique of multiplication which consists in combining identical figures, for example, in *Les Sources tarries* (*Dried-up Springs*, b. 1889) or *Les Troies Ombres* (*The Three Shades*, b. 1886): the juxtaposition of the same gesture, but in different positions, generates 'a redoubling of energy'[110] and a 'rhythmic amplification'.[111] Although the repetitions in Godard's film are never exactly identical, the combination of similar gestures and the repetition of similar shots tend to heighten the energetic quality of the bodies and to amplify the rhythms they produce. Moreover, Steinberg analyses the isolation of 'anatomical fragments'[112] and the emphasis on 'a body's specific gesture'[113] in Rodin's art. Godard's

107 Leo Steinberg, 'Rodin', in *Other Criteria: Confrontations with Twentieth-Century Art* (Chicago: University of Chicago Press, 2007), p. 382.

108 Ibid.

109 Ibid., p. 346.

110 Ibid., p. 355.

111 Ibid., p. 358.

112 Ibid., p. 361.

113 Ibid., p. 362.

framing also fragments the bodies and sometimes isolates the characters' hands in close-ups. Rodin sculpted 150 single hands, detached from the rest of the body, which condense 'the sum of gestures which a whole body can make'.[114] Uncle Jean's hand stroking Carmen's face evokes the plaster *Masque de Camille Claudel et Main gauche de Pierre Wissant* (*Mask of Camille Claudel and Left Hand of Pierre de Wissant*, *c.* 1895) which juxtaposes the portrait of the model with a disproportionate hand (see Figure 3.9).

Rodin inspired filmmakers such as John Cassavetes in *Shadows* (1959)[115] and Eisenstein who, in his theoretical writings, considers his sculptures from a cinematic perspective.[116] According to Rilke, Rodin succeeded in capturing the gestures of his time, which 'have become more and more impatient, nervous and hurried', as well as more 'hesitating'.[117] Echoing Agamben's thesis on the gestural crisis which occurred at the end of the nineteenth century,[118] Rilke's words indirectly draw a parallel between Rodin's sculptures, which capture all the 'innumerable transitions' and 'intervening moments' of the body,[119] and the invention of cinema, which breaks the temporality of ancient images. Unlike photography that freezes movement,[120] Rodin's sculptures represent the development of a gesture by creating a visual sequence of transitory movements and bodily attitudes, which result from the character's premovement (a notion which I shall define in the next section). Rodin considers movement as the transition from one attitude to another.[121] The passage from one attitude to another

114 Ibid., p. 339.

115 See Liandrat-Guigues, *Cinéma et sculpture*, pp. 9 and 69–74.

116 See Didi-Huberman, *Le Danseur des solitudes*, p. 113.

117 Rainer Maria Rilke, *Rodin*, trans. by Jessie Lemont and Hans Trausil (London: Grey Walls Press, 1946), p. 31.

118 Agamben, 'Notes on gesture', pp. 48–52.

119 Rilke, *Rodin*, p. 31.

120 However, as Liandriat-Guigues explains, Rodin liked working with photographs, but without copying the image they show. The development of the different phases of the gesture links Rodin's sculpture to chronophotography. See Liandrat-Guigues, *Cinéma et sculpture*, p. 73.

121 Auguste Rodin and Paul Gsell, *Rodin on Arts and Artists*, trans. by Romilly Fedden (New York: Dover Publications, 1957), p. 32.

involves the coordination of all the body parts. Each attitude sets the whole body in motion, and the transitory movements depicted by Rodin involve complex connections. For example, when someone walks, the feet move in coordination with the knees and the swinging of the arms, as well as with all the uncountable micromovements of the body schema. If someone hails a taxi by waving, the transition from the walking attitude to the waving attitude impacts on the position of the feet and legs, and the movement of the arm changes the equilibrium of the body in space. If a gesture is transitory by nature, its measure depends on the linkage between plural bodily movements and postures. Rodin emphasises the ideas of passage and shifting in sculpture:

> It is, in short, a metamorphosis of this kind that the painter or the sculptor effects in giving movement to his personages. He represents the transition from one pose to another – he indicates how insensibly the first glides into the second. In his work, we still see a part of what was and we discover a part of what is to be.[122]

The figuration of the passage of time in the body echoes Deleuze's definition of the everyday attitude in film that he associates with a time-image embodying the shifting between 'the before' and 'the after', as discussed in Chapter 2.[123] In his interview with Rodin, Paul Gsell notes when contemplating *L'Age d'Airain* (*The Age of Bronze*, 1877): 'The subject of this sculpture is exactly that – the passage from somnolence to the vigor of the being ready for action.'[124] By showing the transition from somnolence to awakening, from torpor to action, the sculpture, according to Rilke, 'indicates in Rodin's work the birth of gesture'.[125]

Premovement and the Birth of Gestures

The fundamental notion of premovement, which enables us to consider the relationship between sculpture and cinema and the transition from posture to gesture, has been conceptualised by the dancer and

122 Ibid., pp. 32–3.
123 Deleuze, *Cinema 2. The Time-Image*, p. 195.
124 Rodin and Gsell, *L'Art*, p. 33.
125 Rilke, *Rodin*, p. 21.

scholar Hubert Godard in dance studies. The latter analyses a scene from Vincente Minnelli's *Ziegfeld Follies* (1946) in which Gene Kelly and Fred Astaire make the exact same gestures. Yet, the way they perform the choreography looks very different, on account of the premovement which is peculiar to each dancer.[126] The premovement anticipates the attack of the gesture and mostly depends on the weight of the body, which shapes the individual's attitude towards gravity.[127] Therefore, it is the attitude that not only preexists the birth of the gesture – for example, in the way an individual stands – but also produces the expressive impulsion of the performed gesture. The same gestural form varies in accordance with the premovement which involves the continuous nonconscious action of the body schema.[128] Hubert Godard's definition of premovement, which focuses on all the imperceptible motions which enable the body schema to find its equilibrium in relation to gravity, evokes this sentence of Rilke: 'Even stillness, where there was stillness, consisted of hundreds and hundreds of moments of motion that kept their equilibrium.'[129] Moreover, posture, through the activity of the muscular system, does not result from a purely mechanical force, but from emotional, affective and often unintentional fluxes of energy which give its unique quality to the human gesture. Hubert Godard's concept echoes Rudolf von Laban's theories on dance. As the latter writes, each bodily movement, according to the body's weight and its environment, reveals one's inner life and 'originates from an inner excitement of the nerves, caused by [...] sense impression', resulting 'in the voluntary or involuntary inner effort or impulse to move'.[130] The premovement gives its impulsion to the gesture. The flow of vital energy (or 'the flow of movement', to use Laban's terminology)[131]

126 Hubert Godard, 'Le Geste et sa perception', in Isabelle Ginot, Marcelle Michel and Hubert Godard (postface), *La Danse au XXe siècle* (Paris: Larousse-Bordas, 1998), p. 225.

127 Ibid., p. 224.

128 Ibid.

129 Rilke, *Rodin*, p. 4.

130 Rudolf von Laban, *The Mastery of Movement*, revised by Lisa Ullmann (Plymouth: Northcote House, 1988), p. 19.

131 Ibid., p. 18.

shapes the body through effort (like the effect of 'three-dimensional "sculpting"'[132] according to Dee Reynold's expression), in relation to its environment and in interaction with others.

Premovement often structures the mise-en-scène of post-New Wave films. In *L'Enfant secret* (*The Secret Son*, 1979), Philippe Garrel films the birth of gestures, from the stasis of the body to its movement, in long shots which focus on the premovement for a long time, following Bresson's recommendation: 'Be sure of having used to the full all that is communicated by immobility and silence.'[133] Such a method of mise-en-scène enables the filmmaker to create a sense of escalation, to intensify the slightest gestures and to amplify the characters' feelings through their bodily rhythms. Considering the significance of the musical notion of weak beat ('temps faible') in Akerman's *Je, tu, il, elle* and *Prénom Carmen*, Damien Truchot demonstrates how both filmmakers emphasise premovement by extending the time preceding the birth of the characters' gestures.[134] He draws a parallel between the musical anacrusis and the notion of premovement to highlight the role of breath in the expression of gestures. The purpose of the anacrusis consists in giving an impulsion to the musical phrase.[135] In *Prénom Carmen*, the musical attack, which mirrors the attack of the bank itself,[136] highlights the emergence of the musicians' gestures, who suspend their bow in the air before attacking a new phrase. In the String Quartet n°10 (Op. 74), which is rehearsed during the sequence of the bank robbery, the attack of the main theme is repeated several times and escalates during the first movement. The violinist takes a deep breath, positions himself in front of the musical score and gives a stroke of the bow, which brings in its wake the rest of the quartet (see Figures 3.10, 3.11 and 3.12).

132 Dee Reynolds, *Rhythmic Subjects* (Alton, Hampshire, England: Dance Books), p. 8.

133 Bresson, *Notes on the Cinematograph*, p. 16.

134 Damien Truchot, 'Sur le temps faible: Akerman/Godard', in *Sur le geste*, ed. by Suzanne Liandrat-Guigues (Le Havre: De l'incidence, 2006), p. 156.

135 Ibid., p. 146.

136 Critics have often mentioned the parallel between the musical attack and the bank attack in *Prénom Carmen*. See Jean-Luc Godard, Guy Scarpetta and Dominique Païni, 'Jean-Luc Godard la curiosité du sujet', *Artpress*, p. 13; Alain Bergala, *Nul mieux que Godard* (Paris: Cahiers du cinéma, 1999), p. 116.

Figures 3.10–3.12. *Prénom Carmen*: The violinist takes a deep breath and starts to play.

Waves and Seascape: The Fluidity of Gestures

Finally, the emergence of the gestural flows in *Prénom Carmen*, as well as their sculptural dimension, needs to be considered in relation to the visual and aural motifs of the seascape. In *Prénom Carmen*, the stream of life – the 'torrents de vie' as violist Claire says in reference to Beethoven's *Tagebuch* – emerges through the co-presence of gestures, music and natural elements, which enter into dialogue with one another through the audiovisual medium, giving birth to the image in the spectator's eyes. According to Pethő, Godard uses the metaphor of ebb and flow in his cinema to stress the idea that '[t]he blank screen becomes the shore of a cinematic ocean where the waves can be either images or sounds […]'.[137] The cinematic screen becomes this liminal space where gesture generates rhythms, forms and traces that circulate in the continuous flow of sounds and moving images. It is through these gestural dynamics of interrelation and intermediality that Godard, as a filmmaker, aims to address the spectator as an active subject.

Throughout the film, the movement of the waves helps understand human gestures and the notion of premovement. The opening shot of the film starts with Carmen saying in voice-over: 'C'est en moi, en toi que se produit des vagues terribles' [It's in me, in you that terrible waves occur]. The water retreats in an inward movement and then springs forward and outward. Godard films numerous shots of waves which, like a life force, constantly revitalise the movement of the sea. Such images evoke the choreography of the string quartet. The two violinists, the violist and the cellist continuously push and pull their bows, creating a tide-like swaying movement that circulates between them. In the perpetual movement of ebb and flow, two opposing forces move the powerful liquid masses of the sea which, before the birth of each new wave, seems to be suspended in a brief, indecisive and never completely still moment of silence. When Didi-Huberman describes the style of the flamenco dancer Israel Galván, he compares his gesture to the encounter between 'deux mouvements affrontés' [two confronting movements], which at their pivotal point creates a 'zone

137 Pethő, *Cinema and Intermediality*, p. 280.

d'arrêt' [stop zone] where the silence of the gesture resounds.[138] Similarly, in Godard's film, the interplay of contradictory energetic fluxes, which is visible in the dynamic shots of the sea, structures the gestural choreography of Carmen and Joseph, for instance, when they are firmly pressing the palm of their hands one against the other. Their gestures of rejection and attraction echo the backwash of the sea. For example, when Joseph, bare-chested, stands close to Carmen, who is looking at the sea through the window, his gestures are hesitant and are suspended halfway while he brushes her green dress. As Carmen encourages him, he abruptly undresses her, in a movement which evokes Rodin's *L'Eternelle Idole* (*The Eternal Idol*, c. 1890–3), but his impulsive gesture, which is interrupted by Carmen, suddenly withdraws.

The interrelation between the music, the seascape and the bodily rhythms draws attention the act of listening. Through the analogy between the characters' and the musicians' gestures, Godard explores what Bergala calls 'la profondeur de l'écoute' [the depth of listening].[139] The filmmaker playfully refers to psychoanalytical theories,[140] for instance, when he compares Carmen to Electra or plays with the resonance between the words *mer* (sea) and *mère* (mother).[141] According to Barthes, modern ways of listening developed with psychoanalysis and the exploration of the unconscious. While listening was historically considered an intentional and conscious act, from this point onwards, there are unknown territories that can be explored:

> [L]istening includes in its field not only the unconscious in the topical sense of the term, but also, so to speak, its lay forms: the implicit, the indirect, the supplementary, the delayed: listening grants access to all forms of polysemy, of overdetermination, of superimposition, there is a disintegration of the Law which prescribes direct, unique listening; by definition, listening was *applied*; today we ask listening to *release* [...][142]

138 Didi-Huberman, *Le Danseur des solitudes*, p. 114.

139 Aumont, *A quoi pensent les films*, p. 270.

140 Regarding Godard's interest in psychoanalysis, see Powrie, 'Godard's *Prénom Carmen* (1984), Masochism, and the Male Gaze'.

141 In *Prénom Carmen*, Godard refers to Giraudoux's *Electre* (1937) and quotes the play in the final dialogue of the film.

142 Barthes, *The Responsibility of Forms*, p. 258.

Barthes's words, particularly the terms 'superimposition' or 'release' (*laisser surgir*), relevantly describe Godard's editing techniques which combine and superimpose heterogeneous visual and aural elements. At the end of the film, in the hotel, while Carmen puts her hand under Joseph's chin before being rejected with a wave of his hand, the call of the seagulls suddenly resounds for a few seconds. Then, Carmen's gang leader enters the room, briefly strokes her hair and kisses her ear before leaving the room again. Joseph bitterly remarks that the man's gesture was not accompanied by the sound of the sea, putting words to his ability to listen to Carmen's body beyond what can be consciously heard.

Revealingly, Rodin's sculptures are often compared to the liquid movement of water and to the swell. Rilke's depiction of Rodin's work is particularly relevant to Godard's film in the way he describes gestures as rushes of water (*jaillissement*). For example, he observes how the gesture in *L'Âge d'airain* 'bursts forth like a spring that softly ripples over this body'.[143] Claire Gheerardyn, who analyses Rilke's metaphorical language by comparing it to Bergson's description of movement, points out the powerful evocation of water in his essay, which underlines the suddenness and momentum of gestures. In the passages quoted by Gheerardyn, gesture takes maritime and aqueous shapes: the terms 'jet d'eau' [water jet], 'vagues' [waves], source, 'ressac' [backwash], and the repetition of the verb 'jaillir' [to gush] evoke the gestural flows in *Prénom Carmen*, especially during the 'Rodin scenes'.[144] For example, during the sequence in Uncle Jean's flat, after Carmen rejects Joseph's gestures by pushing him off-screen, his hand suddenly springs from the off-field space and grips her shoulder (see Figures 3.13, 3.14 and 3.15). The fluidity of his gesture is emphasised by the way Godard turns off the diegetic sounds in favour of Beethoven and the sound of the waves. The sudden and mute apparition of Joseph's hand enables the viewer to perceive the birth of the gesture in the shot. Following this, after having inserted a shot showing the surging of the waves, Godard repeats the exact same take, but instead of editing Beethoven's music, mixes the sounds of

143 Rilke, *Rodin*, p. 21.

144 Claire Gheerardyn, 'Geste révélé, geste révélateur: Rilke face à Rodin', *Fabula / Les colloques*, Penser le mouvement (2015) <http://www.fabula.org/colloques/document2666.php> [accessed 15 April 2017].

Figures 3.13–3.15. *Prénom Carmen*: Joseph grips Carmen's shoulder.

the sea with Carmen and Joseph's dialogue. Again, Joseph's hand springs from the off-camera space and grips her shoulder, while she says: 'Je vous attire' [You're attracted to me]. The cinematic process of repetition makes the characters' gestures resonate with the continuous sound of the waves, and shapes the spectator's perception of gestures.

Similarly to the sculptor who shapes the forms with his two hands, Godard uses only two mixing tracks, because he has 'only two hands to manipulate them'.[145] The metaphor of the gesture of carving occurs repeatedly throughout the film. The filmmaker uses the sculptural motif to forge links between the images of the quartet, of the sea, and of the couple, and the editing to create associations, metaphors or equivalences. 'The view of a violin which is carving [the audible space]' is associated with the 'image of the sea which does the same, carving with waves and crevasses, highs and lows', and finally with the image of the couple 'who will have moments of high and low feeling'.[146] Such a manner of constructing the film and creating cohesion defines cinema according to Godard: 'This is how it all hangs together, completely logically, that's the cinema.'[147]

Conclusion

In the final sequence of the film, Uncle Jean's assistant quotes Beethoven's *Tagebuch* to reveal the film's inner workings: 'L'union parfaite de plusieurs voix empêche, somme toute, le progrès de l'une vers l'autre' [The precise coinciding of several musical voices generally hinders the progression from one to the other.][148] Through the gestures of linkage and detachment, the heterogeneous elements of the films do not merge, but enter into dialogue and communicate.

145 Godard and Bachmann, p. 16.

146 Ibid., p. 17.

147 Ibid.

148 Translation in Maynard Solomon, *Beethoven Essays* (Cambridge, MA: Harvard University Press, 1990), p. 247.

First, in opposition to television which abolishes the necessary distance between the spectator and the image, Godard reveals how gestures in cinema prove to be essential in the process of fabrication and communication of the images. Secondly, the gestures, which shape the forms of the film and give cohesion to its hybrid aesthetics, emphasise the 'gesturality' of the cinematic image. Composed of a series of frames, the moving image captures the constant shifting between 'the before' and 'the after' that characterises the transitory nature of corporeal movements. In *Prénom Carmen*, the gestures create a liminal space between different attitudes, postures, actions, but also visual and aural perceptions. As Deleuze points out, Godard's cinema emphasises the interstice between two elements, '[b]etween two actions, between two affections, between two perceptions, between two visual images, between two sound images, between the sound and the visual'.[149] It is in this sense that Löffler highlights the gestural dimension of the cinematic image in Godard's *Passion*, arguing that 'the images themselves become gestures entering into an exchange throughout the film'.[150]

Finally, gesture is the element which, in *Prénom Carmen*, incorporates and develops the features of the other arts, by highlighting the connection between the gestures of music-making and the gestures of filmmaking, and freeing Rodin's sculptures from their original paralysis. By expanding on Agamben's argument, who postulates that cinema exhibits the 'mediality'[151] or, in other words, the intersubjective and relational qualities of gestures, we can argue, in light of the analysis of *Prénom Carmen*, that Godard's cinema stresses the intermedial nature of gestures. On the one hand, as discussed in Chapter 1, they interact with the technological body of film (including the camera, the editing table and the mixing deck) and, on the other hand, they set in motion and interconnect the features of the other arts.

Referring to Klossowski's work and focusing on the semiotics of gestures in the film *Roberte* (1979), the next chapter explores further the relationship between cinema and the other arts. The *tableau vivant* is a device used by Klossowski and Zucca to problematise the links between the representation, performance and reception of gestures in their film.

149 Deleuze, *Cinema 2. The Time-Image*, p. 180.

150 Löffler, 'Gesturing the Image', p. 32.

151 Agamben, 'Notes on Gesture', p. 58.

CHAPTER 4

The Mystery of Gesture according to Pierre Klossowski: *Tableau Vivant* and Film Performance in Pierre Zucca's *Roberte* (1979)

> Draw from your models the proof that they exist with their oddities and their enigmas.[1]
>
> – Robert Bresson

In a film, the meaning of gestures seems to be immediately intelligible. According to Merleau-Ponty, '[t]he meaning of a film is incorporated into its rhythm just as the meaning of gesture may immediately be read in that gesture: the film does not mean anything but itself.'[2] Yet, as previously seen, gestures sometimes make us wonder about their potential signification, as if they were concealing a secret. Unveiling the characters' conflicting relationship with verbal language, they are the sensitive symptoms of trauma, taboo, pathologies and fantasies. The apparent obviousness of gestures proves difficult to translate into words. As discussed in Chapter 3, the fabrication of cinematic images and the communication of their meanings to the spectator originate in a mysterious dialogue of heterogeneous gestures. In the 1980s, Godard often referred to Christian imagery in order to reflect on the mystery of creation and to criticise 'the spiritual bankruptcy of modern materialism'.[3] For example, in the *tableaux vivants* of *Passion* (1982), which lay emphasis on the corporeality of the cinematic image, models reincarnate masterpieces of European art

1 Bresson, *Notes on the Cinematograph*, p. 16.

2 Maurice Merleau-Ponty, *Sense and Non-Sense* (Evanston, IL: Northwestern University Press, 1966), p. 57.

3 Steven Jacobs, 'Tableaux Vivants 1: Painting, Film, Death and Passion Plays in Pasolini and Godard', in *Framing Pictures: Film and the Visual Arts* (Edinburgh: Edinburgh University Press, 2011), p. 108.

history such as El Greco's *The Immaculate Conception* (1607–13). Resisting against industrial modes of communication in a manner comparable, albeit different to Godard,[4] the writer and artist Pierre Klossowski also draws on theology, iconography and the genre of *tableau vivant* to consider the gestural nature of the image.

As a renowned translator, essayist, philosopher, novelist, prolific author of large format drawings and occasional screenwriter and actor, Klossowski (1905–2001) developed a heterogeneous, and yet very coherent literary and artistic work that influenced a new generation of philosophers in the 1960s and 1970s, among them Foucault and Deleuze. All of his work – including the film adaptations *Roberte* (1979) by Pierre Zucca and, more indirectly, *L'Hypothèse du tableau volé* (*The Hypothesis of the Stolen Painting*, 1978) by Raoul Ruiz[5] – reveals his fascination with the mystery of human gestures. Klossowki was fully involved in the creative process of *Roberte.* His first known project of adaptation dates back to 1966,[6] before his first encounter with Zucca. Klossowski's interest in cinema significantly grew in the mid-1960s. In 1965, he was interviewed in Eric Rohmer's documentary *Le Celluloïd et le Marbre* (*Celluloid and Marble*) in which artists and writers such as Victor Vasarely and Claude Simon were asked to express their views on cinema. At that time, he also played the role of the merchant in Robert Bresson's *Au hasard Balthazar* (1966). In the 1970s, he collaborated with Ruiz on the adaptation of *La Vocation suspendue* (*The Suspended Vocation*, 1978).

Interweaving literature and means of visual expression, such as painting and sculpture, Klossowski's work reveals his 'obsession visuelle du geste muet' [visual obsession with silent gesture].[7] His novels and essays cause

4 Deleuze suggests a parallel between the works of William S. Burroughs, Marshall McLuhan, Klossowski and Godard. For the philosopher, these authors succeed in revitalising ways of thinking about the image, both in theory and in practice. See Gilles Deleuze, 'Lettre à Pierre Klossowski', *Europe*, 1034–5 (2015), 61–2.

5 Although *L'Hypothèse du tableau volé* draws on his literary work, Klossowski did not contribute to the writing of the script.

6 Pierre Klossowski, 'Argument de 1966', in Klossowski and Pierre Zucca, *Roberte au cinéma*, special issue of *Obliques* (Paris: Borderie, 1978), pp. 11–14.

7 Pierre Klossowski, *Tableaux vivants: Essais critiques 1936–1983*, ed. by Patrick Mauriès (Paris: Le Promeneur, 2001), p. 134.

two distinct modes of communication – gesture on the one hand and verbal language on the other – to interact. In *Le Bain de Diane* (*Diana at Her Bath*, 1956) and *Les Lois de l'hospitalité* (1965), Klossowski uses the rhetorical device of ekphrasis to speculate on the potential meanings of gestures in art.[8] The meticulous description and interpretation of bodily movements, attitudes and postures emphasises their unsolvable ambiguity, and suggests the limits of the mediation of language to convey vision.[9] In the early 1970s, Klossowski decided to devote himself almost exclusively to the visual arts. Defining himself as a 'monomane' [monomaniac],[10] Klossowski used various media – including film – to reiterate the same visions, especially those depicting the fantasised heroine named Roberte. In the early 1950s, Klossowski asked his brother Balthus to illustrate *Roberte ce soir* (1953),[11] but, dissatisfied with the result, eventually decided to do it himself, first by making lead pencil drawings that evoke the silvery texture of early silent films, before opting for coloured pencils in 1972.

The character of Roberte is modelled on the physiognomy of Klossowski's wife and muse Denise Morin-Sinclaire. In 1970, the latter posed before Zucca's camera for photographs of *tableaux vivants*, published in Klossowski's essay *La Monnaie vivante (Living Currency)*. In order to compose the pictures, Zucca drew on his experience of still photography, which he actively practiced from the mid-1960s to the mid-1970s on the film sets of directors like François Truffaut (*L'Enfant sauvage* (*The Wild Child*), 1970), Jacques Rivette (*Out* 1, 1971) and Jean Eustache (*Mes petites amoureuses* (*My Little Loves)*, 1974). Acting as a liaison between the New Wave and the post-New Wave generations,[12] Zucca is a filmmaker who reflects on the fabrication of images, exploring a liminal space between

8 See ibid., p. 130.

9 See Alain Fleischer, 'Retours, détours, contours', in *Pierre Klossowski, tableaux vivants*, ed. by Agnès de la Beaumelle (Paris: Gallimard, Centre Pompidou, 2007), p. 47.

10 Pierre Klossowski, 'L'Indiscernable', in *Pierre Klossowski*, ed. by Catherine Grenier (Paris: La Différence, Centre national des arts plastiques; Marseille: Ryôan-ji, 1990), p. 188.

11 See Fleischer, 'Retours, détours, contours', p. 54.

12 See *Pierre Zucca, l'homme, le cinéaste*, dir. Angela Romboni (Carlotta, 2007).

illusion and the real.[13] In his first long feature *Vincent mit l'âne dans un pré* (1976), he depicts a world where falsification, simulation and dissimulation underscore the ambiguous nature of the cinematic image. Reality is experienced as a *trompe-l'oeil* by the characters who are at once captivated by phantasmagorical visions and stuck in the banality of everyday life.[14] Sharing the same passion for the image, Klossowski saw Zucca as the ideal filmmaker to direct *Roberte*. In 1975, the young director shot a black-and-white short film with the cooperation of Klossowski and his wife, in preparation for the long feature.

Roberte's erotic adventures in post-war Paris are recounted in the trilogy *Les Lois de l'hospitalité* (comprising *Roberte ce soir*, *La Révocation de l'Edit de Nantes* (1959) and *Le Souffleur ou le théâtre de société* (1960)), in which the writer tackles the problem of identity. Of Calvinist origins, Klossowski's character Roberte was a member of the Resistance during the Second World War and has become an influential Member of Parliament and chief of the censorship board in the time of the Fourth Republic. She is married to Octave, a Catholic and reactionary upper-class old man, theologian, writer and art collector, who is dismissed from his academic chair for having collaborated during the Vichy era. Octave subjects his wife to the perverse practice called 'les lois de l'hospitalité', defined by Klossowski as the 'prostitution' of the spouse by the husband, or her 'adultération' – a neologism that refers to Octave's willingness to make her wife adulterous.[15] In doing so, Octave hopes to grasp Roberte's authentic identity, which she supposedly conceals in his presence.[16] But Roberte's identity proves indeterminate. She plays incompatible roles that reveal the plurality of her natures. Her dissolute life dissolves the coherence of her selfhood. In the film adaptation this is demonstrated to the spectator through the unintelligibility of her gestures, which take the form of 'hiéroglyphes animés'

13 See Pierre Zucca, Jean-Claude Bonnet, Philippe Carcassonne and Jacques Fieschi, '*Roberte*. Entretien avec Pierre Zucca', *Cinématographe*, June 1978, p. 41.

14 See Pierre Klossowski, 'Simuler le simulateur (*Vincent mit l'âne dans un pré*)', *Cahiers du cinéma*, July–August 1976, pp. 83–4.

15 See Klossowski and Zucca, *Roberte au cinéma*, pp. 11–12.

16 Pierre Klossowski, 'Protase et apodose', in *Klossowski*, ed. by René Micha (Aix-en-Provence: L'Arc, 1970), p. 12.

[animated hieroglyphs], to use Antonin Artaud's expression.[17] Performing Octave's role, Klossowski plays opposite Morin-Sinclaire to the point of creating a troubling confusion between reality and fiction,[18] complicating the problematic staging of male sadomasochistic fantasies played out on the female body.

According to Klossowski, cinema must not imitate painting or literature.[19] Yet *Roberte* is a film that integrates other arts such as painting, photography, theatre and literature. The cinematic specificity of gesture in the film emerges, paradoxically, from the interaction with other media, such as the literary descriptions of *La Révocation de l'Edit de Nantes*, Frédéric Tonnerre's paintings – a fictitious nineteenth-century pompous artist whose ridiculously emphatic and outdated academic style fascinates Octave – and with the drawings made by Klossowski after the shooting of the film. The latter was deeply inspired and fascinated by the living embodiment of his visions on the film set.[20] In his drawings, Klossowski, who fears representing his figures like inert wooden puppets or marionettes, breathes life into the characters thanks to the theatricality of their gestures.[21]

Unlike an actor who performs on stage, a model poses and therefore does not act. For Klossowski, 'the picture [is] an instrument which acts by itself [...].'[22] In his life-size drawings, the image originates in the interrelation between the model's corporeal presence, the artist's inner vision and the work of his hand and gaze.[23] By contrast, the practice of cinema essentially relies on the actors' performances. If Klossowski considers Morin-Sinclaire

17 Antonin Artaud, *Le Théâtre et son double*, in *Œuvres complètes*, 26 vols (Paris: Gallimard, 1956–94), IV (1964), p. 65.

18 See Jérôme Prieur, 'Hospitalité. Pierre Zucca: *Roberte*', in *Nuits blanches, essais sur le cinéma* (Paris: Gallimard, 1980), p. 53.

19 Pierre Klossowski, 'Le Cinéma ne doit pas simuler la littérature', *Les Nouvelles Littéraires*, 15 March 1979, p. 14.

20 See Fleischer, 'Retours, détours, contours', p. 52.

21 Klossowski considers himself a 'playwright'. Cited in Anthony Spira, 'A Pantomime of Spirits', in *Pierre Klossowski*, ed. by Anthony Spira and Sarah Wilson (Ostfildern: Hatje Cantz, 2006), p. 67.

22 Ibid., p. 64.

23 Klossowski, 'L'Indiscernable', p. 185.

as Roberte's 'modèle' even in Zucca's film,[24] she is actually an actor who embodies a character and acts a part. Breaking the unilateral relationship between the artist's gaze and the model's passive body, the shooting becomes the locus of an intersubjective and playful experience where the theatricality of the *mise-en-scène*, the incongruous situations within the narrative, the expressive style of acting and the comical, even *burlesque* tonality of certain scenes bring out the inextricable intertwining of seriousness and hilarity inherent to Klossowski's work, – what Blanchot names 'the hilarity of the serious'.[25]

Film performance in *Roberte* is closely related to Klossowski's original conception of the *tableau vivant*. Popular in eighteenth-century theatre and nineteenth-century Parisian salons, this practice which consists in reproducing the composition of a painting – models hold the pose by precisely imitating the gestures of the painted figures – develops 'a site where the "figural" gives way to the "corporeal" '.[26] By giving life to a pre-existing representation, the models appear like living statues, suspended between stillness and movement, representation and life. For Klossowski, the ambiguous passage from a frozen position to the expression of motion (and vice versa) evokes the mechanically broken-down movements of automatons[27] and the jerky gestures of silent film actors, which deeply fascinated him as a child.[28] If the animation of the *tableaux vivants* in *Roberte* sometimes resembles a mechanical ballet, Zucca also leaves room for the actors' spontaneous reactions. Crucially, the *tableaux vivants* are acted rather than posed. The term *tableau vivant* must be understood literally: the image is at once organised, staged and ritualised like a *tableau* by the director, and living thanks to the actors' singular performances. They imbue the space

24 See ibid.

25 Maurice Blanchot, 'The Laughter of the Gods/Le Rire des Dieux', in Pierre Klossowski and Maurice Blanchot, *Decadence of the Nude/La Décadence du nu*, ed. by Sarah Wilson and intro. by Alyce Mahon (London: Black Dog, 2002), p. 163.

26 Pethő, *Cinema and Intermediality*, p. 381.

27 See 'Entretiens avec Pierre Klossowski', *Les Nuits de France Culture*, France Culture, 12 May 2016 [first broadcast 5–10 June 1972].

28 See Klossowski, 'Le Cinéma ne doit pas simuler la littérature', p. 14.

of representation with emotions and bodily sensations that they at once simulate and experience.[29]

On the one hand, Zucca – as well as Klossowski who contributed to the mise-en-scène by paying close attention to the position of hands and fingers[30] – draws on a repertoire of codified gestures, referring to the body language of figurative painting and the histrionic code of silent cinema. On the other hand, the film simultaneously shows how the actors' performances escape the codification of body language. The camera captures the quivering of their skins, and grasps the impulsive life that agitates their bodies by making their corporeal presence palpable. As will be discussed in the last section of this chapter with reference to Anne-Marie Dardigna's criticism of the misogynistic dimension of Klossowski's *Les Lois de l'hospitalité*,[31] this approach to performance proves highly problematic when the female performer is asked to perform coerced sexual acts in which she expresses spontaneous gestures of discomfort.

Body Language

In his essay 'Klossowski or bodies-language', Deleuze notes the sophisticated relationship between body and language in Klossowski's literary work: 'Klossowski's work is build upon an astonishing parallelism between body and language, or rather on a reflection of one in the other. Reasoning is the operation of language, but pantomime is the operation of the body.'[32] While highlighting their difference, Deleuze analyses the parallel between the two, and the exchange of properties between the

29 Fleischer, 'Retours, détours, contours', p. 52.

30 See Zucca, Bonnet, Carcassonne and Fieschi, '*Roberte*. Entretien avec Pierre Zucca', pp. 40–1.

31 See Anne-Marie Dardigna, *Les Châteaux d'Eros ou Les Infortunes du sexe des femmes* (Paris: F. Maspero, 1980).

32 Gilles Deleuze, *The Logic of Sense*, trans. by Mark Lester (New York: Columbia University Press, 1990), p. 280.

'flexion' of verbal language and the flexion of gestures.[33] In *La Révocation*, the device of ekphrasis animates the body of the female figure depicted by Ingres in *La Grande Odalisque* (1814) and renders the frozen gestures fluid.[34] Language constitutes bodies made of words. Postures, gestures and attitudes articulate sentences, arrange syntax and deploy semantic fields. If Deleuze prefers the portmanteau word 'bodies-language' to conceptualise the language of the body, Klossowski and Zucca often use the more conventional notion of 'body language' (*langage du corps*) to refer to the codification of bodily expression in the realm of aesthetics.[35] Costume, posture, gaze and gesture transmit a code of embedded meanings that are supposedly immediately accessible to the spectator, although the intelligibility of a gestural code and the understanding of its subtleties often require being familiar with its cultural conventions. On this point, the art historian André Chastel notes how modern spectators struggle to grasp the meaning of codified gestures in ancient (especially religious) painting.[36] As Zucca suggests, the coordination of postures, attitudes, hand gestures and looks can potentially articulate the most sophisticated 'sentences'. Drawing on the codes of religious iconography, antique statuary, late nineteenth-century academic painting, early twentieth-century illustrations and silent cinema, Klossowski and Zucca explore how meaning is embodied in body language, and more precisely in the movement of the characters' gestures. By referring to the genre of *tableau vivant*, they show how the corporeal nature of this language – which is not frozen, but living and in motion – imbues the code of gestures with sensations and impulses that unsettle the representation.

Remarkably, Zucca mimics the histrionic code of silent cinema in the ending sequence of *Roberte*, which, in the form of a flashback interspersed with intertitles, narrates the meeting between the wounded German officer Von A. (Jean-François Stévenin) and Roberte, who is working as a nurse for the Red Cross in Rome during the Second World War. The sequence

33 Ibid., p. 286.

34 Klossowski, *Les Lois de l'hospitalité*, p. 22.

35 Pierre Zucca, 'La Double Nature de l'image', in Klossowski and Zucca, *Roberte au cinéma*, p. 8.

36 André Chastel, *Le Geste dans l'art* (Paris: Liana Levi, 2001), p. 22.

establishes a clear correspondence between gestures and feelings. Eloquent gestures also convey the characters' intentions. When the head nurse asks Roberte to exit the room, she indicates the door with her index finger. The tradition of 'eloquent gestures'[37] in silent cinema draws on the histrionic code of theatre. Numerous pedagogues, especially in the United States, appropriated the methods of the French theoretician François Delsarte and developed the 'Delsarte system' or 'Delsartism' in order to codify the gestural expression of emotions and feelings. According to Roberta E. Pearson and Christophe Damour, the codified system of Delsartism largely caricatured and betrayed Delsarte's ideas, actually based on 'the observation of human behaviour' and 'nature' rather than on the imitation of artificial postures: 'Delsarte, it would seem, desired to challenge the hegemony of the histrionic code but the wholesale acceptance of Delsartism perverted its founder's intentions.'[38] Histrionic actors selected 'their gestures from a conventional, standardized repertoire'[39] which was very precisely described and illustrated in acting manuals. The histrionic code is often assimilated into a linguistic system in which each gesture or posture corresponds to an unequivocal meaning. Yet, Pearson notes that this very peculiar semiotics of gesture is not equivalent to verbal language: 'A gesture is not a word or a syllable but a whole phrase which cannot be further broken down.'[40] The combination of different postures and gestures enables the actors to express various meanings, although the 'Delsarte system' encompasses a 'limited lexicon'.[41]

However, in the broader framework of film performance, Nacache argues that establishing a semiology of gestures proves to be 'impossible' or, at least, highly problematic.[42] First of all, Delsartism remains exceptional

37 See Pearson, *Eloquent Gestures*.

38 Pearson, *Eloquent Gestures*, p. 22. See also Christophe Damour, 'L'Influence de Delsarte sur le jeu de l'acteur de cinéma aux Etats-Unis', in *L'Acteur de cinéma: Approches plurielles*, ed. by Vincent Amiel, Jacqueline Nacache, Geneviève Sellier and Christian Viviani (Rennes: Presses universitaires de Rennes, 2007), pp. 19–31.

39 Pearson, *Eloquent Gestures*, p. 21.

40 Ibid., p. 23.

41 Ibid., p. 24.

42 Nacache, *L'Acteur de cinéma*, pp. 157–9.

in film history: not only did it not embrace all the diversity of acting styles during the silent era – for instance, the expression of pathological behaviours in slapstick comedy disrupts any stable gestural code as discussed in Chapter 2 – but the craft of acting considerably evolved with the revolution of talking pictures. With the rise of realism and naturalism, actors progressively developed a 'natural' and fluent style of acting. The understanding of the film tends to rely more on verbal expression than on the codification of gestures. Finally, Nacache argues that any attempt to translate a gesture into words signifies the erasure of the gesture to the benefit of a signification which becomes external to it. There is in gestural expression a *je-ne-sais-quoi* that seems to irreducibly escape verbal translation.[43]

The tension between gesture and language is analysed by Julia Kristeva in her influential article entitled 'Le Geste, pratique ou communication?' She pinpoints the difficulties encountered in kinesics studies to establish a semiology of gestures based on the communicative and linguistic model of verbal language. She argues that gesture should be considered as a practice that generates a semiotic text in the process of being produced.[44] A gesture shows the process of elaborating on a message and exhibits the activity that precedes the formation of meaning.[45] From this perspective, Kristeva argues that gesture is above all 'anaphoric', in the sense that it indicates directions and establishes relations.[46] Kristeva's theory of gesture proves useful to analyse acting. For instance, Peter Brooks draws on Kristeva's argument to explain that mute gestures in melodrama are too indeterminate and unstable to be analysed linguistically 'in terms of signifier and signified': 'Gesture is in fact desemanticized, it is anaphoric, in Julia Kristeva's term, in that it points *toward* meaning.'[47] Gestures in melodrama must be deciphered like hieroglyphs, marks or metaphors that point toward ineffable affects, emotions, desires or moral dilemmas. Similarly, Naremore,

43 Ibid., p. 158.

44 Kristeva, 'Le Geste, pratique ou communication ?', p. 64.

45 Ibid., p. 50.

46 Ibid., p. 53.

47 Peter Brooks, 'The Text of Muteness', in *Melodramatic Imagination: Balzac, Henry James, Melodrama, and the Mode of Excess* (New Haven, CT: Yale University Press, 1976), p. 71.

in his seminal essay on acting, also refers to Kristeva's anaphoric function to analyse gesture in film: 'Meaningless in itself, the anaphora is a purely relational activity whose free play allows meaning to circulate, even when meaning is unintended.'[48]

The gesture of pointing is perhaps the most conventional anaphoric gesture. The French ethologist Boris Cyrulnik has demonstrated the crucial role of this gesture in relation to language. It is only after several months of neurological maturation that a baby starts using his or her index finger to point at things, instead of trying to catch them with opened fingers. This phase usually corresponds to the beginning of the learning of language.[49] The gesture of the index finger paves the way to the articulation of meaning through verbal language. Chastel highlights the recurrence of this anaphoric gesture in painting. By pointing at a figure or an object within the representation, the gesture of 'admonition', to refer to Alberti's terminology, enables the spectator's gaze to circulate within the *tableau* and to make connections between the different components of the picture. The gesture of the index finger exhibits a process of communication that develops between the space of representation and the spectator.[50]

Figures 4.1–4.2. *Roberte*: An extra and Roberte use their index finger to impose silence on other characters.

48 Naremore, *Acting in the Cinema*, p. 23.

49 Boris Cyrulnik, *La Naissance du sens* (Paris: Hachette, 1991), p. 55.

50 Chastel, *Le Geste dans l'art*, p. 38.

By contrast, when it covers the lips of the painted figure, the index finger indicates the muteness inherent to the image. The *signum harpocraticum* suggests the character's desire to stay quiet, or intimates silence to the other figures or to the spectator. In *Roberte*, while preparing for the staging of a *tableau vivant*, a young extra puts his index finger on his closed lips in order to impose silence on his partner and then, by raising his index, points to the door through which Roberte is supposed to appear (see Figure 4.1). Similarly, Roberte's hands 'censurent la parole' [censor speech],[51] as Klossowski writes, when she puts her index on the mouth of her lover Vittorio (Barbet Schroeder) to prevent him speaking (see Figure 4.2). The religious dimension of the *signum harpocraticum* signifies the primacy of vision over speech.[52] By interlacing eroticism and theology, Klossowski explores the perversions and ambiguities of verbal and body language in a transgressive way.[53] According to Barthes, Klossowski borrows scholastic terms in his writings to unveil the taboos of language and sex.[54] By reusing the code of Christian iconography in erotic *tableaux vivants*,[55] Klossowski seeks to communicate the incommunicability of the fantasy through the silent corporeal presence of the characters. In this sense, Zucca suggests that the *tableaux* in *Roberte* can be viewed as rituals of incarnation.[56]

51 Pierre Klossowski, 'L'Idiome corporel est-il un simulacre de communication ?', in *La Ressemblance* (Marseille: Ryôan-ji, 1984), p. 53.

52 Chastel, *Le Geste dans l'art*, p. 67.

53 Obsessed with the moral tension between bodily and spiritual pleasure, Klossowski is considered as a 'theo-pornologer'. See Alyce Mahon, 'Pierre Klossowski, Theo-pornologer/Pierre Klossowski, Théo-pornologue', in *Decadence of the Nude/La Décadence du nu*, ed. by Wilson, p. 38.

54 Roland Barthes, *Œuvres complètes*, ed. by Eric Marty, 3 vols (Paris: Seuil, 1993–5), II (1994), p. 903.

55 For example, Spira argues that '[...] the images of the parallel bars recall the scene of Christ's crucifixion'. See Spira, 'A Pantomime of Spirits', p. 76.

56 Zucca, Bonnet, Carcassonne and Fieschi, '*Roberte*. Entretien avec Pierre Zucca', p. 41.

Intermedial Migrations and Gestural Variations

At once relational and intersubjective, gestures establish a process of communication that, in *Roberte*, fosters the dialogue between the arts. As demonstrated in Chapter 3, intermediality in cinema interrelates diverse modes of expression that can exchange their gestural properties. In *Roberte*, the genre of *tableau vivant*, which Marie-Hélène Mello defines as a bridge between the arts,[57] explores an in-between space where gestural codes circulate from one medium to another. At the beginning of the film, Octave makes a gesture of *admonition* that invites the spectator to contemplate *Lucrèce*, a painting made by the nineteenth-century (fictitious) painter named Frédéric Tonnerre, supposedly a disciple of Courbet (see Figure 4.3). Ironically, Zucca highlights the ambiguous nature of the

Figure 4.3. *Roberte*: Frédéric Tonnerre's painting entitled *Lucrèce*.

57 Marie-Hélène Mello, 'Le Tableau vivant d'après Raoul Ruiz. Une esthétique de l'"inter-image"', in *La Circulation des images: Médiations des cultures*, ed. by Richard Bégin, Myriam Dussault and Emmanuelle Dyotte (Paris: L'Harmattan, 2006), p. 140.

tableau. Standing on the edge of a small stage that is surrounded with sculptures and pedestals, Octave theatrically opens a red curtain to unveil the painting, which paradoxically looks like a coloured photograph of a *tableau vivant* figuring Roberte as a model. It resembles Zucca's photographs illustrating Klossowski's essay *La Monnaie vivante*. Significantly, a sculpture stands next to the characters on the right side of the *tableau*, highlighting the statue-like aspect of the models. The setting of the film and of the painting not only alludes to theatre – numerous scenes in *Roberte* are framed by curtains or balustrades – but also establishes a clear equivalence between the theatrical scene and the space of the *tableau*. While gesturing toward the painting with the index finger of his right hand, Octave interprets the characters' attitudes and deciphers the meaning of the representation. After having read a Latin quotation inscribed at the bottom of the painting, Octave comments on the painted gestures, covering the image with a speculative text. The scene shows the correlation between the gesture of the index finger, which points to the painting, and the articulation of its meanings by speech.

The apparent convergence of different media in the same space paradoxically highlights their divergences. First, Octave's animated gestures contrast with Tarquin's and Lucretia's petrified attitudes; second, the photographic quality of the image emphasises the artificiality of the pose; finally, the 'painted' figures remain deaf to Octave's words. In his writings on literature, drawing and cinema, Klossowski always clearly defines, analyses and compares the specific components of each medium. In contrast to the graphology of his literary texts, Klossowski considers images as hieroglyphs,[58] thus pointing out their gestural dimension – gestures being typically compared to hieroglyphs as we have seen with Artaud, Kristeva and Brooks. He sees a clear opposition, if not a conflict, between verbal and painterly modes of expression. Speech 'semanticises' gestures and makes them speak, while the irreducible muteness of gestures in painting neutralises speech.[59] Literature opens a mental space where speech, description, argumentation and narrative articulate the meaning of gestures and,

58 Klossowski, 'Entretien avec Alain Arnaud', in *La Ressemblance*, p. 102.

59 Klossowski, *Tableaux vivants*, pp. 126–7.

more broadly, of images.[60] Interpreting gestures requires speculating on the meaning(s) that they seem to indicate. Unlike the specular nature of the image, Klossowski considers literature as being essentially speculative. Writing and drawing are thus two distinct modes of expression.[61]

In film, speech and image, word and gesture co-exist in the same space. In that regard, Roberte's first appearance in the film is revealing. The camera does not show her face, but highlights the desk where she writes her diary. Zucca emphasises her ritual of writing. After opening the drawer where she conceals her diary, she starts to write on a new white page with her fountain pen. The white page is the space of graphology and speech. She simultaneously reads in voice-over the sentence that she is writing. At the end of the first sentence, the camera suddenly moves upward, leaves the space of the diary to unveil the mirror that decorates the writing desk. In the mirror appears the phantasmagorical vision of a hand that strokes her breast. In the specular space of the mirror, visions and fantasies are silently conveyed to the spectator. Finally the camera returns to the diary, revolves and shows Roberte, who gazes at herself in the mirror. The fantasmatic vision in the mirror announces the return of haunting images of the past, especially those of her aggression by Vittorio in 1944. In the same way that the troubling memory of the war resurges in Roberte's mind, Vittorio also surprisingly reappears in her life more than ten years later. In contrast to Roberte's earlier fantasy, where she was imagining the sensuous touch of his hand – obliterating the rest of his body including his face – reality manifests itself on the other side of the mirror in a much more brutal way when she meets Vittorio again. At the first opportunity, he grabs her breasts in a violent gesture of possession.

In *tableaux vivants*, gestures apparently buried in the past are reiterated and revived at other places and times. The *tableau vivant* is a porous site of performance that enables Klossowski to model and remodel his visions in different media. In *Les Lois de l'hospitalité*, gestures do not cease to migrate from one site of performance or from one medium to another. From the models' pose to the *tableau*, and from the *tableau* to its ekphrasis, the

60 See ibid., p. 131.

61 Klossowski, *La Ressemblance*, p. 102.

literary description of a painting implies at least two levels of migration. In *Roberte*, not only are gestures remediated from the ekphrasis to the *tableau vivant*, but also, in a cyclical way, they migrate again from the film to the drawings made by Klossowski after the shooting. All these gestural migrations reveal formal recurrences. Indeed, despite the variety of media, the repetition of similar gestures seems to indicate the reproduction of a gestural code that must be deciphered by the spectator. However, although Klossowski reiterates and reconstructs the same scenes, the expression of the characters' gestures is never identical. As Carrie Noland explains, '[...] when gestures change location, when they migrate from one site of performance to another, they in fact confront a different reception and may even be experienced in a new way.'[62] For example, slight, albeit significant variations can be perceived in the sequence of the 'parallel bars' that Roberte recounts in her diary.[63] An aggressor harasses Roberte in the bus and chases her under the arches of the Palais Royal before kidnapping her and dragging her to a gym with the help of an accomplice. Roberte is then tied to parallel bars and assaulted by her agressor who compulsively licks her opened palm. The sequence was reconstructed in Zucca's photographs that accompany Klossowski's essay *La Monnaie vivante* and in the black-and-white short film and full-length feature film in colour shot respectively in 1975 and 1977. Klossowski repeatedly 'painted' this vision of sexual assault in his life-size coloured pencil drawings made before and after the shooting of the two films. Finally, in collaboration with Klossowski, the artist Jean-Paul Réti designed two sculptures that depict key moments of that sequence: the kidnapping of Roberte in the stairs and her rape.

In all these representations, Roberte's hands are endowed with a sexual connotation.[64] Her right hand is opened by force, finger after finger, by the aggressor. Several drawings depict the man holding two of her fingers, while the others remain closed on her palm. In Zucca's photograph, the male character grips Roberte's wrist, but her fingers remain completely opened, as if she were showing no sign of resistance. On the contrary, she

62 Carrie Noland, 'Introduction', in *Migrations of Gesture*, ed. by Carrie Noland and Sally Ann Ness (Minneapolis: University of Minnesota Press, 2008), p. xvi.

63 Klossowski, *Les Lois de l'hospitalité*, pp. 40–5.

64 Klossowski, *La Ressemblance*, p. 53.

strongly squeezes her palm closed in the long feature film: the aggressor must start again twice to force her to open her fingers. Yet, when he grabs her in the stairs of the gym, she simply places her hands on his shoulders, while in the drawings or in the sculpture, Roberte struggles by making expressive arm and hand gestures. Her right and left hands are either opened or closed: she shows the palm of one hand and hides the other. As Deleuze suggests, hands in Klossowski's work express a dilemma and a disjunction.[65] They ambiguously show and conceal, invite and resist, and indicate contradictory directions to the spectator. In all the *tableaux*, whether they are cinematic, pictorial, literary or photographic, the gestural variations demonstrate the malleable rather than frozen nature of body language. Crucially, the staging of sexual violence raises ethical questions that will be addressed in the last sections of this chapter.

The Suspension of Gestures: Puzzling Gestures and Interpretative Vertigo

In Klossowski's graphic work, gestures that suggest different possible meanings are linked with other gestures that potentially indicate other, often contradictory meanings.[66] The linkage of plural gestures that indicate various directions disorientates the spectator and disrupts the intelligibility of the representation. The beholder faces the enigma of the hieroglyphs.[67] Klossowski transgresses the boundaries between the 'dicible' [utterable] and the 'indicible' [unutterable], the 'montrable' [representable] and the 'immontrable' [unrepresentable].[68] Combining opposite stereotypes in the same bodily expression, Zucca obfuscates the meaning of gestures. Rather than clarifying an action in an unequivocal and homogenous way, stereotypes unveil Roberte's contradictions,

65 See Deleuze, *Logique du sens* (Paris: Minuit, 1969), p. 331.

66 Klossowski, *Tableaux vivants*, p. 131.

67 See Pascal Bonitzer, 'Le Silence extérieur', in *Pierre Klossowski*, ed. by Grenier, p. 38.

68 See Klossowski, *Tableaux vivants*, p. 131.

especially in the *tableaux vivants* that intersperse the film.[69] From this perspective, Roberte's gestures become deeply ambiguous. The complex attitude of her hands and fingers manifests the perverse nature of the image.[70]

Klossowski theorises the concept of contradictory gestures in *La Révocation*. In his diary, Octave appropriates Quintilian's definition of solecism which in rhetoric postulates a contradiction between gesture and speech.[71] Octave attempts to understand the extent to which the notion of solecism could be developed in painting despite the muteness of the painted figures. In the opening sequence of *Roberte*, Octave explains how 'la logique du contradictoire' [the logic of the contradictory] animates the painting of Lucretia's rape (see Figure 4.3). Tonnerre depicts a key moment: Tarquin threatens Lucretia with death if she does not consent; feeling ashamed, she then decides to commit suicide. Do Lucretia's right and left hands signify her resistance against Tarquin's assault or, on the contrary, betray a secret pleasure? Not only do her two hands indicate opposite directions, but also, in a more puzzling way, the attitude of each hand ambiguously suggests equivocal meanings. If her right hand appears to reject Tarquin's gaze, its attitude could also be interpreted as a sign of invitation. The palm, which is opened and untightened, is offered in Tarquin's direction. According to Octave, Lucretia's hand gestures show the perfect and absolute simultaneity of moral repugnance and pleasure.

As Daniel W. Smith notes, through the myths of Diana and Actaeon as well as Tarquin and Lucretia, Klossowski's work constantly repeats the same fantasy: 'The woman discovering the presence of her body under the gaze or the violence of a third party, who, whether an angel or a demon, communicates a guilty voluptuousness.'[72] In her erotic (mis)adventures that oscillate in an undecided way between prostitution, adulterous relationship and rape, and even more ambiguously between reality and imagination, Roberte is trapped in *tableaux vivants* which obsessively repeat the same solecism over and over again: she reacts in a contradictory way

69 Klossowski and Zucca, *Roberte au cinéma*, pp. 7–8.

70 Ibid., p. 8.

71 Klossowski, *Les Lois de l'hospitalité*, p. 14.

72 Daniel W. Smith, 'Klossowski's Reading of Nietzsche. Impulses, Phantasms, Simulacra, and Stereotypes', *Diacritics*, 35.1 (2005), 8–21 (p. 14).

to the violent humiliations that men (Vittorio in the chapel, the aggressor in the gym club) make her endure. In his monograph on Klossowski, Ian James interrogates the ethical significance of this 'cliché of male sexual fantasy': 'Roberte always begins by resisting her assailants but then part of her succumbs and begins, despite herself, to experience sexual pleasure in the encounter.'[73] However, as James rightly notes, the solecism does not consist in the successive expression of contradictory feelings (Roberte says no, then yes), but in their simultaneity, which gives to the *tableaux* their 'bizarre' and even 'disturbing' tonality:[74] '[…] it is important to note that it is not a transition from no to yes, that this gesture of the hands evokes rather a simultaneous and paradoxical no and yes which, as will become clear expresses Roberte's difference from herself.'[75] The solecism points to the character's 'lack of self-coherence',[76] to the fracturing of her identity that is disrupted by the 'impersonal movement of desire'.[77] Her gestures, which seem to negate each other, are suspended in an indecisive and unresolved moment that turns the stereotypical code of body language into an enigma and, ultimately, suggests Octave's inability to grasp Roberte's identity.

Finally, Klossowski draws on polytheist theology to develop the notion of solecism. Roberte's contradictions evoke those of the pagan gods who want to be adored in their most immoral and shameful behaviour. Condemned by St Augustine, these gods take pleasure in their own shame.[78] Through the mediation of theatre and scenic games (what Klossowski names *theologia theatrica*), divinities give to human passions a disproportionate and immoderate dimension. Like statues in motion, the actors' gestures are simulacra that incarnate the incommunicable presence of the gods on stage.[79] At the heart of all the representations of Roberte – the goddess

73 Ian James, *Pierre Klossowski: The Persistence of a Name* (Oxford: Legenda, 2000), p. 192.

74 Ibid., p. 170.

75 Ibid., p. 193.

76 Ibid., p. 192.

77 Ibid., p. 193.

78 Klossowski, *Le Bain de Diane* (Paris: Gallimard, 1980), p. 111.

79 Ibid., p. 115.

invented by Klossowski – the silent ritualisation of gestures conveys the persistence of a haunting secret.

With the concept of solecism, Klossowski seems to parody the notion of pregnant moment (*instant prégnant*) theorised by Lessing in painting and used as a dramatic device in eighteenth-century theatre, mainly at the instigation of Denis Diderot, who postulates the equivalence between the theatrical stage and the *tableau* in his writings on dramatic arts, such as *Entretiens sur le Fils naturel* and *De la poésie dramatique.*[80] On stage, actors suspend their gestures in order to convey and intensify the meaning of a climactic scene, sometimes by referring to a well-known painting. As Steven Jacobs explains,

> [t]ableaux thus represent fixed moments that halt the narrative development of the story and introduce stasis into the movement of the play. During a short period of suspended time, the action is frozen at a point of heightened meaning, a point at which the actor's gestures are especially capable of expressing the full significance and all the implications of the story.[81]

The pregnant moment is meant to resolve a contradiction inherent to 'spatial' arts such as sculpture and painting. In order to tell a narrative, the artist must choose one unique moment that will summarise, thanks to the coordination of the characters' gestures, the continuity of an action. As Barthes explains, this instant, which enables the beholder to read the historical meaning of the represented gesture by condensing the present, the past and the future, is by definition artificial and abstract.[82] Because the painting requires interpretation by the beholder, gestures must be intelligible in order to translate an 'ideal meaning'[83] in visual terms: '[…] the meaning is set into the gesture and the co-ordination of gestures.'[84]

80 See Inès Guégo-Rivalan, 'Energie du geste et représentation: Denis Diderot, précurseur d'une "théâtralité" moderne?', *ATALA Cultures et sciences humaines*, 17 (2014), 337–49 (p. 343); Denis Diderot, *Entretiens sur Le Fils naturel: De la poésie dramatique. Paradoxe sur le comédien*, ed. by Jean Goldzink (Paris: Flammarion, 2005).

81 Jacobs, *Framing Pictures*, p. 88.

82 Roland Barthes, 'Diderot, Brecht, Eisenstein', in *Image Music Text*, trans. by Stephen Heath (London: Fontana Press, 1977), p. 73.

83 Ibid., p. 74.

84 Ibid., p. 76.

As the understanding of gestures depends on their accuracy, the artist's task consists in avoiding any ambiguity that could be detrimental to the interpretation of the picture. Indeed, the beholder must be able to reconstruct the trajectory of the painted gestures. However, the fixity of bodily movements often creates ambiguities.[85] For instance, in the article 'Promenades au Louvre', the nineteenth-century art critic Louis Edmond Duranty notices that the titles and descriptions that caption artworks in the Louvre Museum's catalogue contain errors due to a misunderstanding of the painted gestures. The stoppage of a gesture in painting becomes a source of uncertainty, doubt and even misinterpretation.[86] For example, according to the angle chosen by the artist, it may be difficult to distinguish whether an individual respectfully bows down or simply bends down to pick up an object.

In his famous essay entitled 'The Moses of Michelangelo' (1914), Freud, who admits that the most praised masterpieces often remain obscure, reviews all the contradictory interpretations that have been written about Michelangelo's well-known sculpture. By analysing the movements of Moses's gestures as well as details that have never been noticed by art critics, he seeks to reveal their true significance. Freud's method of interpretation is related to psychoanalysis that '[…] is accustomed to divine secret and concealed things from despised or unnoticed features, from the rubbish-heap, as it were, of our observations'.[87] The complexity of Moses's attitude, which conveys a stark contrast between its apparent stillness and the internal turmoil of the character, is articulated by his 'inner emotions'.[88] According to Sarah Wilson, Klossowski became increasingly familiar with

85 See Bernard Vouilloux, 'Le Geste dans le tableau vivant. Des arts de la scène à la photographie', in *Le Tableau vivant ou l'image performée*, ed. by Julie Ramos (Paris: Mare et Martin, Inha, 2014), p. 127.

86 Louis Edmond Duranty, 'Promenades au Louvre. Remarques sur le geste dans quelques tableaux', *Gazette des beaux-arts*, January–June 1877, p. 172.

87 Sigmund Freud, 'The Moses of Michelangelo', in *Writings on Art and Literature*, ed. by Werner Hamacher and David E. Wellbery (Stanford: Stanford University Press, 1997), p. 134.

88 Ibid., p. 129.

psychoanalytical theories from the late 1920s onwards, and was familiar with Freud's essay:

> Klossowski subsequently devoured the complete run of the *Revue Française de Psychanalyse* from 1927 onwards, as editorial assistant on publication. It published Freud's case histories and his *Moses of Michelangelo*, a case of 'applied psychoanalysis', where the work of art becomes the focus of interpretation.[89]

Although the ambiguity of gestures also results from the characters' turmoil in Klossowski's representations, the notion of solecism, based on the simultaneity of two contradictory signs, differs from Freud's psychoanalytical interpretation of *Moses*. Indeed, Freud analyses in detail how Michelangelo depicts the passage from one feeling – anger – to another – calm. In the theory of the pregnant moment, the simultaneous coordination of different gestures and attitudes is supposed to enable the viewer to reconstruct the chronology of the action. By contrast, Klossowski uses the idea of the pregnant moment in the opposite (or perhaps literal) sense: the character's gestures that translate the simultaneity of contradictory impulses are caught in a suspended moment – as if life itself was suspended – that suggests neither a past nor a future nor a present. It is in this sense that Klossowski assimilates painting to the genre of *tableau vivant*. For instance, he notices that the characters depicted in Balthus's paintings often seem to pose, rather than moving, as if the *tableau* was actually the representation of a *tableau vivant*.[90] However, although the *tableau vivant* is a spectacle in which the suspension of gestures corresponds to the suspension of life in a contradictory temporality, the *dispositif* affects the senses of the spectator differently than a painting, due to the models' slight involuntary movements that animate the representation.[91] How does the trembling of the body impact on the spectator's

89 Sarah Wilson, 'Pierre Klossowski: Epiphanies and Secrets', in *Pierre Klossowski*, ed. by Spira and Wilson (Ostfildern: Hatje Cantz, 2006), p. 16.

90 Klossowski, *Tableaux vivants*, p. 115.

91 See Valentine Robert, 'La Pose au cinéma: film et tableau en corps à corps', in *Entre code et corps: Tableau vivant et photographie mise en scène*, ed. by Christine Buignet and Arnaud Rykner (Pau: Presses universitaires de Pau et des pays de l'Adour, 2012), p. 74.

interpretation of the model's gestures? How does the spectator react to the vital expression of the pathos?

In *Roberte*, the medium of cinema complicates the traditional conception of the *tableau vivant*. The effect of suspension inherent to the *tableau* is acted and inscribed in the movement and the temporality of the mise-en-scène. Suspension is imbued with affect, stillness with movement, and representation with life. Gestures thus cannot be contemplated and interpreted like in a painting or a sculpture. According to Andrew Klevan, the 'fluency' in film performance generates a 'form of interpretative insecurity': '[o]ne posture morphs into another quickly and continuously, making it difficult to track the variations and separate meanings,' he argues.[92] The furtive movement of one gesture, when associated with other bodily expressions, can be difficult to grasp. Gestures constantly transform, distort or shift meanings that can thus be 'suspended, ambiguous, amorphous, generalized, embedded, in-between, transitional, becoming, developing and overlapping.'[93] While Klevan argues that gestures nonetheless continue to make sense, Noland, by contrast, suggests that the gestural expression of affective forms can 'overflow' the process of meaning-making:

> Gesture can indeed transmit a predetermined, codified meaning, but it can also – and simultaneously – convey an energetic charge or 'vitality affect' that overflows the meaning transmitted. To some extent, all iterable signs possessing material (graphemic, phonic, phenomenal) supports 'overflow' their conventional meanings. However, gestures dramatize this extra-semantic dimension of signs, dependent as they are upon actual living bodies charged with eros, affect, and corporeal materiality.[94]

Affects, emotions and corporeal forces modulate the performance of gestures and potentially suspend their interpretation, especially in melodrama, where, as Brooks suggests, '[...] some gestures exist wholly in the medium of ineffability, as marks of an appalling significance beyond the power of interpretation.'[95]

92 Andrew Klevan, 'Living Meaning, the Fluency of Film Performance', in *Theorizing Film Acting*, ed. by Aaron Taylor (New York: Routledge, 2012), pp. 34–5.

93 Ibid., p. 45.

94 Noland, 'Introduction', p. xiv.

95 Brooks, *Melodramatic Imagination*, p. 76.

In his essay on Nietzsche, Klossowski wonders: 'What then is it that will free us from a given signification and restore us to *uninterpretable existence*?'[96] According to him, the intrinsic properties of the cinematic medium tend to suspend the spectators' faculties of interpretation to the benefit of an immediate perception of pathos. Unlike the reading of a novel and the contemplation of a painting, which allow the reader and the beholder to take their time to interpret the meaning of the text and the image, a film triggers an emotional response that immediately reaches the unconscious of the film spectator, as Klossowski explains.[97] His definition of film reception echoes more recent theoretical discussions on 'the invisibility of the medium' that suggests 'a direct contact with the world and no sense of mediation'.[98] This apparently 'raw' and unmediated reality, albeit constructed and staged, thus generates an emotional shock that directly affects the spectator. In this sense, the film *Roberte* enables the viewer to immediately feel and see how the characters, through the singular performance of the actors, experience the scenes and endure the pose, without having the time to interpret the meaning of their slightest gestures. For example, when Roberte is immobilised in a *tableau vivant* by two aggressors named F. and X. who hold her tightly, she intensely reacts to the violence of the situation. She covers her underwear with her left hand, while her right hand resists against F.'s attempt to steal her glove. The quivering of her body, the nervous agitation of her hands and the movements of the camera disrupt the 'reading' of the solecism. Filmed in a medium shot, her gestures result from a state of vivid emotion that strikes the spectator. The process of codification is overwhelmed by the immediate expression and perception of the pathos of the scene.

96 Klossowski, *Nietzsche and the Vicious Circle*, trans. by Daniel W. Smith (London: The Athlone Press, 1997), p. 172.

97 Klossowski, 'Questions aux romanciers. Pierre Klossowski', *Cahiers du cinéma*, December 1966, p. 97.

98 Pethő, *Cinema and Intermediality*, p. 57.

The Cinematic Practice of *Tableaux Vivants* and the Fabrication of the Image

In modernist cinema, filmmakers like Godard, Resnais, Pier Paolo Pasolini, Varda or Rohmer appropriate the genre of *tableau vivant* to reflect on time, death, stillness, slowness, memory and more broadly on the place of cinema in art history.[99] According to Jacobs, the effect of arrested time in a *tableau vivant* imbues the representation with a morbid impression of petrification: 'Not unlike Barthes's famous description of the photograph, tableaux present bodies or poses arrested in time – though the tableau vivant realises this arrest with the help of real but seemingly lifeless bodies.'[100] *Tableaux vivants* reveal the tension between 'animation and mortification' that is often associated with the cinematic art.[101] Strikingly, the last *tableau vivant* in *Roberte*, entitled *La Belle Empoisonneuse*, ritualises the poisoning of Octave by Roberte. As the latter dies, all the protagonists, Roberte, her nephew Antoine (Martin Loeb) and Vittorio hold the pose to the point of looking frozen (see Figure 4.4). For the first and last time in the film, no perceptible movement animates or disrupts the representation: the effect of *tableau* is accomplished in death. The photographic quality of the shot, the period costumes, the painted background of the setting and the eloquent gestures emphasise the excess of theatricality. As Vouilloux suggests, with the advent of instantaneity in the late nineteenth century, the photographs of *tableaux vivants* heightened the artificiality of the posed gestures.[102] The frozen gestures in the shot of Octave's death oddly contrast with the disjunctive effect of suspension and animation which structures Zucca's mise-en-scène in the rest of the film.

99 See Jacobs, *Framing Pictures*, pp. 91–6.

100 Ibid., p. 96.

101 Ibid.

102 Vouilloux, 'Le Geste dans le tableau vivant', p. 132.

Figure 4.4. *Roberte*: The characters hold the pose for the last *tableau vivant* of the film.

While a painter conveys a synoptic representation of movement and time, a camera, by contrast, records each phase of movement in its temporal continuity. Contrary to the photographic or painted *tableau vivant*, cinema shows how the models endure the pose.[103] The cinematic *tableau vivant*, which is, in a sense, a visual solecism, highlights the simultaneity of movement and stasis within the shot. To a certain extent, it reverses the logic of painting and sculpture. While expressivity in sculpture tends to suggest movement, film stresses the statue-like aspect of the figures, and, through the models' poses, highlights what Vouilloux calls 'le tremblement de l'immobilité' [the tremor of stillness].[104] The tension between stillness and movement restores the 'antinomic polarity' of still images, as defined by Agamben:

103 See Vouilloux, 'Le Tableau vivant, entre genre et dispositif', in *Entre code et corps*, ed. by Buignet and Rykner, p. 98.

104 Vouilloux, 'Le Tableau vivant, entre genre et dispositif', p. 99.

> On the one hand, images are the reification and obliteration of a gesture (it is the *imago* as death mask or as symbol); on the other hand, they preserve the *dynamis* intact (as in Muybridge's snapshots or in any sports photograph).[105]

Although the models' poses are reified in a *tableau vivant*, their bodies can slightly tremble, suggesting the potential awakening of the gesture.

Zucca connects the genre of *tableau vivant* with a practice that is often overlooked in film studies, but nonetheless crucial in the film industry. He argues that film stills, which are used for commercial purposes and displayed in the windows of film theatres, create an effect of *tableau*. As Jacobs explains, film stills that must be distinguished from film frames or photograms 'have more in common with painting than photography', in the sense that they put the theory of pregnant moment into practice: 'In contrast with the film frame, which is drawn from a succession of moments, both a painting and a still are a constructed or fictitious moment, a kind of image synthesis of an entire action.'[106] Contrary to the instantaneity of photography that captures only one phase of movement and thus fails, according to Zucca, to convey the real meaning of a gesture, stills require operations of mise-en-scène that construct the image like a *tableau vivant*. After the shooting of a scene, the still photographer asks the actors to reconstruct the action by posing (without staring at the lens of the camera) rather than acting. Although '[s]ometimes, the gestures and positions of the actors differ from the way they are shown in the film',[107] stills must create the illusion that they have been extracted from the film itself. If the *tableaux vivants* in *Roberte* do not resemble photographs – except for the representation of Octave's death – they exhibit the processes of preparation, rehearsal and staging that fundamentally define the craft of the still photographer.[108] Similarly to Godard's *Passion*, the *tableaux vivants* in *Roberte* are shown in their process of elaboration and composition. All the phases of stoppage and movement, immobilisation and reaction are

105 Agamben, 'Notes on Gesture', p. 54.

106 Jacobs, *Framing Pictures*, p. 137.

107 Ibid., p. 132.

108 Pierre Zucca, 'La Photographie du plaisir', in *Images du cinéma: Photographies de plateau réalisées par Pierre Zucca* (Paris: Alain Moreau, 1980), p. 10.

ritualised and acted in the sequences. Although the camera remains invisible, Zucca seeks to unveil the built nature of the image.[109] He suggests that any photographic or cinematic image is constituted of a double and inseparable nature, at once real and imaginary. Overcoming the distinction between documentary and fiction, two poles respectively personified by the Lumière brothers and Georges Méliès, Zucca points out the duality (or 'double-jeu')[110] of the photographic and cinematographic picture, which imposes a frame and a mise-en-scène on the represented event. For example, in the first shot of *Roberte*, the camera shows the decrepit façade of an *hôtel particulier* (specifically the Hôtel d'Albret), in which Octave and Roberte are supposed to live – then the camera moves through the seemingly abandoned entrance hall, crosses corridors and rooms which are too dilapidated to be liveable, and eventually arrives on the edge of a stairwell, freshly repainted in bright yellow and illuminated by an artificial lighting effect. In this long take that depicts a liminal and ambiguous space between 'reality' and 'illusion', the camera shows a room that is interestingly described in the screenplay as the workshop of a shutdown factory (the Hôtel d'Albret was occupied by artisans until the mid-1970s),[111] which is certainly not neutral for Klossowski who considers cinema as 'un procédé industriel' [an industrial process].[112] In this shooting location, which has been partially refurbished for the purpose of the film, the characters get ready for their role. Antoine's private tutor – playfully embodied by Zucca himself – falls down the stairs, brutally dismissed from his post and immediately exits the field of vision – ironically, Zucca needs to return to his place behind the camera. Later, the servant Justin (Michel Berto) sticks fake sideburns on his cheeks (see Figure 4.5), while Roberte tries different hats on in front of a mirror, as if they were getting ready for appearing on stage.

Crucially, the actors of the film, when they are not writers like Klossowski or Alfred Kern, are often filmmakers (Barbet Schroeder, Daniel Schmid, Jean-François Stévenin and Juliet Berto) or even set designers (Max Berto). They embody characters who, like directors or film technicians,

109 Klossowski and Zucca, *Roberte au cinéma*, pp. 6–7.
110 Ibid., p. 3.
111 Ibid., p. 25.
112 See Klossowski, 'L'Indiscernable', p. 185.

Figure 4.5. *Roberte*: The servant Justin sticks fake sideburns on his cheeks.

organise the action and coordinate the mise-en-scène in a fictional world that is represented like a film set. The terms used by Zucca to define his skills as a still photographer – choreographing gestures and gazes, creating contrasts and relationships, stylising – eloquently describe the characters' gestural operations.[113] For example, in a *tableau vivant* dreamt by Antoine, two of his male friends named F. and X. (played by two women including Juliet Berto) devise a scenario to steal Roberte's glove. As she enters the vestibule, a groom in a red costume clumsily handles a teapot and spills tea on her shoes. While two shoeshine boys start to clean them, F. and X. turn off the light and take their places in order to assault Roberte. Before the latter makes her entrance, Berto's character supervises the preparation of the *tableau*. Silently and gently, she touches, manipulates and immobilises the other characters, adjusting their attitudes, such as the position or the angle of their arms, suspending their gestures as if they were models (see Figure 4.6). They seem to rehearse the rituals of a secret ceremony. When Roberte appears, the *tableau* comes to life. While the models perfectly

113 See Zucca, *Images du cinéma*, p. 11.

Figures 4.6–4.7. *Roberte*: Two boys polish Roberte's shoes.

execute the scenario, Roberte is trapped in a chain of events that highlights the choreographed, almost mechanical quality of her behaviour and gestures. When the groom spills tea, she looks at her foot without reacting to the action. In the screenplay, it is mentioned that she is indifferent to the accident.[114] Later on, when she gazes at herself in the mirror and waits for the boys to polish her shoes, Zucca's mise-en-scène underlines the automatism of her attitudes (see Figure 4.7). After turning the light off, F. and X. immobilise Roberte by seizing her arms and feet. Like in the previous *tableaux* that punctuate the film, Roberte's body is paralysed by force. The suspension of her gestures turns out to be an act of violence.

(Re)acting in the Frame of the Representation and Responding to the Common Use of Stereotypes

The notions of machine and automaton are central in Kossowski's narratives.[115] Roberte criticises how her husband depicts her as an automaton trapped in a game.[116] By acting like an automaton in a preconceived scenario, she becomes the main character of a machination that neutralises her will. In the first flashback that takes place in a Roman chapel in 1944, she is aware of performing a role and executing gestures that have been decided for her. Wearing a carnival costume, a purple cape and a black domino mask, she plays a character and executes instructions. As if in a spy film, she must collect hidden documents.[117] Roberte confesses her delight ('sensation délicieuse') at performing her part. Such a sensation of pleasure quickly evolves into apprehension.[118] In the film, she anxiously looks around, for fear of being caught. Emanating from the obscurity of the confessional, a male voice warns her: 'N'oubliez pas votre rôle …'

114 Klossowski and Zucca, *Roberte au cinéma*, p. 55.

115 Prieur, *Nuits blanches*, p. 52.

116 See Klossowski, *Les Lois de l'hospitalité*, pp. 65–7.

117 Ibid., p. 18.

118 Ibid., p. 19.

[Don't forget to play your part ...] The notions of acting, performance and role underline the theatricality of Zucca's mise-en-scène. Roberte is conceived as a character who reacts to circumstances in already known or evolving situations.[119] More than in the drawings, Morin-Sinclaire's performance in *Roberte* renders the spontaneous reactions which modulate the character's behaviour, perceptible.

From this perspective, the character of Roberte can be considered as an allegory representing the Western conception of the image, based on the paradoxical union of the unique and the reproducible.[120] On the one hand, Roberte should be seen like an image that is framed by her husband's imagination.[121] Octave projects onto her physiognomy the image of a fictional Roberte. She is framed in scenarios that obsessively reproduce the same schemas with slight variations. On the other hand, because she is a singular living being, Roberte experiences these situations in an idiosyncratic way. 'What makes every individual a "singular case" or an "idiosyncrasy" is the unique constellation of impulses of which it is constituted,' Smith explains.[122] The turmoil of her gestures unveils the contradiction between the incoherence of her impulsive life and the coercive frame in which she has to perform.[123] Revealing the tension between the stereotypical code of gestures and the impulsiveness of the body, the *tableaux vivants* show how life manifests itself in the frame of the representation (i.e. the *tableau*).

In this sense, Roberte's character in Zucca's film reveals the disjunction between the stereotypes that convey conventional representations of women in Western culture, and the character's singular way of experiencing these stereotypical situations, through the actor's performance. According to Richard Dyer, stereotypes provide a codified vision of the world and

119 See Françoise Levaillant, 'Des Moments suspendus. Aspects de la temporalité dans l'œuvre dessinée de Pierre Klossowski', in *Traversées de Pierre Klossowski*, ed. by Laurent Jenny and Andréas Pfersmann (Geneva: Librairie Droz, 1999), p. 129.

120 See Giorgio Agamben, 'Klossowski et la question de l'image', *Europe*, 1034–5 (2015), 59–60 (p. 59).

121 See Klossowski and Zucca, *Roberte au cinéma*, p. 7.

122 Smith, 'Klossowski's Reading of Nietzsche', p. 9.

123 Pierre Zucca, 'Autour de la notion de signe unique', in *ça cinéma 14* (Paris: Albatros, [n.d.]), p. 5.

society by creating categories 'grounded in social power'.[124] In Klossowski's thinking, stereotypes are the remains of simulacra that, emptied of their fantasmatic content, enter into the common code of representation and expression.[125] Institutionalised, schematic and customary, they belong to '[…] "the code of everyday signs" – which express the gregarious aspect of lived experience in a form already schematized by the habitual usages of feeling and thought (the herd)'.[126] Styles are formed in response to the common use of stereotypes. Klossowski plays with stereotypes both in his literary and visual styles of expression. He attempts to bring out the incongruity of lived experience that stereotypes institutionally conceal and censor. In order to do this, he exacerbates stereotypes to excessiveness. Drawing on a large repertoire of stereotypical gestures (reminiscent of silent cinema, Renaissance painting, nineteenth-century academic painting or early twentieth-century popular illustrations), Klossowski problematises the conventional representation of women in society and inscribes it in the long-term memory of art history. By critically interrogating the obsessive appropriation of the female body by the male gaze, he emphasises and ritualises the violence that is usually neutralised in the academic representation of the nude.[127] As Spira explains about his drawings,

> [h]e unveils the abuse, rape, kidnapping, assault and deception that form part of the collective unconscious at the heart of the European tradition. Underlining their absurdity and ridiculousness, his scenes and situations are mostly borrowed from elsewhere. Like the authors of Greek comedy, he chose theatrical stereotypes, heightened against a vague and undefined backdrop, to demonstrate exemplary human attributes.[128]

124 Richard Dyer, 'The Role of Stereotypes', in *Media Studies: A Reader*, ed. by Paul Marris and Sue Thornham, 2nd edn (Edinburgh: Edinburgh University Press, 1999), p. 12.

125 Klossowski, *Tableaux vivants*, p. 132.

126 Smith, 'Klossowski's Reading of Nietzsche', p. 16.

127 See Pierre Klossowski, 'Decadence of the Nude/La Décadence du nu', in *Decadence of the Nude/La Décadence du nu*, ed. by Wilson, pp. 103–23.

128 Spira, 'A Pantomime of Spirits', p. 76.

The revival of ancient stereotypes in Klossowski's work evokes Waburg's vision of art history, which stresses the constant resurgence of immemorial and ritualised gestures from Antiquity to present times. In the *Mnemosyne Atlas* that juxtaposes heterogeneous reproductions of Renaissance paintings, classical Greek sculptures and news photographs, Warburg observes 'the continuity of the same gestures, the same human attitudes, and the same intensity of feeling throughout history'.[129] His concept of *Pathosformel* refers to the 'formes affectives primitives' [primitive affective forms][130] that symptomatically resurface in the expression of gestures and inhabit the body with an impersonal and anachronistic force that challenges the concept of identity.[131] While echoing the Nietzschean concept of the eternal return, the *dispositif* of *tableau vivant* in Klossowski's work puts Warburg's ideas into practice. The models do not simply imitate a painting, but reincarnate the gestures of the models who initially posed for the painter.[132] The tremor of gestures in the *tableaux vivants* – which symptomatically renders the intensity of the *Pathosformel* apparent – reveals a conflict between codes and impulses.[133]

According to Klossowski, by spreading mass-produced stereotypes that are consumed by spectators to the point of permeating their manner of living and perceiving reality, cinema breaks with the traditional notion of style, which in art reveals the singular sensitivity of the artist or of a small group of artists in response to the rules of representation of a society.[134] As an 'instrument d'analyse' [analytical tool],[135] cinema can overcome this industrial phenomenon on the condition that it critically examines the use of stereotypes, notably those forging the representation of women in society. In her seminal essay 'Visual Pleasure and Narrative Cinema' (1975), Laura Mulvey eloquently demonstrates how 'the unconscious of patriarchal society' moulds the image of women in cinema, more particularly in

129 Raoul Ruiz, *Poetics of Cinema*, trans. by Carlos Morreo (Paris: Dis voir, 2005), p. 51.

130 Didi-Huberman, *L'Image* survivante, p. 212.

131 Eric Van Essche, 'Le Geste survivant. Mouvements de mémoire et mémoires en mouvement chez Georges Didi-Huberman', *DITS*, 12 (2009), 50–65 (p. 63).

132 See Ruiz, *Poetics of Cinema*, p. 51.

133 See Didi-Huberman, *L'Image survivante*, p. 234.

134 See Klossowski, 'Questions aux romanciers', pp. 97–8.

135 Ibid.

Hollywood cinema.[136] The female body, which is highlighted in its sexual difference (the lack of penis), causes within the male unconscious a castration complex, that in Hollywood cinema (which mostly embraces the male point of view) is overcome through the sadistic and/or fetishist representation of women. The fetishisation of the woman's image (which is inherent to the cult of the star) produces stereotypes that not only turn her into an object, but also become the repository of male fantasies.[137]

In *Roberte*, Zucca reproduces and deconstructs these mechanisms of representation. Although the mise-en-scène stresses the violence of the male gaze, the director also highlights the heroine's subjectivity. While Roberte takes possession of secret documents concealed in the tabernacle of the chapel, the camera slowly gets nearer to Vittorio who, dressed like a Swiss Guard, insistently watches her from the back of the nave. Roberte intentionally drops the chalice in order to provoke him. Punishing her for this sacrilege, the Swiss Guard removes her domino mask and purple cape and, while firmly holding her by the wrists, lights her corset and her naked flesh with a torch. The *tableau vivant* ambiguously highlights the conflict between Roberte's agency and the male power that wants to direct her gestures and control her body, her image and her narrative by force. She is at once humiliated by a representative of the Catholic authority and subjected to his scopophilia. At first sight, the motif of the torch appears to be a metaphor for the complicity between the mechanical eye of the camera and the male gaze; however, in this scene, the camera starts to move backwards when Vittorio lights Roberte's body and thus distances itself from the Swiss Guard's viewpoint. Furthermore, in the *tableau vivant* depicting Roberte's aggression by F. and X., even though the camera follows the movement of the torch that slides along her body, the androgyny of the aggressors disrupts the normative schema of sexual differences.[138]

136 Laura Mulvey, 'Visual Pleasure in Narrative Cinema', in *Film Theory and Criticism: Introductory Readings*, ed. by Leo Braudy and Marshall Cohen (New York: Oxford University Press, 1999), p. 833.

137 See ibid., p. 840.

138 Klossowski discusses the Sadean theme of androgyny in his essay 'Le Philosophe Scélérat' (1967). See Pierre Klossowski, *Sade mon prochain; précédé de Le Philosophe scélérat* (Paris: Seuil, 2002).

In destabilising binary gender representations, Zucca and Klossowski distort the common use of stereotypes. Their 'vision "disproportionnelle"' [disproportionate vision][139] imbues the code of everyday signs with fantasmatic apparitions. According to Elizabeth Cowie, fantasy is an imagined and distorted 'mise en scène of desire'.[140] While in his graphic work Klossowski exaggerates the imbalance of proportions and distorts the reproduction of stereotypes, Zucca's camera reproduces reality through a 'regard gullivérien' [Gulliverian lens],[141] changing proportions and isolating parts of the body. In *Roberte*, the mechanical effect of amplification tends to codify gestures in an incongruous manner. For example, when Octave and Antoine examine a sequence of black-and-white photographs representing a mundane episode of Roberte's public life, Octave shows a particular interest for the manner that she puts on her leather glove – he ambiguously reverses the order of the pictures, giving the deceptive impression that she removes the glove (see Figure 4.8). Antoine notes the incongruous position of the thumb, without being able to explain the origin of his trouble. In *La Révocation*, Roberte's thumb is sexually connoted. When she describes the effect of sexual pleasure on her body, Roberte writes that '[son] attribut se développa jusqu'à atteindre l'épaisseur de [son] pouce' [her 'private parts' grew until they reached the size of her thumb].[142] The linguistic stereotype 'attribut', which is usually used to refer to male genitals, is used by Klossowski to pinpoint the incongruous proportion of Roberte's clitoris, which protrudes like a penis.[143] The stereotype covers and uncovers the intensity of the fantasy in the text, in the same way that the glove, which circulates from hand to hand in the film, exchanged and traded like a fetish, covers and uncovers her palm and thumb. This codified gesture, often filmed in close-up, takes a fantasmatic dimension in the *tableaux vivants*. In Antoine's dream, Roberte offers her hand to X. who, having removed the glove, lights her naked palm and her erect thumb with the torch.

139 Klossowski, 'Protase et Apodose', p. 9.

140 Elizabeth Cowie, *Representing the Woman: Cinema and Psychoanalysis* (Basingstoke: Macmillan, 1997), p. 133.

141 Klossowski, 'L'Indiscernable', p. 185.

142 Klossowski, *Les Lois de l'hospitalité*, p. 69.

143 See Klossowski, 'Protase et apodose', pp. 15–20.

Figure 4.8. *Roberte*: The character puts on her leather glove.

Furthermore, the camera amplifies reflexes, reactions and small movements which escape codification, giving unexpected proportions to the characters' slightest gestures. In 'The Work of Art in the Age of Mechanical Reproduction', which Klossowski translated into French in 1936, Benjamin conceptualises the 'optical unconscious' of the camera in a way that evokes the idea of the disproportionate vision. According to Benjamin, the medium of cinema gives access to the unconscious of gestures by showing, more precisely than in real life, their most imperceptible details, for example, thanks to the technological process of enlargement.[144] By capturing the split second of a stride or the manner that an individual grasps a lighter, the camera magnifies minuscule gestural variations and fluctuations. When Octave and Antoine scrutinise Roberte's photographs, Zucca highlights the corporeal presence of the teenager, who sits in the foreground of the shot. While holding his right wrist, his left hand and fingers gradually

144 Walter Benjamin, 'L'Œuvre d'art à l'époque de sa reproduction mécanisée', trans. by Pierre Klossowski, *Zeitschrift für Sozialforschung*, 5.1 (1936), 40–68 (p. 60).

impart nervous movements and show signs of agitation. Do these minute gestures betray Antoine's reaction to the vision of Roberte? Or do they reveal the actor's malaise in front of the camera? The scene emphasises the difference between photography, which dissects and freezes each phase of gesture (and allows the viewer to examine them) and cinema, which renders the excess of impulsive gestures perceptible.

Finally, imagination exaggerates the characters' experience. By giving a fragmented rendering of reality and reproducing operations of the unconscious in the form of flashbacks or dream sequences, the discontinuity of the sequences mirrors the 'discontinuité morale' [moral discontinuity] of Roberte's attitudes and behaviour.[145] Narrated in flashback, the sequence of the parallel bars does not consist in the accurate reproduction of the experience, but rather in an imaginary evocation.[146] Symptomatically, the aggressor appears from all quarters of the Palais Royal, like a demonic presence who inhabits Roberte's imagination. He waits for her to follow him into the obscurity of a gallery. Her body is tense, and the fingers of her right hand are opened wide. After a moment of hesitation, she deliberately follows the aggressor, as if she knew what was going to happen. Morin-Sinclaire, who performed the sequence twice before Zucca's camera in 1975 and 1977, shares the character's memory of the incident. When she strolls under the arches of the Palais Royal, her hesitating gait is imbued with a sensation of *déjà-vu*. The mise-en-scène renders a disproportionate vision of the event, while emphasising the discrepancy between stereotypes and life through the actor's performance.

The representation of women in Klossowski's controversial work has been studied in contrasting ways. In her book *Les Châteaux d'eros*, Anne-Marie Dardigna discusses the misogynistic dimension of Klossowski's work, especially in *Les Lois de l'hospitalité*, in which Roberte is subjected to fantasies of male domination as well as to the violence of the male gaze. She points out that her desire is nothing but a response to the men's desire for her.[147] Whereas Dardigna highlights the misogynist aspect of Klossowski's

145 See Klossowski, 'L'Indiscernable', p. 186.

146 Jean Decottignies, *Pierre Klossowski: biographie d'un monomane* (Villeneuve-d'Ascq: Presses universitaires du Septentrion, 1997), p. 72.

147 Dardigna, *Les Châteaux d'Eros ou Les Infortunes du sexe des femmes*, p. 14.

writing and art in which the woman's body is under attack,[148] other scholars and critics – as highlighted in this section – posit that Klossowski is a writer and artist who recycles stereotypes of sexual violence in critical, self-reflexive, ironic and parodic ways. As James explains,

> [o]n one level it is arguable that he does reproduce traditional schema of the reification of the female body and its appropriation by a violent desire. Yet in exaggerating these schema, in self-consciously playing upon them, his writing articulates a suspension of the very movement of violence itself.[149]

From a similar perspective, Zucca argues that Klossowski's intention is critical.[150] The director describes his own mise-en-scène as a playful reflection on representation, which parodies and distorts the conventions of a traditional 'bourgeois' narrative in an uncanny way.[151] Yet, by analysing Klossowski and Zucca's approach to film performance from a post-Nietzschean perspective, the following section will reveal how the performance of gesture in the staged sexual acts of *Roberte* blurs the line between parody and lived experience in a highly problematic way. Unlike literature and visual arts such as painting, the practice of cinema relies on the actors' performance. As gesture is endured by the performer's body, its performance in cinema raises ethical questions that will be addressed in the last section of this chapter, in particular with regard to the female performer's subjection to coercive sexual acts performed by the male actors.

Performance and the Mystery of Existence

From the mid-1960s, Klossowski develops a particular interest in film performance. He plays the role of the cynical merchant in Bresson's *Au hasard Balthazar*, and acts in several of François Weyergans's short

148 Ibid., p. 23.

149 James, *Pierre Klossowski*, p. 217.

150 Zucca, Bonnet, Carcassonne and Fieschi, '*Roberte*. Entretien avec Pierre Zucca', p. 39.

151 Ibid.

and long feature films between 1967 and 1972. In her autobiographical novel *Jeune Fille* (2007), Anne Wiazemsky, who embodies Marie in Bresson's film, recounts her experience during the shooting and describes Klossowski's difficulties in complying with the director's demands.[152] Unable to move his body according to Bresson's instructions, Klossowski had to repeat the action until he correctly performed the gestures of his character. As discussed in Chapter 1, Bresson seeks to prevent his models from overthinking their words and gestures in order to convey the 'automatism' of human behaviour: 'I ask that the meaning comes from them, from their own impulse, in the moment when [...] I let them loose in the world of the film.'[153] Klossowski certainly shares Bresson's preoccupation for the impulsivity of life and spontaneity, as well as the desire to grasp the model's idiosyncrasy or '*substance*',[154] defined by Keith Reader as 'something like the kernel of his or her being, akin to Christian conceptions of the uniqueness of the individual soul'.[155]

However, while Bresson develops a method of directing opposite to theatre, Klossowski's approach to acting is theatrical. He explores a liminal space where simulation and spontaneity, performance and life intertwine. In the 1950s, Klossowski used to rehearse *Roberte ce soir* with his wife Morin-Sinclair and friends Georges Perros and Michel Butor, in line with the eighteenth-century tradition of the *théâtre de société*. In a letter addressed to Klossowski, Butor remembers the unbearable sensation of malaise that permeated the rehearsals to the point of triggering a fit of laughter.[156] This reaction is due to Klossowski's style, which, according to Agamben, lies on the verge of the laughable,[157] and consciously uses comedy despite the

152 Anne Wiazemsky, *Jeune Fille* (Paris: Gallimard, 2007), p. 203.

153 Robert Bresson, 'To Create Life without Copying It', in *Bresson on Bresson: Interviews 1943–1983*, ed. by Mylène Bresson, trans. by Anna Moschovakis (New York: New York Review Books, 2016), p. 169.

154 Bresson, *Notes sur le cinématographe* (Paris: Gallimard, 1988), p. 41.

155 Keith Reader, *Robert Bresson* (Manchester: Manchester University Press, 2000), p. 129.

156 Michel Butor, 'Souvenirs sur le théâtre de société', in *Pierre Klossowski*, ed. by Andréas Pfersmann (Paris: Centre Georges Pompidou, 1985), p. 28.

157 Giorgio Agamben and Thierry Tremblay, 'Un auteur messianique. Entretien avec Giorgio Agamben', *Europe*, 1034–5 (2015), 9–11 (p. 10).

apparent seriousness of the prose. The malaise described by Butor also highlights the nervousness of the amateur performers who spontaneously express their embarrassment toward the situations within the narrative. Comparing *Roberte* with the 'domestic eroticism' of Andy Warhol's amateur early films, the curator and art critic Catherine Millet pinpoints, '[t]his [impression of amateurism] is largely due to the touching awkwardness of the non-professional actors and a makeshift set.'[158] Simulation, falsity, exaggeration, theatricality, clumsiness and malaise define the mode of performance in Zucca's film. Far from his austere performance in *Au hasard Balthazar*, Klossowski excessively accentuates the tone of his voice and the expressivity of his gestures.

Klossowski's research on performance is profoundly indebted to Nietzsche's philosophy. Translator of *The Gay Science* (1882), the writer has published several articles and essays on Nietzsche since the 1930s, including the well-known monograph *Nietzsche et le cercle vicieux* (*Nietzsche and the Vicious Circle*, 1969). Although James and Smith have eloquently dissected and enlightened his '[p]ost-Nietzschean thinking of the body',[159] they have not specifically addressed the question of acting. In *The Gay Science*, Nietzsche discusses the 'problem of the actor' several times, especially in the aphorism 361. The German philosopher defines acting in those terms:

> Falseness with a good conscience; the delight in pretence erupting as a power that pushes aside, floods, and at times extinguishes one's so-called 'character'; the inner longing for a role and mask, for an *appearance* (*Schein*); an excess of capacities for all kinds of adaptation that can no longer be satisfied in the service of the nearest, most narrowly construed utility – perhaps all of this is distinctive not *only* of the actor?[160]

Klossowski comments on this passage in his article 'Nietzsche, le polythéisme et la parodie', discussing the concept of existence through

158 Catherine Millet, 'Klossowski our Neighbour', in *Pierre Klossowski*, ed. by Spira and Wilson (Ostfildern: Hatje Cantz, 2006), p. 55.

159 Ian James, 'Klossowski, Nietzche and the Fortuitous Body', *Romance Studies*, 19.1 (2001), 59–70 (p. 61); see also Smith, 'Klossowski's Reading of Nietzsche', 8–21.

160 Friedrich Nietzsche, *The Gay Science*, ed. by Bernard Williams and trans. by Josefine Nauckhoff (Cambridge: Cambridge University Press, 2001), p. 225–6.

the notions of role and acting.[161] A role not only implies falsity and simulation, but also casts doubt on any stable identity. A role, which is a role among many others, either fortuitous or chosen, incorporates the possibility of a difference into the body.[162]

While major acting theoreticians of the twentieth century postulate 'a stable locus of selfhood' in performance,[163] Nietzsche's concept of the actor questions the fiction of identity. For example, according to Philip Auslander, '[Stanislavski] insists on the need for logic, coherence, and unity – "the unbroken line" – in acting.'[164] Besides, studies in film performance often point out the consistency of the great actors' gestures from one film to another, to such an extent that they mould the perception of their characters according to their own originality, giving stability and coherence to their persona despite the variety of their roles.[165] According to Klevan, in film '[c]haracter and performer are inextricably intertwined; they coalesce', whereas '[t]he separation of character and performer is explicitly part of theatrical expression'.[166] Yet Youri Lotman suggests the possibility of a tension, even a conflict between the character and the film actor.[167] When actors play against type, like Seyrig in *Jeanne Dielman* (see Chapter 2), they create an interval between their character and their conventional image by changing their habit of acting. For example, in *Vincent mit l'âne dans*

161 Pierre Klossowski, 'Nietzsche, le polythéisme et la parodie', *Revue de métaphysique et de morale*, 63.2–3 (1958), 325–48.

162 Ibid., p. 342.

163 David Kornhaber, '"The Art of Putting Oneself on Stage before Oneself": Theatre, Selfhood, and Nietzsche's Epistemology of the Actor', *Theatre Research International*, 36.3 (2011), 240–53 (p. 242).

164 Philip Auslander, *From Acting to Performance. Essays in Modernism and Postmodernism* (New York: Routledge, 1997), p. 30.

165 See Luc Moullet, *Politique des acteurs* (Paris: Ed. De l'Etoile, Cahiers du cinéma, 1993). Focusing on the gestural style of several major Hollywood stars, Luc Moullet analyses the stylistic features of Cary Grant's gestures and notices among other examples his singular way of bending or raising his finger.

166 Andrew Klevan, *Film Performance: From Achievement to Appreciation* (London: Wallflower, 2005), p. 4.

167 Iouri Lotman, 'Le Problème de l'acteur de cinéma', in *Sémiotique et esthétique du cinéma*, trans. by Sabine Breuillard (Paris: Editions sociales, 1977), p. 158.

un pré, starring Michel Bouquet and Bernadette Lafont, Zucca succeeds in revealing the characters' singularity by provoking apparently unwilled gestures ('quelque geste spontané') that would not be anticipated by the actor, in order to highlight the difference, or even the disjunction between the characters' idiosyncrasy and the actors' persona.[168]

Klossowski moulds Roberte's character like an actor who simultaneously plays opposite roles. She acts as the substitute mother of a teenager who is not hers, as an austere woman of power working in a patriarchal society and as a wife torn between her will to emancipate herself and her husband's will to control her sexual adventures and fantasies. The possibility of changing masks calls her identity into question. Deleuze explains, 'Klossowski's entire work moves toward a single goal: to assure the loss of personal identity and to dissolve the self.'[169] Roberte endures ordeals that exacerbate the contradictions between her different roles, to the point of dissolving her sense of self. Her gestures manifest a lack of self-coherence. For example, during a session with the censorship board, Roberte advocates the ban of Octave's manuscript *Roberte ce soir* which portrays her in a scandalous way. With eloquent gestures, she points out the incriminating passages with a red pencil before sensuously caressing the pencil in a suggestive way.

Morin-Sinclaire finds herself in the same position as that of her character, performing different roles in situations (especially the *tableaux vivants*) that are imposed on her. The actor's reactions in the environment of the film set and in fictional situations that contrast with her own life are ambiguous and unpredictable. In a problematic manner, Klossowski wishes to capture her unwilled reactions, especially in difficult sequences that involve the simulation of sexual assault.[170]

To imagine the sequence of the 'parallel bars', Klossowski very loosely drew his inspiration from an incident that Morin-Sinclaire actually experienced. One day, while going to her workplace located at the Palais Royal, a man approached her on the rear platform of the bus, touched her hand

168 Klossowski, 'Simuler le simulateur', p. 84.

169 Deleuze, *The Logic of Sense*, p. 283.

170 Klossowski, 'L'Indiscernable', p. 186.

and, when she tried to avoid him, followed her inside the bus. However, unlike the aggressor in the film, the man never sat down near her and did not follow her in the galleries of the Palais Royal. When Morin-Sinclaire acted the scene, she could thus feel the discontinuity between her fictitious role and the memory of her own experience, as she explains in Fleischer's documentary *Pierre Klossowski, un écrivain en images* (1996). It is this ambiguous and simultaneous relation of resemblance and distance between the 'real' person of Morin-Sinclaire and Roberte's fictitious roles that Klossowski attempts to stage in the film. By highlighting the multiplicity of roles and identities in the same physiognomy through exaggerated effects of theatricality, Klossowski hopes to reveal the bodily manifestation of existence in Roberte/Morin-Sinclaire's gestures.

Expanding on Nietzsche's aphorism, Klossowski argues that a role is a simulacrum that manifests a possibility of being and, for that reason, unveils the fortuity of existence. A role reveals existence through the actor's physiognomy.[171] As James explains, Klossowski's post-Nietzschean thinking postulates the embodiment of existence. Klossowski distinguishes 'le corps propre' [the proper body] and 'le corps fortuit' [the fortuitous body]. The proper body gives the illusion of a cohesive and stable self, while existence is 'an ungraspable flux or becoming, a becoming without end, without meaning or purpose'.[172] The proper body filters through consciousness and language the random, impersonal and meaningless impulses of the fortuitous body, which is abstract, invisible and chaotic. The linguistic code gives 'a fallacious interpretation of the random drives which constitute bodily existence'.[173] In acting, the simulation of a role implies a process of falsification that at once conceals and reveals the incoherence of existence, in the sense that a role – apparently stable and coherent – indicates a possibility of difference and multiplicity within the individual. As Deleuze puts it, [t]he dissolved self opens up to a series of roles, since it gives rise to an intensity which already comprehends difference in itself, the unequal in itself, and which penetrates all others, across and within multiple bodies.'[174]

171 Klossowski, 'Nietzsche, le polythéisme et la parodie', p. 342.
172 James, 'Klossowski, Nietzche and the Fortuitous Body', p. 63.
173 Ibid., p. 64.
174 Deleuze, *Logic of the Sense*, p. 298.

Drawing on Klossowski and Nietzsche to analyse Philippe Grandieux's cinema, Chamarette argues that the fortuitous body 'cannot take an embodied corporeal form in the shape of human bodies',[175] and thus cannot be represented as such in a film. The chaos of impulses is by definition incommunicable and non-representable. Yet Klossowski seeks to grasp the ungraspable. By introducing a contradiction in the apparent self-coherence of the body and by dissolving identity, he hopes to see and feel, through the simulacrum of the actor's gestures, the embodied manifestation of existence. As he argues, gestures show the passage from the chaotic life of impulses to meaning – and to paraphrase Deleuze[176] – from intensity to intentionality.[177] The improvised, unwilled and spontaneous gesture, which is first meaningless, simulates impulses that, once interpreted, are charged with meaning.

Through the simulation of Roberte's gestures, the ungraspable and impossible representation of the vision (or fantasy) that originates from the obscurity of the fortuitous body becomes palpable.[178] Although the impulses remain indiscernible, they manifest themselves in the actor's corporeal presence and become a source of tactile sensations for the spectator. Klossowski points out the impossibility of differentiating the emotions feigned by the 'model' from the emotions that she spontaneously experiences during the shooting of the film. The indiscernible quality of her gestures and expressions – which reveals the indiscernibility of embodied existence – rightfully mirrors the ambiguity of Roberte's reactions in the narrative, especially as the character has been indivisible from Morin-Sinclaire's '"style" physiognomique' [physiognomy] since its creation.[179] The actor, who must act in front of the technical crew and sometimes before anonymous passers-by, potentially performs the erotic scenes with reluctance and embarrassment. Small gestures and facial expressions seem to betray her repugnance, and perhaps her *jouissance* to perform, potentially mirroring Roberte's feelings of shame and pleasure.[180] Morin-Sinclaire's physiognomy

175 Chamarette, *Phenomenology and the Future of Film*, p. 211.
176 See Deleuze, *Logic of the Sense*, p. 298.
177 Klossowski, 'Nietzsche, le polythéisme et la parodie', pp. 323–4.
178 Klossowski, 'L'Indiscernable', p. 186.
179 Ibid., p. 185.
180 Ibid., p. 187.

enables the indiscernible to be seen and felt.[181] The 'palpability' of existence, which is a crucial idea for Klossowski, is also discussed by Deleuze in his essay on Francis Bacon. The intensity of the fortuitous body (or the 'body without organs') stimulates levels of sensation and vibration that manifest in flesh and nerves: 'the body without organs is flesh and nerve; a wave flows through it and traces levels upon it; a sensation is produced when the wave encounters the forces acting on the body [...].'[182] The forces that animate the body affect the nervous system and produce sensations that become haptic or, in other words, tactile and palpable.

In the same way that Warburg considers the historian as a 'seismograph' who records the obscure movements of memory in bodily expression,[183] Klossowski defines himself as 'the seismograph of the life of the impulses'.[184] According to James, 'Klossowski's writing [...] simulates a fortuitous body within a semiotic which grounds itself in the un-grounding of chaotic flux and affect.'[185] In *Roberte*, the gestural code is retranslated into a constellation of reflexes through the actors' performances. The vital force of the body creates a myriad of micro-gestures that nervously disrupt the codification of body language. For example, when Roberte, Octave and the bank clerk (Frédéric Mitterand) are having dinner, they conform to the protocols of politeness. Their gestures are codified: Octave introduces Roberte to the bank clerk with a hand sign, then the bank clerk greets Roberte with a hand kiss and waits for her to sit first. When the valet serves food in a heavy silence, the bank clerk's malaise becomes more and more perceptible. The fingers of his right hand nervously play with the inside of his slice of bread. In a comical way, he suddenly cleans his glasses instead of eating. Unwilled, compulsive or impulsive gestures appear in almost all the scenes of the film. When Roberte angrily discusses Antoine's education with Octave, the angle of the camera highlights the exaggerated nervous swing of her

181 Ibid.

182 Gilles Deleuze, *Francis Bacon: The Logic of Sensation*, trans. by Daniel W. Smith (London: Continuum, 2003), p. 45.

183 See Van Essche, 'Le Geste survivant', p. 62; Didi-Huberman, *L'Image survivante*, p. 137.

184 Cited in Smith, 'Klossowski's Reading of Nietzsche', p. 13.

185 James, 'Klossowski, Nietzsche and the Fortuitous Body', p. 68.

leg and the impulsive choreography of her fingers, while Eric Demarsan's improvised jazz music covers the characters' dialogue.

Finally, when the aggressor licks Roberte's palm while she is attached to the parallel bars, the fingers he uses to immobilise her hand are also nervously agitated. Roberte opens or closes her eyes, gazes in the direction of the man or looks away. Her face moves from one side to the other, while her thigh and knee impart slight movements. The camera records her reflexes, reactions and her indiscernible movements of hesitation, revulsion, and/or of pleasure.[186] All these micro-gestures (reflexes, titillation) constitute a complex constellation of signs. The ambiguity and uncertainty of the gestures and the irreducible hesitation that emanates from the actors' performance take a perverse dimension:

> What is perverse is precisely this objective power of hesitation in the body: this paw which is neither left nor right; this determination by fits and starts; this differentiation never suppressing the undifferentiated which is divided in it: this suspense which marks each moment of difference; and this immobilization which marks each moment of the fall.[187]

The ambiguity of gestures creates shifts and ruptures that assemble and disassemble meaning. During the dinner with the bank clerk, Roberte gently pushes and brushes his right hand to grab the ladle on the table. Similarly, at the end of the film, while she leaves Von A., who sleeps in his hospital bed, her hand almost imperceptibly touches the man's arm: the latter suddenly wakes up and grabs Roberte by the waist. There is a discrepancy between the intention of Roberte's most mundane actions (grabbing an object, standing up) and the expressivity of her gestures, which produces a friction between two bodies and renders the intensity of the fantasy graspable. By capturing the actors' slightest gestures, the camera grasps unexpectedly the enigmatic manifestation of bodily existence.

Through the effects of his mise-en-scène which exhibit the staged and constructed nature of the image – as demonstrated in the previous sections – Zucca establishes a critical distance that questions the stereotypes

186 Klossowski, 'L'Indiscernable', p. 187.

187 Deleuze, *Logic of the Sense*, p. 281.

of male domination and sexual violence. Yet, the analysis of performance in this section shows the limits of Zucca's mise-en-scène. Indeed, the director himself confesses that his approach to mise-en-scène, which relies on exaggeration, distortion and parody, ceases to work when the female performer is supposed to actually experience her character's feelings, especially during the sequence of the parallel bars where the boundary between the 'reality' of lived experience and the illusory nature of film performance is intentionally blurred.[188] Occupying a voyeuristic position during the shooting (like his fictional character Octave), Klossowski seeks to observe the expression of spontaneous gestures of discomfort or pleasure in Morin-Sinclaire's face and body while she is subjected to coercive sexual acts performed by the male actors, notably in the sequence of the parallel bars. While it may be questionable the extent to which the actor really experienced pleasure in this sequence, it is clear that it was a deliberate choice on the part of Klossowski to create discomfort for the female performer during the sadomasochistic restraint scenes to the extent that her body would express involuntary gestures and uncontrolled reactions. By blurring the line between film performance and lived experience (i.e. between performed and spontaneous gestures), the film raises ethical questions regarding the performance of the female actor, since the latter was expected to endure gestures of discomfort during the staging of sexual scenes.

In line with Agamben's ethical conception of gesture (discussed in Chapter 2), Cowie explains that '[e]mbodied, and of the body and not of thought, gesture is the performing of the body as a living being in specific time and space and social context'.[189] At once embodied and endured, gesture is thus ethical in the sense that it bears responsibility.[190] This ethical dimension of gesture is particularly central in film aesthetics as the performance of gesture oscillates between life and representation as demonstrated throughout this book and, more precisely, in this chapter. Although Zucca's mise-en-scène stages stereotypes of sexual violence in a

188 Zucca, Bonnet, Carcassonne and Fieschi, '*Roberte*. Entretien avec Pierre Zucca', p. 41.

189 Elizabeth Cowie, 'The Time of Gesture in Cinema and its Ethics', *Journal of Cultural Research*, 19.1 (2015), 82–95 (p. 83).

190 Ibid., pp. 85–7.

critical way, the analysis of performance in *Roberte* reveals the exploitation of male power over a female performer during the filmmaking process, echoing Dardigna's criticism of the problematic representation of women in Klossowski's work.[191]

Conclusion

The notion of the *tableau vivant* in Klossowski's work opens a liminal space between sense and sensation, intentionality and intensity, the voluntary and the involuntary, which problematises the conceptualisation of gesture in film. On the one hand, Zucca and Klossowski reproduce codified gestures that originated in painterly and theatrical traditions. In line with Klossowski's novels and artworks, they put the emphasis on stereotypical gestural signs that indicate equivocal directions to the spectator. On the other hand, the migration of frozen gestures into the moving image accentuates the instability of the representation. The simultaneity of movement and stillness is revealing of the ambiguous nature of gestures that can communicate codified meanings and express the impulsivity of the body at the same time. In this sense, *tableaux vivants* contradict the distinction made by Kendon between gesture as a voluntary act of communication and non-gestural motions such as uncontrolled and nervous movements.[192] The vitality of the body – visible through the trembling of gestures – can disrupt the stability and the fixity of the code of body language. The models as well as the actors who pose and perform do not have an absolute control over their body. The slightest motion can potentially affect the spectator's perception of the scene. In *Roberte*, the ambiguity of gesture raises aesthetic and ethical questions about film performance, the nature of the cinematic image, as well as the process of film reception.

By expanding on the idea of simultaneity, the following chapter will show the extent to which human gestures interweave heterogeneous lines.

191 See Dardigna, *Les Châteaux d'Eros ou Les Infortunes du sexe des femmes*.

192 See Kendon, *Gesture: Visible Action as Utterance*, p. 8.

As discussed throughout the book, not only do gestures reveal the heterogeneity of the cinematic medium in its interaction with other media and arts, but also the heterogeneity of behaviours, ways of being and existential lines within society. At once individual and collective, conditioned and singular, gestures raise questions about how, beyond their differences, people live together within a community, in interaction with others and their environment – even when at first glance these social groups can look homogeneous and ideologically conditioned by the same social codes. By analysing Godard and Miéville's, Deligny's and Rivette's works, Chapter 5 will discuss the relation between the straight line of social conditioning and the serpentine line that animates human gesture.

CHAPTER 5

Gestural Lines

> As walking, talking and gesticulating creatures, human beings generate lines wherever they go.[1]
>
> – Tim Ingold

In Raoul Ruiz's *L'Hypothèse du tableau volé* (*The Hypothesis of the Stolen Painting*, 1978) – in which an art collector attempts to interpret several *tableaux vivants* reproducing Frédéric Tonnerre's paintings – the narrator asserts that 'tout mouvement effectué par un être humain laisse un tracé imaginaire assimilable à une courbe' [any movement performed by a human being leaves an imaginary trace comparable to a curve]. This commentary invites the spectator to envision gesture, no longer as a figurative form of representation, but as a dynamic and virtual trace of movement, namely a curved line. According to Maxine Sheets-Johnstone, the 'linear design' of bodily movement refers to the 'linear contours of the body', while the '[l]inear pattern describes the trajectory or trajectories that a living body creates in moving'.[2] When someone is gesturing, his or her linear pattern is most often not perceivable, but only imagined:

> The patterns emerge in the form of imagined trajectories that a moving body draws in the process of moving. [...] What are imaginatively constituted in all instances are *lines*. Lines are clearly spatial entities, whether actually drawn and perceived or whether imaginatively followed and constituted.[3]

1 Tim Ingold, *Lines: A Brief History* (Abingdon: Routledge, 2007), p. 1.

2 Maxine Sheets-Johnstone, 'The Imaginative Consciousness of Movement: Linear Quality, Kinaesthesia, Language and Life', in *Redrawing Anthropology: Materials, Movements, Lines*, ed. by Tim Ingold (Abingdon: Routledge, 2011), p. 115.

3 Ibid., p. 116.

Resulting from 'our imaginative consciousness of movement',[4] the kinetic lines are at once spatial, temporal and dynamic. Significantly, Sheets-Johnston explains that '[linear patterns] are always qualitatively distinct by virtue of the dynamic reality of movement itself'.[5] In other words, a line is not a gesture, but a way to envision or map its trajectory. For example, in Laurence Sterne's *Tristram Shandy* (1759–67), Corporal Trim draws a serpentine line in the air with his stick in order to gesturally express the freedom lost by men once they get married.[6] Sterne reproduces the linear pattern of Trim's flourish in the form of a line, which is a synthesis and an abstraction of the gesture, translating its free trajectory into a 'dynamic and temporal' trace.[7] The line, which is not straight but serpentine, results from the improvised movement of the hand, 'free to go where it will for movement's sake'.[8]

If film enables the spectator to see the linear design of gestures, linear patterns remain most of the time invisible. In a series of artworks entitled *Following the Right Hand of ...* (2008–9), the French artist Pierre Bismuth follows the gestural trajectories of iconic Hollywood actors with a black marker, translating their visual perception into black lines drawn on a plexiglass sheet and superimposed on a film still. As Erika Balsom explains, '[t]he scribbled line indexes Bismuth's viewing of the film, its nervous energy pointing to a thorough redirection of attention away from the narrative progression and towards the movements of an actress' right hand.'[9] Giving a tangible form to the visual impulse produced by the actor's gestures within the spectator's mind and body, the line therefore materialises the spectator's kinesic engagement with the film. Moreover, the lines form an abstract expressionist drawing evoking the process of light painting photography. Before being used by artists like Matisse, Man Ray and Picasso, the device

4 Ibid.
5 Ibid., p. 126.
6 See Laurence Sterne, *Tristram Shandy* (London: Everyman's Library, 1991), pp. 148–9 (volume 3).
7 Ingold, *Lines*, p. 72.
8 Ibid., p. 73.
9 Erika Balsom, *Exhibiting Cinema in Contemporary Art* (Amsterdam: Amsterdam University Press, 2013), p. 121.

was originally invented with a scientific purpose in the field of motion studies. Entitled *Pathological Walk from in Front* (*c.* 1889), the first light painting photograph shows the inscription of an irregular, discontinuous and serpentine line of movement on a black surface. Etienne-Jules Marey's assistants Georges Demenÿ and Bernard Quénu managed to capture the movement of walking by fixing incandescent bulbs on the subject's body. The adjective 'pathological' is revealing of a line that is not straight, but tangled and confused.

Furthermore, Giorgio Agamben draws a parallel between Gilles de la Tourette's footprint method and the scientific inventions that announce the birth of cinema at the end of the nineteenth century, including chronophotography.[10] In his method of imprint, Tourette used the straight line as an instrument to observe and study the manner of walking of his subjects. As Janet Harbord explains:

> Tourette's method was to attach a roll of white paper to the floor and draw a line down the centre whilst his subjects, their feet smeared with iron sesquioxide powder, were required to walk the line to the best of their abilities. The resulting footprints provided a trace of movement that could be calibrated and compared according to length of step, cadence, direction, symmetry and so forth.[11]

Tourette's method evokes a recurring gag in Jacques Tati's films. In *Les Vacances de monsieur Hulot* (*Monsieur Hulot's Holiday*, 1953) and *Mon oncle* (*My Uncle*, 1958), Monsieur Hulot leaves, in spite of himself, the mark of his footprints on the ground (see Figure 5.1). The line, which is not straight but digressive, manifests the character's disorientation, hesitations, clumsiness and wandering.

'[...] [T]he living being is characterised by the undulous or serpentine line, [...] each being has its own way of undulating, [...] the object of art is to render this undulation distinctive,' Bergson writes, drawing on a passage of Leonardo da Vinci's *A Treatise on Painting*.[12] The serpentine

10 Agamben, 'Notes on Gesture', pp. 48–50.

11 Janet Harbord, *Ex-centric Cinema. Giorgio Agamben and Film Archaeology* (New York: Bloomsbury Academic, 2016), p. 64.

12 Henri Bergson, *The Creative Mind*, trans. by Mabelle L. Andison (New York: Philosophical Library, 1946), p. 272.

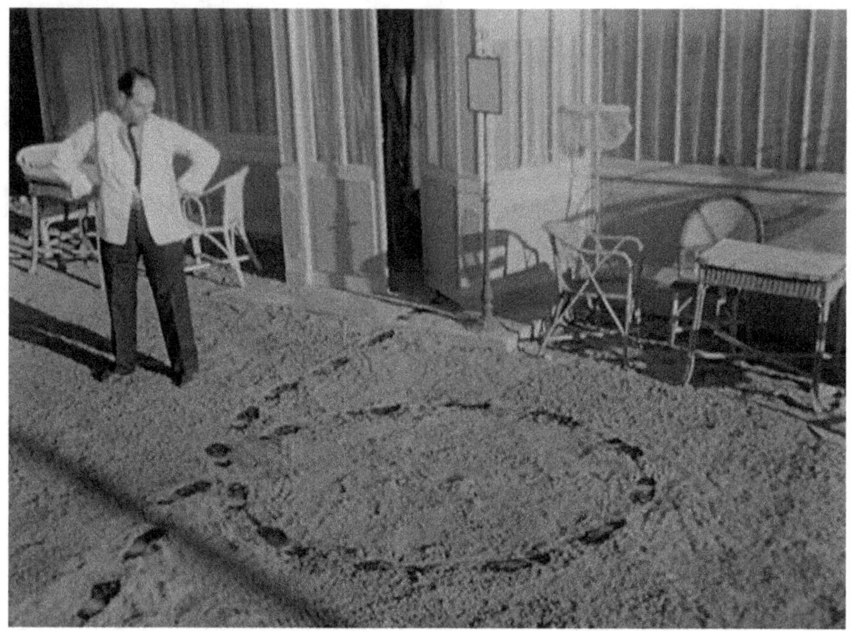

Figure 5.1. *Les Vacances de monsieur Hulot*: The character leaves the mark of his footprints on the ground.

line, which is not necessarily visible, emanates from a virtual centre ('centre virtuel'),[13] beyond the linear pattern of the body. In Loïe Fuller's famous choreography *Serpentine Dance*, which was filmed by several filmmakers, including the Lumière brothers, the serpentine movement of the dancer's draperies produces volumes and surfaces in motion, expanding the virtual lines of her gestures beyond the corporeal limits of the body. In a similar vein, when Artaud analyses the choreographic style in Balinese theatre, he insists on the lines produced by the actors' costumes and gestures, which make them look 'like huge insects full of lines'.[14] 'Each of their movements

13 Georges Didi-Huberman, 'La Danse de toute chose', in Laurent Mannoni and Didi-Huberman, *Mouvements de l'air: Etienne-Jules Marey, photographie des fluides* (Paris: Gallimard, Réunion des musées nationaux, 2004), p. 283.

14 Artaud, *The Theatre and Its Double*, trans. by Mary Caroline Richards (New York: Grove Press, 1958), p. 64.

traces a line in space,' Artaud notes.[15] When gestural lines are captured in the act of their performance, they are often associated with dance. While Didi-Huberman sees the expression of a dance in Marey's graphs, light painting photographs and chronophotographs, Kandinsky in his writings on abstract art also connects the line with the dynamic movement of the dancing body.[16] In Degas's drawings of dancers, the linear pattern of movement, which exceeds the figurative contour of the body, becomes perceivable when the artist corrects the drawing: the trace of the dancer's gesture appears in the lines, which like a trail, overflow the boundaries of the linear design, giving the impression that the movement is broken down, like in a chronophotographic sequence.

The serpentine line is commonly opposed to the straight line. Ingold points out the ideological dimension of the straight line, a product of authority, control and power as the word 'ruler' reveals: 'A ruler is a sovereign who controls and governs a territory. It is also an instrument for drawing straight lines.'[17] As Foucault demonstrates in the well-known essay *Surveiller et punir* (1975), the straight line indeed becomes – in the disciplinary grid-pattern of society – an instrument to discipline the body and condition gestures.[18] In the context of growing industrialisation, the straight line establishes itself as an 'icon of modernity',[19] especially in constructivist art and architecture, and the grid, as a tool to rationalise movement, space and time. While the straight line evokes rationality, convention, norm and order, the serpentine line, especially in the eighteenth and nineteenth centuries, becomes the emblem of fancy (*fantaisie*), freedom, oddity, *flânerie*, digression, madness and feeling.[20] The dichotomy between the straight and

15 Ibid.

16 See Didi-Huberman, 'La Danse de toute chose', in *Mouvements de l'air*, pp. 177–316; Wassily Kandinsky, *Point and Line to Plane*, trans. by Howard Dearstune and Hilla Rebay (New York: Dover Publications, 1979), p. 100.

17 Ingold, *Lines*, p. 160.

18 Michel Foucault, *Surveiller et punir: Naissance de la prison* (Paris: Gallimard, 1975), pp. 173 and 179.

19 Ingold, *Lines*, p. 167.

20 See Bernard Vouilloux, *Ecritures de fantaisie: grotesques, arabesques, zigzags et serpentins* (Paris: Hermann, 2008).

the serpentine line highlights the tension between conditioned behaviours and idiosyncratic gestures, determinate trajectories and indeterminate impulses, gestural codification and the detours of wandering.

By examining the tension between serpentine and straight lines, this chapter aims to explore the notion of gestural line in post-New Wave cinema from cinematic, philosophical, political and ideological perspectives. Throughout the 1970s, line becomes a central notion in Godard's reflection on gesture and conditioning, in Fernand Deligny's research on education, everyday life and autism, and in Jacques Rivette's approach to improvisation and film acting. In the television series *France/tour/détour/deux/enfants* (1977), Godard and Anne-Marie Miéville explore how the linear pattern of the body is conditioned by society. How can gestures disrupt the predictability of programmes in a capitalist society structured by Taylorism? By focusing on the education of two children, the filmmakers dissect the power of the norm and the potential resistance of gestures, in a way that not only evokes Foucault, as Michael Witt has already demonstrated,[21] but also Deleuze and Guattari's conceptualisation of the line. Around the same time, the educator and writer Fernand Deligny developed an alternative method of education on the fringe of psychiatric institutions. Deligny was involved in several film projects, such as *Le Moindre Geste* (1962–71) and *Ce Gamin, là* (1975), which both highlight the gestural trajectories of marginal characters and neurodiverse persons. The two films bring out the multiplicity of lines (traces, threads, knots, customary and wandering lines) that take root in the characters' slightest gestures. Finally, the practice of improvisation in Rivette's *Out 1: Noli me tangere* (1971), made in the context of the political crisis resulting from May 1968, questions the notions of spontaneity, freedom and deconditioning. The gestural lines are no longer conditioned and planned in the script, but result from the actors' agency.

21 Michael Witt, 'Altered Motion and Corporeal Resistance in *France/tour/détour/deux/enfants*,' in *For Ever Godard*, ed. by James Williams, Michael Temple and Michael Witt (London: Black Dog, 2003), pp. 200–13.

Breaking Down Gestural Lines in the Social Grid: Godard and Miéville's *France/tour/détour/deux/enfants* (1977)

In the television series *France/tour/détour/deux/enfants* produced by Antenne 2 – loosely inspired by the school book *Le Tour de la France par deux enfants* (1877), written by G. Bruno and used in the schools of the Third Republic – Godard and Miéville reflect on the ideological dimension of education and on the impact of social conditioning on everyday life. Interviewing and filming two children named Camille and Arnaud at home, at school or in the street, Godard and Miéville, who allude to scientific motion studies of the late nineteenth and early twentieth centuries, use the device of slow motion in order to scrutinise their gestures. Developing a 'type of antitelevision',[22] they distort and play with television conventions. Although structured in twelve episodes of 26 minutes that replicate the same standardised structure, their programme leaves room for irregularity, detours, digressions and improvisation. As David Sterritt argues, '[…] the standardized shape of each episode serves the same function as the underlying chord structure of a bebop composition.'[23] In the rigid grid of television, the directors attempt to reveal lines of movement that escape or resist the predictability of the programme.

When the journalist Robert Linard (performed by Godard himself) interviews the children, he introduces the notion of line on several occasions. In the same way that 'programme' and 'grid' are terms that both define the working of television and social conditioning, line is also a polysemic word that, in Godard and Miéville's film, can refer to: the linear pattern of human movement, the city map, the lines of Camille's exercise book, and, ultimately, the TV image itself, which is indeed constituted of lines.[24] In the second episode ('Mouvement 2'), Godard asks Arnaud if he travels

22 Philippe Dubois, 'Video Thinks What Cinema Creates. Notes on Jean-Luc Godard's Work in Video and Television', in *Jean-Luc Godard, Son + Image 1974–1991*, ed. by Bellour and Bandy, p. 174.

23 David Sterritt, *The Films of Jean-Luc Godard: Seeing the Invisible* (Cambridge: Cambridge University Press, 1999), p. 257.

24 From 1949 to 1983, French television adopted the 819-line high-definition system E.

rather in straight lines or in curved ones. The boy answers that he moves in a straight line when he walks along the street, and that he moves in a curve when he turns a corner. He thus envisions the trajectory of his walking according to the outline of the city map and the pattern of the streets.

Furthermore, Godard encourages the child to understand the difference in nature between a point (immobility) and a line (movement):

ROBERT LINARD:	Est-ce qu'on pourrait dire que tu es un point immobile dans l'espace?
ARNAUD:	Non, je suis plutôt un point qui bouge dans l'espace. […]
RL:	Et entre les deux points – celui où tu étais avant et celui où tu es maintenant – ça fait une ligne?
A:	Oui, j'ai fait une ligne.
RL:	Et est-ce que tu fais partie de cette ligne ou tu fais seulement partie des points où tu étais et des points où tu es?
A:	Je crois plutôt que je fais partie de cette ligne.
[ROBERT LINARD:	Are you a motionless point in space?
ARNAUD:	No, I'm rather a moving point in space. […]
RL:	And between the two points – where you were before and where you are now – does that make a line?
A:	Yes, I made a line.
RL:	And are you part of this line or are you just part of the points where you were before and the points where you are now?
A:	I think I'm part of the line.]

Crucially, by altering the tape speed, Godard and Miéville break down (*décomposer*) the line of movement into a series of points. Like scientists, they observe particles of gestures. 'On numerous occasions in *France/tour*, we are suddenly conscious that the human body, whether in isolation or viewed as part of a crowd is being scrutinised in precisely the same way that a scientist examines particle motion through a microscope,'[25] Witt explains, comparing Godard and Miéville's use of video with Muybridge's and Marey's chronophotography. The two directors highlight Camille's and Arnaud's everyday gestures such as: undressing before going to bed,

25 Witt, 'Altered Motion and Corporeal Resistance', p. 207.

turning the TV on or playing in the school playground with friends. They also use the device of slow motion to break down the urban movement of the crowd, for example, showing people coming out of the escalator of the Parisian metro in 'Mouvement 2', people and cars crossing the street in 'Mouvement 3' or cars and trucks driving on the highway in 'Mouvement 8'. Just as in Perec and Queysanne's *Un homme qui dort* (*The Man Who Sleeps*, 1974), which also reflects on social conditioning (see Chapter 1), the crowd is named 'the monsters'. The reflection on the relationship between people, machines, automatons and programmes permeates all the episodes of the series which, through the metaphor of the monsters, plays with the codes of dystopian fiction (recalling Godard's 1965 film *Alphaville*, for example).

In line with Foucault's thought, '[t]he series examines the conditioning of the human infant as a docile subject of capitalism.'[26] School is viewed as a place of 'enforced incarceration'[27] that is ruled by 'the power of the Norm'.[28] In *Surveiller et punir*, Foucault, who analyses how power coerced the body during the eighteenth century, demonstrates the extent to which the slightest gesture becomes the result of a process of social codification. The social machine breaks down and recomposes the body in order to condition the quality of its gestures (in terms of trajectory, amplitude or precision):

> The human body was entering a machine of power that explores it, breaks it down and rearranges it.[29]

> The act is broken down into its elements; the position of the body, limbs, articulations is defined; to each movement are assigned a direction, an aptitude, a duration; their order of succession is prescribed. Time penetrates the body and with it all the meticulous controls of power.[30]

26 Ibid, p. 208.

27 Ibid.

28 Foucault, *Discipline and Punish: The Birth of the Prison*, trans. by Alain Sheridan (New York: Vintage Books, 1995), p. 184.

29 Ibid., p. 138.

30 Ibid., p. 152.

The calibration and the control of the body supposedly guarantee a better gestural efficiency. In the nineteenth and twentieth centuries, the criteria of efficiency, energy waste and productivity were central concerns in motion studies. By breaking down movement, Marey aimed to improve the quality of gesture by reducing fatigue, and '[increasing] productivity in almost all areas of social life'.[31]

Similarly, in the wake of Taylorism, the American scientists Frank and Lillian Gilbreth, who were both pioneers in time and motion study, used different media such as film, light painting photography and three-dimensional models to measure and improve the gestural sequences executed by workers in factories, offices and hospitals. They sought to eliminate waste motions, simplify gestures and rationalise the number of movements for each task. In their trials, gestures were precisely timed with a chronometer, before a grid-pattern backdrop. Altered motion speed was sometimes used to enhance the perception of gestures. Gilbreth's films highlight the likeness between the working of the assembly line and the cinematic machine that breaks down movement into a series of frames in order to mechanically reproduce it. Analysed, calibrated and rationalised, the line of gestures is segmented and divided into a series of points. Segmentation enables better control and a better motion efficiency in order to avoid irregularities, inconstancies and hesitations. According to Ingold, '[o]nce the trace of a continuous gesture, the line has been fragmented – under the sway of modernity – into a succession of points or dots.'[32] If the process of segmentation multiplies the possibilities of recomposition – through the creation of new programmes, new forms of life and new experiences – Citton also points out the risk of losing the *élan vital* that animates human life.[33]

In *France/tour/détour*, Godard and Miéville focus on the segmental lines that codify everyday behaviours, gestures and rhythms in late 1970s France. Assimilating segmental lines from birth, people reproduce certain patterns that, from generation to generation, divide an individual's life into different segments, such as home-school; school-military service;

31 Cited in Harbord, *Ex-centric Cinema*, p. 65.

32 Ingold, *Lines*, p. 75.

33 Citton, *Gestes d'humanités*, p. 271.

work-retirement. Conceptualised by Deleuze and Guattari, the notion of segmental line, which echoes Foucault's concept of biopower, defines social ordering and its impact on the body. According to Deleuze,

> The first kind of line which forms us is segmentary – of rigid segmentarity (or rather there are already many lines of this sort): family – profession; job – holiday; family – and then school – and then the army – and the factory – and then retirement. And each time, from one segment to the next, they speak to us, saying: 'Now you're not a baby any more'; and at school, 'You're not at home now'; and in the army, 'You're not at school now' … In short, all kinds of clearly defined segments, in all kinds of directions, which cut us up in all senses, packets of segmentarised lines.[34]

The segmental line frames the social but also intimate life of an individual. When Godard and Miéville film Camille in the bathroom of her home in the opening sequence of 'Mouvement 1' (see Figures 5.2–5.7), the sequence brings out such segmental lines. The directors slow down the tape speed to scrutinise Camille's gestures while she is undressing before putting her nightshirt on. Significantly, the tiles of the bathroom wall form a grid pattern in the background of the image, which is reminiscent of Gilbreth's motion studies. Embodying authority at home, Camille's mother can be heard off-screen. Firstly, she asks her daughter whether she has already prepared her school bag for the next day; secondly, she wonders what Camille is doing in the bathroom: 'Qu'est-ce que tu fais Camille? Qu'est-ce que tu fais?' [What are you doing, Camille? What are you doing?] Camille answers that she is taking her vest off; finally, her mother asks her several times to hurry up. Camille must execute this everyday gestural sequence with a temporal constraint. The voyeuristic gaze of the camera highlights the lack of intimacy: Camille is a surveyed subject; her slightest gestures are under control, rooted in the segments home-school. As Witt suggests, it seems that '[a] contagious Taylorisation has spread far beyond the factory, infecting all gesture, from the most mundane (washing up) to the most intimate (love-making)'.[35]

34 Gilles Deleuze and Claire Parnet, *Dialogues II*, trans. by Hugh Tomlinson and Barbara Habberjam (New York: Columbia University Press, 2007), p. 124.

35 Witt, 'Altered Motion and Corporeal Resistance', p. 209.

Figures 5.2–5.7. *France/tour/détour*: The camera scrutinises Camille's gestures.

Yet the process of slow motion, which invites the spectator to look at Camille's gestures more closely, stresses their lack of efficiency, especially when she struggles to put her nightshirt on. She makes a lot of unnecessary and irregular motions to perform a simple action. Like the choreographed movements of draperies in Fuller's *Serpentine Dance* or Marey's *Etude de mouvements de danse et de draperie* (1886), her gestures give unexpected forms to the nightshirt. The rhythmicity and amplitude of Camille's gestures resist the Taylorist imperative of efficiency. In the 1970s and 1980s, Godard was preoccupied with the potential resistance of gestures to social conditioning. In *Sauve qui peut (la vie)* (*Every Man for Himself*, 1980), he refers to the sociologist and communist activist Robert Linhart[36] who condemns the excessive rationalisation of workers' gestures in factories while pointing out the existence of small margins of bodily resistance:

> Quelque chose, dans le corps et dans la tête, s'arc-boute contre la répétition et le néant. La vie: un geste plus rapide, un bras qui retombe à contretemps, un pas plus lent, une bouffée d'irrégularité, un faux mouvement […]
>
> [Something in the body and in the mind arches its back against routine and void. Life: a quicker gesture; an arm moving up and down – off beat; a slower step forward; a gust of air; a startled gasp; a wrong move […]][37]

In *France/tour/détour*, Camille's gestures, which are not standardised, reveal margins of individual interpretation within the social grid. According to Witt, 'Neo-Foucauldian denunciation of the disciplinary regulation of the body gives way to a systematic search for glimpses of the fissures and disjunctions – sudden and mysterious points of corporeal resistance – concealed beneath superficial homogeneity and continuity.'[38] Clumsiness, irregularity, confusion and hesitation prove that Camille's gestures are not conditioned by segmental lines only, but are also made up of other lines.

'Whether we are individuals or groups, we are made of lines and these lines are very varied in nature,'[39] Deleuze insists, distinguishing three different kind of lines: segmental lines, molecular lines ('ligne moléculaire') and lines of flight ('lignes de fuite'). In contrast with segmental lines,

36 In the wake of May 1968, Robert Linhart was employed in a Citroën factory based in Paris, at La Porte de Choissy. He shares his experience in *L'Etabli* (Paris: Minuit, 1978).

37 Translation in the DVD of *Sauve qui peut (la vie)/Slow Motion* (London : Artificial Eye, 2005).

38 Witt, 'Altered Motion and Corporeal Resistance', p. 211.

39 Deleuze and Parnet, *Dialogues II*, p. 124.

molecular lines, which are much more flexible and unpredictable, result from the *élan vital*: 'They trace out little modifications, they make detours, they sketch out rises and falls.'[40] The words *tour* [tour] and *détour* [detour] in the title *France/tour/détour* point out the tension between the codified system of segmentary lines and the idiosyncratic expression of molecular lines. Finally, the line of flight is a line of rupture and of *deterritorialisation* which, like 'a sort of delirium', disrupts the code and deviates from the furrow.[41]

As we have seen with Walter Benjamin in Chapter 4, the 'optical unconscious' of the camera is able to grasp the slightest impulses, urges and nervous reactions of disgust or attraction that manifest on the surface of the body. By breaking down Camille's gestures, the technique of slow motion scrutinises her mood swings with precision. As Godard notes, '[…] even when she was doing extremely banal things, you'd go suddenly from profound anguish to joy a split second later.'[42] By contrast, Godard admitted to having been less interested in the boy's gestures, which seem to be much more conditioned by segmental lines: 'Between each image was always the same guiding line.'[43] For example, at the beginning of movements 2 and 3, Arnaud and Camille are respectively filmed in the street going to school. On the one hand, Arnaud prepares himself, energetically putting his jacket and schoolbag on. The process of slow motion highlights a certain determination and will in all his motions that do not deviate from everyday routine. On the other hand, when Camille is shown running in the street, she traces a straight line before making a detour. Indeed, she slows down, changes trajectory and jumps on a bench. The detour is a useless digression and a loss of time. In the segment of her itinerary (going from a point A (home) to a point B (school)), Camille creates new lines, other lines, her own lines. '[W]atch someone walking down the street and see what little inventions he introduces into it, if he is not too caught up in his rigid segmentarity, what little inventions he puts there,' Deleuze writes.[44] Camille improvises,

40 Ibid.

41 Ibid., p. 40.

42 Cited in Witt, 'Altered Motion and Corporeal Resistance', p. 201.

43 Ibid.

44 Deleuze and Parnet, *Dialogues II*, p. 128.

reacting to her environment and following her *élan vital*. Jumping on the bench is a playful gesture. The breakdown of her movement emphasises the great diversity of her corporeal and facial expressions, which change very quickly. She also moves at different speeds, slowing down her running before speeding up again. The alteration of the tape speed stresses the changes of rhythm and the irregularities in Camille's gestures.

For Godard, slow motion is a tool that reveals the unexpected and unknown in bodily movements that are supposed to be known, codified, calibrated, segmented and classified:

> All the possible permutations between these 25 images represent thousands of possibilities. I concluded that when you change the rhythms, and analyse a woman's movements, even movements as simple as buying a loaf of bread for instance, you realise that there are loads of different worlds inside the woman's movement.[45]

The process of slow motion does not fragment the gestural line into segments, but rather turns the line into an irregular dotted line which, according to the mathematician Gilles Châtelet, is different from the line and the dot. The dotted line gives to the image a virtual dimension.[46] In Godard and Miéville's work, the dotted line generates new possibilities of perception which, by defamiliarising the most ordinary gestures, reveal a constellation of fleeting motions and emotions. It makes unexpected gestural potentialities visible.

While Godard and Miéville focus on social conditioning and gestural resistance in normative education, the educator Deligny explores new ways of living with and educating children on the fringe of society. In the late 1960s, by working with children and teenagers with behavioural, psychological and mental troubles, he developed exploratory research on gestural lines, which significantly influenced Guattari, Deleuze and Certeau. In the Cévennes, Deligny attempted to create a community in which autistic people and educators could co-exist together in spite of their gestural differences.

45 Cited in Witt, 'Altered Motion and Corporeal Resistance', p. 201.

46 Gilles Châtelet, *Les Enjeux du mobile: Mathématique, physique, philosophie* (Paris: Seuil, 1993), p. 33.

The Knotting of Heterogeneous Gestural Lines in *Le Moindre Geste* (1962–71) and *Ce Gamin, là* (1975)

Deligny, who deliberately occupied the margins throughout his lifetime, remains little known in France and abroad despite the republication of a large part of his writings in 2007.[47] After the Second World War, Deligny experimented with new ways of working and living with children and teenagers, who most often had neurodevelopmental disorders. In 1946, while working for the educative association *Travail et Culture* in the North of France, he met André Bazin and Chris Marker, two central figures in the history of post-war French cinema. On the advice of Bazin, François Truffaut contacted Deligny in the 1950s, while he was finishing the script of *Les Quatre Cents Coups* (*The 400 Blows*, 1959). According to Toledo, Deligny suggested to the young director the idea of Antoine Doisnel (Jean-Pierre Léaud) running towards the sea at the end of the film.[48] In the 1960s and 1970s, Deligny and Truffaut regularly corresponded;[49] Deligny requested Truffaut's help several times to produce his own film projects. From the 1950s to the 1980s, Deligny used the film camera as a pedagogical tool.[50] He did not consider himself a filmmaker and never 'made' films in the conventional use of the term. But he was involved in several significant projects: *Le Moindre Geste* was filmed by his assistant Josée Manenti in 1962–5 and edited by Jean-Pierre Daniel in 1968–70 (without Deligny's participation) with the material support of Chris Marker and his production company SLON/ISKRA; the documentary *Ce Gamin, là* was directed by Renaud Victor between 1972 and 1974 and co-produced by Truffaut's production company Les Films du Carrosse. These films document Deligny's ideas about gestural lines.

47 Fernand Deligny, *Œuvres*, ed. by Sandra Alvarez de Toledo (Paris: L'Arachnéen, 2007).

48 Toledo, 'Le Moindre Geste', in *Œuvres*, ed. by Toledo, p. 599.

49 Bernard Bastide, 'Correspondance François Truffaut-Fernand Deligny', *1895. Mille huit cent quatre-vingt-quinze*, 42 (2004), 77–110 <https://journals.openedition.org/1895/281> [accessed 19 August 2018].

50 See Deligny, 'La Caméra outil pédagogique', in *Œuvres*, pp. 414–17.

Territory, Line, Trace and Thread in Le Moindre Geste

Deligny's ideas about the line, which he developed from the late 1960s, are already prefigured in *Le Moindre Geste*. If the film is perhaps a film without any author,[51] it is ultimately, according to Daniel, Deligny's film,[52] even though the latter did not direct the film in the strict sense of the term. In charge of the shooting, Manenti explains that he was often present during the process of filmmaking, but mostly stayed in the background.[53] Although Deligny was not directly engaged in the act of filmmaking, the film credits acknowledge and stress his paternity over the work. At the beginning, Deligny introduces the main character, Yves, in voice-over. Diagnosed with a neurodevelopmental disorder, Yves has lived with Deligny and Manenti for several years. Like a game without strict rules, the film offers Yves the possibility not only to move freely, followed by Manenti's mobile camera, but also to speak. The images and his speech, which was recorded on a tape recorder during the shooting, are desynchronised, heightening the fragmented quality of the editing. The film shows him gesturing, being in the world, getting lost, roaming alone and interacting with others, often with difficulty.

The narrative loosely draws on a minor news item that reports the wandering of a bullock in the streets of Paris, having escaped from the slaughterhouse of La Villette. Deligny turns the news item into a fable: two teenagers, Yves and Richard, escape from the psychiatric institution in which they are educated and wander in the Cévennes. After Richard falls into a hole, Yves tries to save him by looking for a rope, but progressively forgets him. At the end of the film, Valérie, a young woman who lives in a village nearby, brings him back to the asylum. For Daniel, the loose narrative is a pretext to see Yves's gestures.[54] Yves responds to the environment of the shooting – the mountains, the quarry, the river, the paths, etc. – which,

51 Jean-Pierre Daniel in '*Le Moindre Geste:* Autour de Fernand Deligny', *L'Image, le monde*, 2 (2001), 33–65 (p. 57).

52 Ibid., p. 59.

53 Josée Manenti in '*Le Moindre Geste.* Autour de Fernand Deligny', p. 58.

54 Daniel in '*Le Moindre Geste.* Autour de Fernand Deligny', p. 59.

like a playground, becomes an inexhaustible source of potential actions and unpredictable gestures.[55]

According to Ingold, the world and the body are made of lines that are not only abstract, virtual or imaginary, like latitude and longitude for instance, but also real and observable, for example, in designs, in the palm of our hands, in the mud-cracks or in the paths which are traced by the recurring passages of human beings and/or animals. Lines can be of different natures, such as traces, cracks and threads. The trace is 'any enduring mark left in or on a solid surface by a continuous movement'[56] while the thread is 'a filament of some kind, which may be entangled with other threads or suspended between points in three-dimensional space'.[57] *Le Moindre Geste* brings out the leitmotivs of the trace and the thread. First of all, at the beginning of the film, Yves traces simple human figures on a sheet of paper. Like in Henri-Georges Clouzot's *Le Mystère Picasso* (*The Mystery of Picasso*, 1956) in which Picasso paints for the camera, the black lines are filmed as they are drawn by Yves. Although Yves's hand appears through the sheet, the camera mostly focuses on the line itself rather than on the gesture. The prologue stresses Yves's creativity and gestural freedom. After escaping the asylum, though he is constrained by his immediate environment and by his encounters with other characters, he can freely draw his own lines of movement. Full of agency and inventiveness, he is presented by Deligny as the essential creator of the film rather than as the guinea pig of a pedagogical experiment.

Secondly, the characters move in a territory that is constituted by a network of paths, roads and railway lines. Rather than walking along these lines, Yves, most often, crosses them. While escaping, Yves and Richard deviate from the path to wander in wild nature. Yves's impulse to cross the line also manifests itself when he exits the frame on several occasions. As Comolli explains, the freedom of movement that defines Yves's performance makes him difficult to frame – he often escapes the field of view.[58]

55 Deligny, 'Quand même il est des nôtres', in *Œuvres*, p. 634.

56 Ingold, *Lines*, p. 43.

57 Ibid., p. 41.

58 Jean-Louis Comolli, 'L'Evadé. *Le Moindre Geste*, de Fernand Deligny, Jo Manenti et Jean-Pierre Daniel, 1959–1970', in *Voir et pouvoir: l'innocence perdue: cinéma, télévision, documentaire* (Lagrasse: Verdier, 2004), p. 586.

At the end of the film, when Yves is returning to the asylum with Valérie, he walks on the main road, which signifies the end of his free wandering.

Finally, the film weaves another sort of line: the thread. Yves is a character who experiences great difficulty in making knots. He clumsily manipulates his shoelaces and struggles with ropes (see Figures 5.8–5.11). The leitmotiv of the thread, which has been purposely stressed in the editing of the film, mirrors Daniel's difficulty in forging links between the different narrative fragments of the film. Deligny, who often compares cinematic images with chips (*copeau*, *éclat*), is aware of the discontinuous nature of the cinematic medium.[59] The difficulty in knotting (or tying together) the threads of the narrative is also symptomatic of Yves's struggle to develop relationships with others. The threads can be potentially abandoned and unknotted. Yves's wandering develops in the margins of the fiction. His

Figures 5.8–5.11. *Le Moindre Geste*: Yves manipulates shoelaces and ropes.

59 Deligny, 'Camérer', in '*Le Moindre Geste.* Autour de Fernand Deligny', p. 65.

gestures gravitate around a forgotten centre, that is, the hole in which Richard has fallen. Moreover, Valérie and Yves's respective lines fail twice to be tied. The first time, Valérie observes Yves and then runs away; the second time, she tries to touch him, but Yves rejects her and continues to wander on his own. In the epilogue of the film, Yves drops his rope to follow Valérie. Although he first keeps his distance, both characters eventually walk next to each other, holding hands and following the same line. Their trajectories separate when Yves returns to the asylum.

Wandering Line, Customary Line and Community in Ce Gamin, là

Beyond his difference, Yves is shown as being part of a community. '[I]l est des nôtres' [He is one of us], Deligny writes.[60] However, *Le Moindre Geste*'s fragmented editing emphasises the lack of interrelation between the different social groups that inhabit the territory in which Yves is wandering. How can a common territory, shared by residents, workers, educators and neurodivergent people be constituted? In the late 1960s, a few years after the shooting of *Le Moindre Geste*, Deligny's preoccupation with common spaces grew. He wanted to invent a space where the gestures of wandering and the gestures of dwelling could co-exist.[61] He thus created a network in the Cévennes, bringing together autistic children, non-professional educators, farmers and workers.[62] The network established an ecological mode of existence in which multiple lines of existence and heterogeneous forms of life could interrelate in the same territory. According to Marielle Macé, the ideas of network and cohabitation are at the core of ecological thinking.[63] By stimulating the interconnection between heterogeneous lines of existence, Deligny attempted to revitalise the notion of community through the emergence of a common

60 Deligny, 'Quand même il est des nôtres', in *Œuvres*, p. 635.

61 See Toledo, 'Le Moindre Geste', in *Œuvres*, p. 606; Toledo, 'Ce Gamin, là', in *Œuvres*, p. 1036.

62 Toledo in '*Le Moindre Geste.* Autour de Fernand Deligny', p. 41.

63 Macé, *Styles*, pp. 111–12.

body ('corps commun').[64] In its political dimension, the notion of line can thus be defined as a device to see and analyse singular manners of dwelling in a territory and within a community.

In 1969, Deligny developed a system of maps in order to trace the gestures and movements of autistic children who lived under his team's care. Through the notions of *ligne d'erre* (wandering line) and *ligne coutumière* (customary line), *gestes d'erre* (wandering gestures) and *gestes coutumiers* (customary gestures), he distinguishes, on the one hand, the autistic children's unpredictable trajectories and, on the other, the adults' everyday activities.[65] Deligny understands the word 'erre' in the same way as 'errer' (to wander).[66] While the wandering line indicates a certain way of being that deviates from the main paths and randomly drifts at the margins, the customary line refers to the everyday reiteration of subsistence gestures, such as making bread, doing the dishes, peeling potatoes and sewing. Thanks to the practice of cartography, Deligny observes how both lines intertwine at once in the children's and the adults' gestures. The lines are the graphic trace of all the gestures and movements repeated by the community every day. The map is a medium that makes it possible to see what would otherwise go unnoticed, by bringing out the interconnection of everyday trajectories, reiterated patterns and unexpected detours. By using their kinesic intelligence, the persons who traced the map from memory or in the field needed to be attentive to their own gestures and to the gestures of the autistic children who they were taking charge of (see Figures 5.12 and 5.13).

While the customary lines and gestures form a pattern ('trame') that structures the autistic children's life and orientates their movements thanks to identifiable landmarks,[67] the children weave another sort of line, which Deligny compares to a spiderweb. The ideas of 'inné' [innate], 'agir' [doing

64 Deligny, *Les Détours de l'agir ou le moindre geste*, in *Œuvres*, p. 1333.

65 See Gilles Deleuze and Félix Guattari, *A Thousand Plateaus: Capitalism and Schizophrenia*, trans. by Brian Massumi (Minneaopolis: University of Minnesota Press, 2005), p. 202; Deligny, *Les Détours de l'agir ou le moindre geste*, in *Œuvres*, pp. 1247–344; Fernand Deligny and Isaac Joseph, *Cahiers de l'immuable 1/ voix et voir*, in *Œuvres*, pp. 847–59.

66 See Deligny, *Cahiers de l'immuable*, in *Œuvres*, p. 811.

67 Deligny, *Nous et l'innocent*, in *Œuvres*, p. 714.

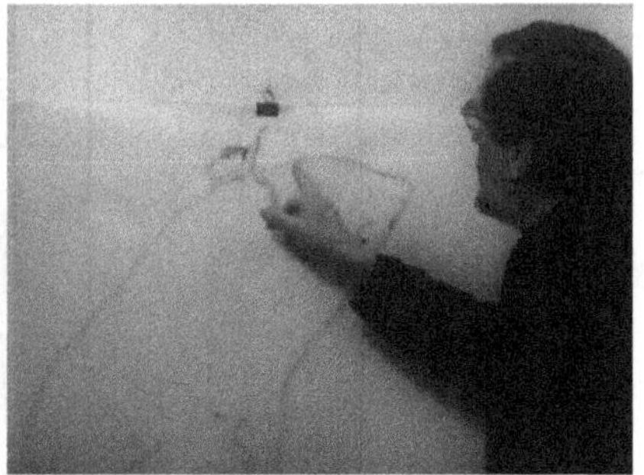

Figures 5.12–5.13. *Ce Gamin, là*: Deligny and one of his co-workers use a system of maps to observe the gestural lines of autistic children.

something], 'détour' [detour], 'échappée' [breakaway] and 'résistance' [resistance] define the concept of 'arachnéen' [arachnean], which is the distinctive feature of the wandering line, as Ogilvie explains: 'Le modèle analogique de ce réseau, qui évoque évidemment la guerre et la résistance, mais pas seulement, est la toile d'araignée, "l'arachnéen", ce tissage obstiné qui offre l'image d'une échappée, d'un dehors, d'un "pas de côté" […]'[68] [The analogical model of this network, which evokes war and resistance – but not only – is the spiderweb, the 'arachnean'. This obstinate weaving offers the image of a breakaway, of an outside, of a 'sidestep' […]]. According to Deligny, the permanence of human life is visible in the innate gestures of autistic people, who are able to execute elementary gestures that prove essential in the everyday life of a community. Deligny distinguishes the adults' gestures of making (*faire)* and the autistic children's gestures of doing (*agir*).[69] Indeed, if the adults intentionally gesture to make something, the children repeat customary gestures without being preoccupied with the purpose of the action.[70] They react to the adults' routine, attracted by the trace of their customary lines. Their gestures, which are not driven

68 Bertrand Ogilvie, 'Vivre entre les lignes', in Fernand Deligny, *L'Arachnéen et autres textes* (Paris: L'Arachnéen, 2008), p. 246.

69 See Deligny, *Les Détours de l'agir*, in *Œuvres*.

70 Deligny, *Singulière ethnie*, in *Œuvres*, p. 1453.

by projects and intentions and can lack self-control, are often less efficient than the adults' ones. They are not subjected to the imperative of efficiency.

In the network, customary and wandering lines are closely interwoven. Deligny observes that the autistic children's presence influences the adults' slightest gestures, which are modulated by the wandering lines.[71] Through the constant co-presence of multiple lines of existence, the network thus enables the emergence of a common body.[72] It is in this sense that Deligny's network inspired Deleuze and Guattari's concept of rhizome. The rhizome is a cartographic model of thought, which, rather than organising elements according to a hierarchical and arborescent system, fosters the interconnection, crossing and interweaving of a multiplicity of heterogeneous lines.[73] According to Deleuze and Guattari, 'Deligny opened his lines of writing to life lines. The lines are constantly crossing, intersecting for a moment, following one another.'[74] The autistic children's wandering gestures not only weave lines of flight, but actually interweave several heterogeneous lines: '[...] *a line of flight, which is already complex since it has singularities; and there a customary or molar line with segments; and between the two (?), there is a molecular line with quanta that cause it to tip to one side or the other.*'[75]

But to what extent can the wandering lines traced by the adults translate all the indeterminacy of the autistic children's gestures? Barbara Formis criticises the process that consists in obliterating the indeterminacy of gestures by turning them into an abstract trace, a metaphor or an image, like a line for example.[76] For instance, the serpentine line in *Tristram Shandy* paradoxically freezes a spontaneous and 'free' gesture in a determined and fixed form. In the late 1970s, Deligny progressively abandoned the practice of mapping in favour of the film camera. Contrary to maps, film and video enabled Deligny, as well as the parents' children, to see the children's gestures directly in their immediate environment. However, in contrast to

71 Deligny, *Acheminement vers l'image*, in *Œuvres*, p. 1684.

72 Deligny and Joseph, *Cahiers de l'immuable*, in *Œuvres*, p. 852.

73 Deleuze and Guattari, *A Thousand Plateaus*, pp. 3–25.

74 Ibid., p. 203.

75 Ibid. (emphasis in original).

76 Formis, *Esthétique de la vie ordinaire*, p. 118.

the maps, the filmic medium cannot give a synoptic and comprehensive understanding of the territory in which the children and adults cohabit. In the documentary *Ce Gamin, là*, the map and the moving image, which make it possible to see the trace of gestures differently, dialogue with each other and prove to be complementary. Although Certeau questions the relevance of the trace and the line to grasp the gesture of walking, given that '[t]he trace left behind is substituted for the practice',[77] he refers to Deligny's wandering line as a notion to rethink the manners of moving in modern cities and to revitalise the ways of looking at people's gestures.[78] While walking or exploring a city, people can indeed wander and traverse the rational grid of society by making unpredictable trajectories and meaningless detours, as previously seen in *France/tour/détour*.

Impressed by *Le Moindre Geste*, the filmmaker and communist activist Renaud Victor decided to make a documentary on Deligny's network in 1972. Truffaut, who produced *Ce Gamin, là*, asked Deligny to write a commentary and read it in voice-over. Due to a lack of money, the shooting of the film was sporadic. Even when he could not actually film for lack of reel, Victor could plan the shooting without any difficulty, due to the monotony of the network's life.[79] *Ce Gamin, là* focuses more particularly on the life of the young autistic Janmari, who was a constant source of questioning and interest for Deligny. The medical profession considered Janmari as being incurable and impossible to live with. At the beginning of the film, Deligny criticises the living conditions in psychiatric hospitals where the perception of the outside world is reduced to walls and window bars. With the network, Deligny attempted to create a countermodel of existence where Janmari could live outside, within a community, and manifest a sense of belonging by walking, wandering and gesturing.

The film traces the progressive evolution of Janmari's behaviour, year after year. At first, Janmari spends most of his time spinning around and swaying. He does not spin around himself, but around an absent centre: an

77 Certeau, *The Practice of Everyday Life*, p. 97. See also Doina Petrescu, 'The Indeterminate Mapping of the Common', *Field*, 1.1 (2007), 88–96 (p. 93).

78 Certeau, *The Practice of Everyday Life*, pp. xviii and 34.

79 Cited in Toledo, 'Ce Gamin, là', in *Œuvres*, p. 1035.

absence of will, language, project, intention and, ultimately, subject.[80] Like in *Le Moindre Geste*, the symbolism of the knot expresses the autistic children's difficulty to live as subjects. According to Deligny, a knot is a project that would be the proof of the existence of the subject.[81] He observes that autistic people, who are not conditioned by the structures of verbal language and the code of social interactions in the same way as others, are not able to make knots by themselves.[82] In order to make knots, the autistic children, similarly to Yves in *Le Moindre Geste*, need a third hand, that is, the hand of one of the adults who live with them. The knots, which interweave wandering and customary lines, structure the mode of existence of the network.[83] Gradually, through contact with the adults, Janmari starts to take part in the life of the community by reiterating essential gestures, like making bread or chopping firewood. His gestures manifest his sense of belonging. Contrary to Yves, he is no longer isolated: the film shows him progressively living and wandering in co-presence with others.

If gestures of knotting are essential to the development of a community, they are also crucial to weave storylines in narrative cinema. As suggested in Chapter 3, the issues of cohesion, co-existence and co-presence are not only political but also narrative. In *Out 1: Noli me tangere*, Rivette emphasises at once the difficulty to constitute a cohesive group of characters and to build a narrative in the political context of post-May 1968. The film, which was entirely improvised by the actors, raises questions that are also relevant to *Le Moindre Geste*: how not to lose the thread of the narrative? How to forge links between the scattered fragments of gestures and the disconnected trajectories of the characters? How to make knots through gestures of contact?

In *Un homme qui dort* and *Jeanne Dielman* (1975), Perec, Queysanne and Akerman direct their actors' gestural lines by imposing on them specific gestures and postures (see Chapters 1 and 2). The characters' alienation mirrors the actors' own alienation during the shooting. Albeit performing in

80 See Jean-Louis Comolli, 'Un cinéma hors de lui', in *Corps et cadre: cinéma, éthique, politique, 2004–2010* (Lagrasse: Verdier, 2012), p. 439.

81 Deligny, *Les Détours de l'agir*, in *Œuvres*, p. 1315.

82 Ibid., pp. 1314–15.

83 Deligny, *Nous et l'innocent*, in *Œuvres*, p. 786.

different contexts and manners, Jacques Spiesser and Delphine Seyrig both struggle to invent their characters' gestures in the very rigid grid imposed by the directors. By contrast, Rivette uses improvisation to break with the constraining frame of the script, which like a programme, tends to condition the actors' slightest gestures. Influenced by Jean Rouch's improvised film *Petit à Petit* (*Little by Little*, 1971),[84] he develops an intuitive style of filmmaking which originates in the actors' improvised lines of movement.

Improvising the Line

Liberating the Line during the Post-New Wave

The Soviet filmmaker Eisenstein was used to sketching his characters' 'lines of movement' before shooting, and to plan their 'spatial inscriptions' in the shot.[85] Fascinated by 'la dynamique des lignes et la dynamique de la "marche"' [the dynamics of lines and the dynamics of 'walking'],[86] Eisenstein was convinced that any director had to be able to perform the characters' gestures, even approximately, in order to rightly plan their lines of movement.[87] From this perspective, the invention of gestures thus fundamentally results from the director's rather than from the actor's agency. In the lesson on mise-en-scène entitled 'Mise en Jeu and Mise en Geste' (1948) in which he adapts the end of Dostoevsky's *The Idiot* (1869), Eisenstein describes the trajectories of the characters' slightest gestures. He envisions their gestural lines (or what he calls elsewhere the zigzag of expression),[88] in a very expressive style, close to a drawing: 'The right

84 See *Les Mystères de Paris: 'Out 1' de Jacques Rivette revisité*, dir. by Robert Fischer and Wilfried Reichart (2015).

85 Eisenstein, *Mise en Jeu and Mise en Geste*.

86 Eisenstein, 'Comment j'ai appris à dessiner', *Change*, 5 (1970), 21–3 (p. 23).

87 Eisenstein, 'L'Art de la mise en scène', p. 35.

88 Eisenstein, 'Dramaturgie de la forme filmique', trans. by Danièle Huillet, in *Cinématisme: Peinture et cinéma*, ed. by François Albéra (Dijon: Les Presses du réel, 2009), p. 28.

hand sketches rapid zigzags of refusal in the air.'[89] In this expressive mise-en-scène, the character's interiority is transposed into lines of movement decided by the filmmaker himself. Yet Eisenstein is aware of a certain margin of individual interpretation, if not improvisation, from the actor who can perform fortuitous gestures.[90] The notion of fortuity, already explored in Chapter 4, reveals the porous boundary between performance and life. Even when they are sketched and rehearsed in advance, gestural lines can be subjected to small, sometimes infinitesimal variations.

In *France/tour/détour*, Godard and Miéville explore how margins of individual improvisation exist within the sociopolitical frame of everyday life. Through the process of slow motion, the characters' gestures reveal the entanglement of segmental, molecular and rupture lines. Similarly to the approach to performance in *Roberte*, the television series questions how gestures can react idiosyncratically in a codified frame. While using different methods and having different aims, Godard/Miéville and Zucca/Klossowski attempt to grasp the fortuitous expression of life, either by filming young children, who, without any experience of film acting, perform their everyday life in front of a television camera, or by choosing a non-professional actor to perform the main part in *Roberte*. In both cases, constraint, framing and sociocultural conditioning stimulate spontaneous reactions which might be the signs of a corporeal resistance.

When Godard returned to fiction films in the late 1970s, he explored the tension between the characters' determined trajectories and the indeterminate detours of their gestures. In the short essay film *Scénario de 'Sauve qui peut (la vie)'* (1979), made in preparation for his new long feature, Godard expresses the desire to weave the threads of the narrative from the gestural lines produced by the actors during the shooting. While the arc of a screenplay (the storyline) is conventionally generated by dialogue (the lines), Godard attempts to orientate the storylines by looking more carefully at the gestures themselves. By slowing down the scenes and giving one more time to see, 'on peut trouver un changement de direction dans

89 Eisenstein, *Mise en Jeu and Mise en Geste*. Before shooting a film, Eisenstein drew the composition of the shots, as well as the characters' gestures.

90 Eisenstein, 'L'Art de la mise en scène', p. 36.

l'histoire et comment diriger l'histoire' [we can find a change in the direction of the story, and how to direct the story], Godard argues. Looking at the gestures of waitresses (extracted from the 'Mouvement 4' of *France/tour/détour)* and of young people playing football, Godard uses slow motion to see – in the breakdown of their bodily movements – potential storylines and narrative trajectories, which could be developed in the editing. 'Que la ligne du récit parte de ce qui s'est produit, que ce qui se diffuse parte de ce qui se produit' [The narrative arc should take off from what has been seen, what has happened. The plot should flow out of what has happened], Godard explains.

During the post-New Wave era, preoccupations with conditioning and deconditioning led directors such as Philippe Garrel (*Marie pour mémoire* (*Mary for Memory*), 1967), Jacques Rozier (*Du Côté d'Orouët*, 1973), Rouch (*Petit à petit*) and Rivette (*Out 1*) to develop methods of filmmaking fundamentally based on improvisation, inviting the actors, either professional or not, to invent their lines of movement by themselves.[91] By contrast, according to Mouëllic, most of the New Wave directors did not use the technique of improvisation (or only exceptionally in certain scenes of their films). If Godard's practice of filmmaking can evoke improvisation in *A bout de souffle* (*Breathless*, 1960), he did not let the actors improvise in the proper sense of the term.[92] During the shooting of *A bout de souffle*, Godard broke with the conventions of traditional shootings by developing last-minute ideas, day after day, while following a script which was already well structured.[93] Although they could occasionally be put in a limited situation of improvisation, the actors followed Godard's precise indications.

The development of smaller and more mobile cameras (especially in television and live broadcast)[94] enabled filmmakers to follow more freely the actors' trajectories and gestural lines, like in *Le Moindre Geste* for example. Jean Rouch advocated filming with a movie camera in hand and

91 See Gilles Mouëllic, *Improviser le cinéma* (Crisnée: Yellow Now, 2011), pp. 86–98.

92 Ibid., p. 45.

93 Alain Bergala, *Godard au travail, les années 60* (Paris: Cahiers du Cinéma, 2006), p. 47.

94 See Mouëllic, *Improviser le cinéma*, p. 48.

improvising in collaboration with the performers.[95] Such a dynamic improvisation leads to better interaction between the cinematographer's gestures and the characters' filmed gestures.[96] In this sense, as Citton explains, the camera is not a machine which follows a programme and calibrates the actors' gestural lines, but an apparatus which can record something that has not been predicted and envisioned beforehand.[97]

Like in *France/tour/détour and Le Moindre Geste*, the camera in Rivette's *Out 1*, which is manipulated by the cinematographer Pierre-William Glenn, leaves room for indeterminacy, accidents, improvised gestures, and follows the characters' serpentine lines.

Eccentric Lines, Broken Lines and Spiderweb in Out 1: Noli me tangere

Co-written with Suzanne Schiffman, *Out 1: Noli me tangere*[98] was entirely improvised by the actors, including Jean-Pierre Léaud, Juliet Berto, Michael Lonsdale, Bulle Ogier, Jean-François Stévenin and Bernadette Lafont. Rather than directing their gestures by following the script as in a traditional shooting, Rivette gave them the freedom to invent their role and lines. Loosely inspired by Balzac's *Histoire des Treize* (*The Thirteen*, 1833–9), the narrative follows the wanderings of two marginal characters, named Colin (Léaud) and Frédérique (Berto) in Paris, as well as the rehearsals of two distinct theatrical troupes that perform exercises of improvisation in view of staging Aeschylus's plays, *Seven Against Thebes* and *Prometheus Bound*. The film follows the creative (and also destructive) dynamics within and between the different groups. As Rivette has suggested several times, the progressive erosion of the groups can be analysed in the context of the crisis that came after May 1968.[99] The film shows

95 Jean Rouch, 'La Caméra et les hommes', in *Jean-Rouch ou le ciné plaisir*, ed. by René Prédal (Condé-sur-Noireau: Corlet; Paris: Télérama, 1996), pp. 43–4.

96 Ibid.

97 Citton, *Gestes d'humanités*, p. 265.

98 The version entitled *Out 1: Noli me tangere*, released in 1971, is constituted of eight episodes and lasts almost 13h in total. In 1972, Rivette edited a shorter version of 4h20, entitled *Out 1: Spectre*.

99 See *Les Mystères de Paris*, dir. by Fischer and Reichart.

the disenchantment that results from the failures of political utopian projects. Coincidentally, Lonsdale practiced improvisation with Peter Brook during the events of May 1968 in Paris. He remembers the dissension within the troupe, constituted of American, English and French actors.[100] In *Out 1*, Lonsdale draws on this experience to embody and improvise the role of Thomas, a stage director who struggles to create cohesion in his own troupe.

Improvisation in film is often studied in relation to the other arts, such as dance, music, writing or painting. *Out 1* has been compared to Ornette Coleman's free jazz,[101] Trisha Brown's experimental dance[102] or Julian Beck and Judith Malina's Living Theatre.[103] The exploratory research on gesture remains the common denominator of all these artistic practices. Yet, distinctions must be made between, on the one hand, improvisation in dance and theatre, which is most often practiced in preparation for a performance and thus implies a level of reiteration, and, on the other hand, improvisation in film, which aims to capture the unique occurrence of an unpredictable gesture, impossible to envision in advance.[104] Theatre occupies a central position in *Out 1*: the characters are shown performing exercises of improvisation which above all aim to forge links and cohesion within the group. These exercises are not intended to be reiterated as such in the final performance. The two troupes dissolve before they actually start rehearsing Aeschyllus's text. Rivette uses theatre as a way to critically explore the limits of improvisation: the lack of text, the lack of coordination between the actors and, ultimately, the risk of a rupture within the group, the narrative line and the overall creative process are aspects of improvisation which are questioned throughout the film. Following each session,

100 Michael Lonsdale, *Abécédaire* (Paris: L'œil, 2012), p. 57.

101 See Jonathan Rosenbaum, '*Out 1* and Its Double', <https://www.jonathanrosenbaum.net/2017/05/out-1-and-its-double/> [accessed 9 May 2018].

102 See Francesca Dosi, *Trajectoires balzaciennes dans le cinéma de Jacques Rivette: 'Out 1', 'La Belle Noiseuse', 'Ne touchez pas la hache'* (La Madeleine: LettMotif, 2013), p. 69.

103 Ibid., p. 85.

104 Gilles Mouëllic, 'Performance et improvisation dans *L'œuvre de l'art*', in *La Pensée esthétique de Gérard Genette*, ed. by Joseph Delaplace, Pierre-Henry Frangne and Gilles Mouëllic (Rennes: Presses Universitaires de Rennes, 2011), pp. 227–8.

the characters, especially in Thomas's troupe, share their impressions and reactions, analysing their creative process that is based on intuition, playfulness, abandon and failure. The characters' improvised gestures weave serpentine, eccentric and broken lines.

The lack of collective cohesion is suggested in the title, *Out 1: Noli Me Tangere*. In opposition to the word 'in', used as a synonym for 'trendy' by young French people in the 1960s, 'out' means 'en dehors'.[105] While 'in' people are insiders, integrated in a group respecting certain norms, values and cultural codes, 'out' people refuse or struggle to belong to a group or to constitute one. The relationship between outsider and insider characters, between the 'I' and the 'We', and between the individual and the group is usually defined from the perspective of the centre rather than of the margin. For example, as Mary Ebbott argues, 'Greek tragedy includes many types of marginal figures, characters who are outsiders from the perspective of the Athenian centre [...].'[106] Yet, in *Out 1*, all the characters gravitate around an absent centre. The group of Thirteen, which has been dissolved, becomes Colin's obsession; two central characters of the group, named Pierre and Igor, remain absent and haunt the narrative like ghosts; finally, the absence of script and indications from the director disrupt the actors' habits of acting (in this sense, it is significant that both troupes rehearse and improvise without using Aeschyllus's text, keeping it at a distance). The lack of centre(s) in the narrative creates a sense of instability that blurs the lines between the outsider and insider characters: the outsiders' wandering reflects the loneliness, the marginalisation and the anxieties of the insiders who are not able to successfully forge a group. Thomas ends up alone and 'out' at the end of the film, isolated and abandoned by his partners.

More than 'outsiders', Colin and Frédérique can be considered as eccentrics: they are literally off-centre. Colin expresses his eccentric behaviour through the fanciful and serpentine line of his gestures. He allows himself a certain freedom of movement, either in the privacy of his

105 Stéphane Tchalgadjieff, 'Note du producteur Tchalgadjieff', in *Out 1 et son double/ Out 1 and its Double* (Paris: Carlotta, 2015), p. 6. Booklet included in the box set of Rivette's *Out 1* [on DVD].

106 Mary Ebbott, 'Marginal Figures', in *A Companion to Greek Tragedy*, ed. by Justina Gregory (Malden: Blackwell Publishing), p. 366.

bedroom or in public spaces, including streets, shops or cafés. Analysing the notion of 'fantaisie' [fancy] in post-romantic nineteenth-century literature, Vouilloux sees a convergence between the notion of eccentricity and the wandering lines of 'fantaisie', which can cross the border between reason and irrationality.[107] The thin boundary between eccentricity and madness is perceptible in Léaud's gestural lines and zigzag trajectories. In the last episode of the film, Colin meets two ex-members of the group of Thirteen, Warok (Jean Bouise) and Lucie (Françoise Fabian), in a bourgeois Parisian flat which starkly contrasts with the lack of comfort of his *chambre de bonne*. As he confesses, his search for the truth about the enigmatic and fantasised group turned into a nightmare that brought him to the brink of madness and death. While speaking, Colin zigzags around the dining table and spins around, sketching serpentine lines that recall Corporal Trim's flourish. Framing Warok and Lucie in the foreground, the camera moves right and left to follow Colin's trajectory; his eccentric way of being decentres the shot.

The second part of the title, *Noli me tangere*, is inspired by Giotto's painting representing Christ's refusal to be touched by Mary Magdalene on the morning of his resurrection.[108] *Noli me tangere* can be translated as 'do not touch me' or 'stay away from me'.[109] The title, which emphasises the sense of touch and the refusal of contact, suggests, on a gestural level, the difficulty of working collectively. Rivette and Schiffman structured the film around the encounters and interactions between the characters. They designed a diagram to frame the conditions of improvisation.[110] The actors were constrained by the space and the environment in which they were playing, as well as by their interactions with the other members of the cast (even though Léaud and Berto often improvised alone in their room or in the street). In *Out 1*, the entanglement of trajectories (Colin meets Thomas, Thomas meets Sarah, Sarah meets …, and so forth) multiplies the narrative potentialities and the possibilities of contact and rupture between the characters and within the groups.

107 Vouilloux, *Ecritures de fantaisie*, p. 162.
108 Dosi, *Trajectoires balzaciennes*, p. 101.
109 Tchalgadjieff, 'Note du producteur Tchalgadjieff', p. 5.
110 Schiffman cited in Dosi, *Trajectoires balzaciennes*, p. 66.

The literature on Rivette's cinema, and more particularly on *Out 1*, explores a constellation of notions evoking Deligny's work, such as itineraries, trajectories, fluxes, lines and spiderweb. In Rivette's films, the camera maps the characters' trajectories and gestural lines in the shot, and records the trace of human fluxes in the filmic space.[111] When the actor Bernadette Lafont describes her experience on the shooting of *Out 1*, she uses the words 'toile' [web], 'fil' [thread] and 'écheveau' [skein].[112] According to her, all the actors had to weave their own piece of spiderweb on the film set.[113] Similarly, Francesca Dosi, who draws on Balzac's essay *Théorie de la démarche* (1833), analyses the lines that animate the actors' gestures, comparing *Out 1* to a network and a spiderweb.[114]

In the film, the gestural lines are creative but also potentially destructive, continuous but also threatened with fragmentation and dissolution. For example, in Episode 1, Thomas's troupe performs different exercises of improvisation. First, in order to forge connections between themselves, the actors play the game of the mirror, which is a classic exercise of ensemble building. Working in pairs, they closely interact with each other, trying to perform the same gestures. Béatrice (Edwine Moatti) champions the game's beneficial qualities, which enable them to make contact with each other. Then, in the second part of the session, the characters lie on the ground and, in a regressive manner, start to moan and gesticulate, making convulsive and aggressive gestures, including fighting and biting. They play simple-minded children or disabled persons, without feet or arms, blind or mute. Going into a trance, they progressively merge together, forming a formless collective body, which continuously aggregates and disintegrates according to their initiatives (see Figures 5.14–5.17). In contrast with the game of the mirror, which aims to develop human contact and kinesic intelligence, their regressive gestures express their struggle to form a cohesive group together.

111 Didier Coureau, 'Jacques Rivette, poétique des flux', in *Jacques Rivette: Critique et cinéaste*, ed. by Suzanne Liandrat-Guigues (Paris: Lettres modernes; Caen: Minard, 1998), p. 56.

112 Bernadette Lafont, *Le Roman de ma vie: Souvenirs* (Paris: Flammarion, 1997), pp. 152–4.

113 Bernadette Lafont, *La Fiancée du cinéma* (Paris: Olivier Orban, 1978), p. 133.

114 Dosi, *Trajectoires balzaciennes dans le cinéma de Jacques Rivette*, p. 575.

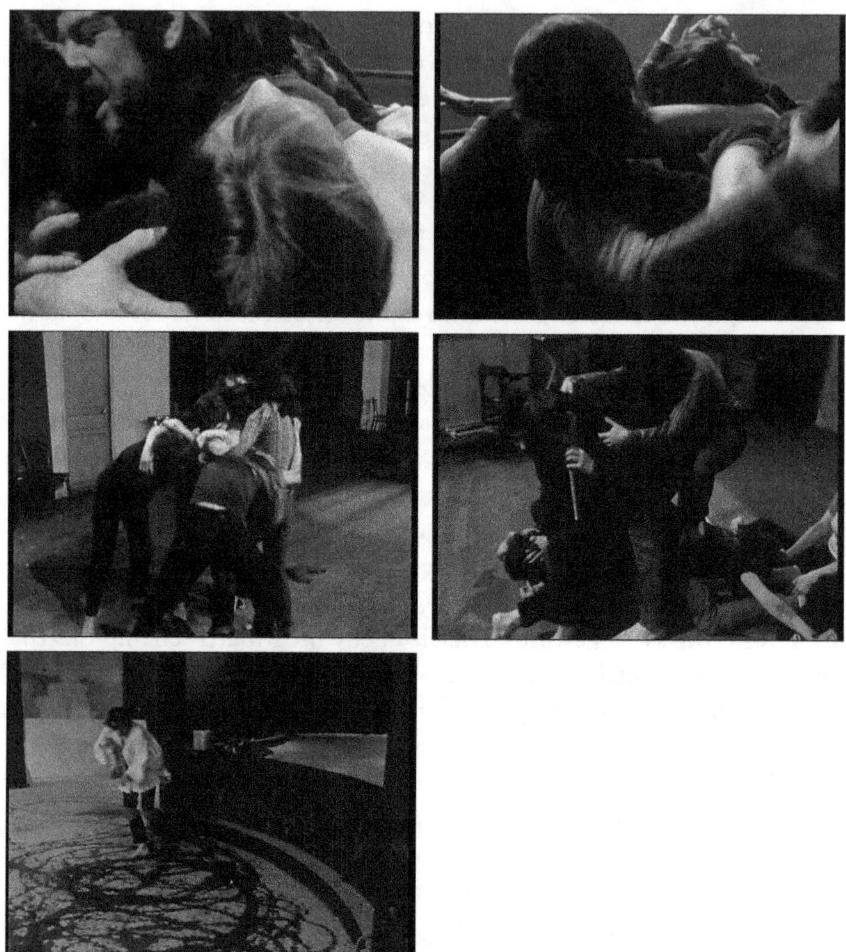

Figures 5.14–5.18. *Out 1*: Rivette films the actors' improvised gestures.

The gestural lines are not clearly visible or readable, but rather entangled and confused like in Jackson Pollock's action painting. A reference to the painter's drip technique appears briefly in a shot of *Out 1* when an actor in Lilly's troupe drips water on the ground (see Figure 5.18). In the same way as Dosi and Lafont compare Rivette's film to a spiderweb, Allan

Kaprow uses the same metaphor to describe the skein of lines and splashes in Pollock's artworks.[115] Like other contemporary avant-garde artists, both Rivette and Pollock put the emphasis on the gestural process of creation.[116] Through the improvised gestures of the actors, *Out 1* takes the form of a work in progress: the narrative unfolds as they invent their gestural lines. Hubert Damisch compares the aesthetics of 'déroulement' [unfolding] at the core of Pollock's action painting to John Cassavetes's 'acting cinema', which is partly based on improvisation.[117] The lack of straight line defines the unpredictability of acting cinema.[118] Instead of filming the performance of Aeschyllus's plays, Rivette, in response to Pollock's non-representational aesthetics, focuses on the muddled, shapeless, intuitive, discontinuous and chaotic lines that emerge during the rehearsals.

To a certain extent, the session of improvisation in Episode 1 also evokes Henri Michaux's drawings and paintings. The latter painted to decondition himself from his verbal culture.[119] Michaux, who started at first to draw random lines on paper – 'ligne somnambule' [sleepwalking line], 'ligne [...] qui erre' [wandering line] – notes that this process often led him to failure, encouraging him to explore other paths.[120] In *Out 1*, the actors of Thomas's troupe also seek to decondition themselves from a verbal culture that reproduces codified patterns of thinking. At the start, their confused gestures are accompanied by unarticulated sounds, like grunts and groaning. Improvisation becomes a means to express a lost spontaneity. As Frédéric Pouillaude explains, the dichotomy of nature vs. nurture feeds a certain ideal of improvisation.[121] The fantasy of spontaneity leads Thomas's troupe to an illusory freedom. Far from being deconditioned from linguistic and social codes, the characters progressively start to articulate vowels and consonants,

115 Cited in Formis, *Esthétique de la vie ordinaire*, p. 155.

116 Ibid., p. 145.

117 Hubert Damisch, *Ciné fil* (Paris: Seuil, 2008), pp. 81–4.

118 Mouëllic, *Improviser le cinéma*, p. 83.

119 Henri Michaux, *Emergences-Résurgences* (Genève: Flammarion, 1972), p. 5.

120 Ibid., pp. 8–9.

121 Frédéric Pouillaude, 'Vouloir l'involontaire et répéter l'irrépétable', in *Approche philosophique du geste dansé: De l'improvisation à la performance*, ed. by Anne Boissière and Catherine Kintzler (Villeneuve-d'Ascq: Presses Universitaires du Septentrion, 2006), p. 151.

then words and finally sentences extracted from Aeschylus's play. Intention, will, artificiality and cultural references interfere with the actors' search for gestural spontaneity. If they are 'free' in the sense that their gestures are not dictated by the director, that does not mean that their gestures are necessarily free or spontaneous. 'Those who work in improvisation have the chance to see with frightening clarity how rapidly the boundaries of so-called freedom are reached,' Peter Brook, who practiced improvisation in theatre, explains.[122] One of the risks of free improvisation is to reiterate certain clichés and patterns to the point of contradicting the impulse of life and hindering creativity. By trying to be spontaneous and avoid the conventions of the histrionic code, '[the actor] is reaching inside himself for an alphabet that is also fossilized, for the language of signs from life that he knows is the language not of invention but of his conditioning.'[123]

The lack of structure and cohesion constitutes another pitfall in improvisation. In his theories on theatre, Stanislavski points out the actors' crucial need for a continuous line in order to build their character. The 'disjointed exercises' of improvisation, which are 'useful in classroom work', break the continuity of the line of action.[124] Actors need a text and a 'superobjective' to develop their characters' inner lines: 'It is only when he comes to a deeper understanding of his part and a realisation of its fundamental objective that a line gradually emerges as a continuous whole.'[125] Stanislavski argues that every art must develop an 'unbroken line'.[126] For example, someone who 'make[s] certain unrelated movements with his arms, head and body' cannot be considered a dancer due to the lack of coordination and harmony of his or her gestures.[127] For the same reason, 'some accidental and unrelated lines on a piece of paper' cannot be called a design.[128] In contrast to the modernist aesthetics of fragmentation and discontinuity in Brecht's

122 Brook, *The Empty Space*, p. 125.

123 Ibid.

124 Konstantin Stanislavski, *An Actor Prepares*, trans. by Elizabeth Reynolds Hapgood (London: Geoffrey Bles, 1937), p. 275.

125 Ibid., p. 253.

126 Ibid., p. 254.

127 Ibid., p. 253.

128 Ibid., p. 253–4.

theatre, Stanislavski's preoccupation with coherence echoes the ideal of wholeness in classical sculpture: 'Break up a beautiful statue and the small scraps of marble cannot be overwhelming in their effect,' Stanislavski explains.[129] The unbroken line, which requires a certain self-coherence (as mentioned in Chapter 4), drives the character's emotions and desires, and thus shapes the quality of his or her gestures throughout the play. All the 'short lines'[130] and small objectives converge 'into one superobjective':[131]

> The superobjective and through action are the inborn vital purpose and aspiration rooted in our being, in our mysterious 'I'. Every play, every role, has concealed in it a superobjective and a line of through action which constitute the essential life of the individual roles and of the whole work.[132]

The line coordinates the multiplicity of actions, conflicts and obstacles that the character experiences in interacting with other characters. If the actor deviates from the line, he or she will fail to embody his or her character.

It is due to a lack of superobjective and unbroken line that Bernadette Lafont experienced great difficulty embodying her character during the shooting of *Out 1*. When Rivette offered her a role in the film, the shooting had already started. She knew nothing about her character, except her first name Sarah, her profession of writer and her affiliation with the enigmatic group of Thirteen.[133] Thomas, a past lover, asks Sarah to join his troupe in order to take part in the sessions of improvisation. At first, Lafont did not know how to deal with the vagueness of her character's identity, feeling a sense of disconnection and powerlessness.[134] The actor's difficulties, which mirror her character's struggle to improvise with Thomas's troupe, are highlighted in Episode 7.

129 Ibid., p. 275.
130 Ibid., pp. 255–6.
131 Ibid., p. 274.
132 Konstantin Stanislavski, *Creating a Role*, trans. by Elizabeth Reynolds Hapgood (London: New English Library, 1970), p. 70.
133 Lafont, *Le Roman de ma vie*, pp. 151–2.
134 Ibid., p. 153.

All the actors, including Sarah, work on an exercise that aims to develop their attention skills. In the session, they perform twelve different situations. Each time Thomas names a new actor, the troupe must freeze in order to interrupt the action and let the designated comedian initiate a new situation. Bergamotte (Bernadette Onfroy) plays hopscotch, then Quentin (Pierre Baillot) plays a marionette, then Achille (Sylvain Corthay) imitates a monkey, and so forth. Their gestural lines are constantly diverted, interrupted and subjected to sudden changes of direction and arbitrariness. The actors need to adapt to these new situations by performing together in a playful and even childlike manner. When the comedians collectively analyse their performance at the end of the rehearsal, Sarah is criticised for having played against the rules, to the point of putting the cohesion of the group in jeopardy. For instance, when Béatrice takes the lead, Achille starts singing a Russian chant which, like an incantation, encourages the troupe – except Sarah, who disappears off-camera – to improvise the ritualised gestures of an esoteric ceremony (see Figures 5.19–5.21). With the complicity of another actor, Sarah runs, puts her hand on Achille's mouth and prevents him from singing and moving. Her aggressive gestures suddenly interrupt the situation. Achille reproaches Sarah for having introduced a new theme in an ongoing situation, only because she was personally irritated by the game. In the same session, Sarah interrupts another situation (see Figures 5.22–5.24). Rose (Christiane Corthay) gathers the comedians one by one by joining their hands together in order to forge links between them: their gestural lines form a knot which is immediately unknotted by Sarah. Instead of joining the circle, she refuses to play the game and to move. When Rose encourages her, she deliberately falls on the ground. Once again, the action is brutally interrupted. Sarah's gestures of interruption and refusal manifest a corporeal resistance.

'When a line of physical action "dies", one possible cause is that the actor has forgotten the contact with his partner,' the theatre director Thomas Richards explains.[135] The attention to their partners and the ability to keep contact and react accordingly, 'within a fixed line of actions', are constraints which enable the actors to gesture more spontaneously.[136]

135 Richards, *At Work with Grotowski on Physical Actions*, p. 81.

136 Ibid.

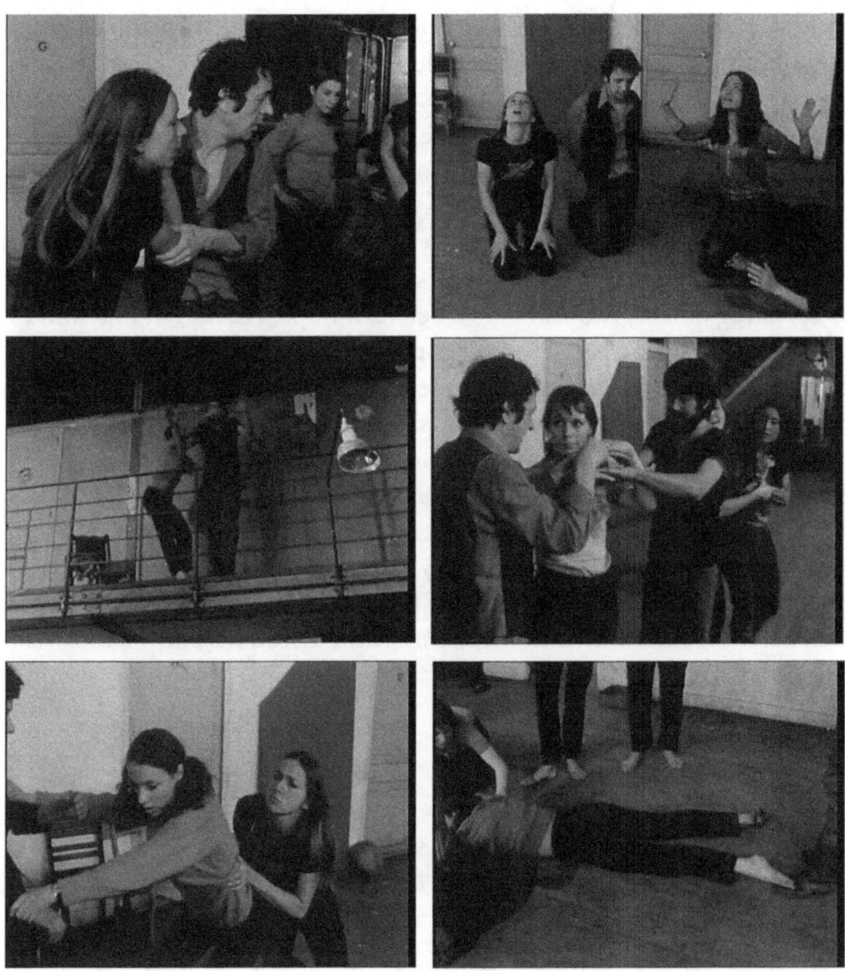

Figures 5.19–5.24. *Out 1*: Bernadette Lafont disrupts the exercises of improvisation.

Furthermore, according to the director and theorist Jerzy Grotowski, if the actor overthinks or does not know what to do, they will be paralysed: '"What to do next?" – *is* the paralysis. "*What to do next?*" This is the question that makes all spontaneity impossible.'[137] During the shooting,

137 Cited in ibid., p. 82.

Lafont, Ogier or Léaud often wondered what to do next. Their lack of inspiration or spontaneity, their wanderings, their moments of doubt and hesitation and their anxieties, which can be seen in their verbal and gestural exchanges, were integrated by Rivette in the editing.[138] As Lafont tells, the filmmaker turned the moments of panic and sterility into moments of dramatic tension. For example, at one point, Lafont and Bulle Ogier were so little inspired before starting a new scene that the latter just asked Lafont to give her a slap in order to create a situation of tension.[139] The anecdote is revealing of the great difference between improvisation in film and in theatre. The editing process enables the director to rearrange the scenes, and to weave, even loosely, the fragmented threads of the narrative by constructing a certain continuity of plots, motifs, postures and gestures. Even when the actors' gestures lack spontaneity or result from an impulse that is apparently disconnected from the narrative – 'out' the line of actions – they become the expression of a mysterious tension between the characters, feeding the atmosphere of conspiracy at the core of the film. The scattered fragments of the shooting eventually form a knot of heterogeneous fluxes and narrative lines which expand in multiple directions like a spiderweb.

Conclusion

In Godard and Miéville's series, Deligny's work and Rivette's research on improvisation, the concept of line opens new ways of approaching the notion of gesture in film. Gestural lines, which can be visible, imaginative or metaphorical, manifest themselves in different forms and manners. First, the line can be the result of an act of perceptive imagination, which consists in visualising the trajectory of gestures as they are performed by the characters in their immediate environment; secondly, the line can be a visible gestural trace filmed by the camera, such as a pathway, the outline of a map or a drawing. Thirdly, the line can take the multidimensional

138 Lafont, *La Fiancée du cinéma*, pp. 152–3.

139 Ibid., p. 135.

form of threads, knots and spiderwebs: the metaphors of knotting and weaving not only reveal the characters' relations to their environment and others, but also highlight the role of gestures in the development, the spinning and the editing of narrative lines.

Furthermore, through their intersection with spatial, ideological and narrative lines, such as the Taylorist grid in *France/tour/détour* or the plot in *Out 1*, gestural lines map a liminal space in between borders and margins, determined and indeterminate trajectories, social conditioning and idiosyncratic behaviour and, more broadly, in between the collective and the individual. While gestural lines appear to be programmed through social conditioning in *France/tour/détour*, they also reveal margins of bodily resistance, invention, initiative and improvisation, in spite of the rectitude and the constraint of the social grid. In contrast, although gestural lines in *Out 1* do not follow the programme of a conventional script, they reveal the actors' difficulties in freeing themselves from their conditioned behaviours to act spontaneously.

Finally, the liminal nature of lines strikingly appears in Deligny's network, in which the reiterated and determined trajectories of everyday life are interwoven with the indeterminate trajectories of wandering. The customary lines delineate a territory, with its pathways and landmarks, which structures the autistic children's existence while offering them the space to drift. In contrast to the fixity of borders, gestural lines prove to be dynamic forms of life, which are essentially characterised by multiplicity and movement. The concept of gestural line in post-New Wave cinema thus makes it possible to consider the notions of heterogeneity, co-existence and community, from both political and aesthetic perspectives.

Conclusion

When Citton describes gesture as a knot of contradictions that mirrors the complexity of human life, he points out the impossibility of defining the notion in a definitive and exhaustive way.[1] In this book, I regarded gesture as a concept *in movement* which resists the fixity of strict definitions and generalisations. Transitory and codified, ephemeral and culturally shaped, singular and conditioned, existential and ideological, human gesture shifts meanings, temporalities, categories and notions. Circulating and migrating between disciplines, media and art forms, gesture fundamentally embraces the movement of human life, in its physiological, imaginative, emotional, sensual, artistic, intellectual, sociocultural, ethical and political dimensions.

First, I have showed how gesture in post-New Wave cinema occupies an intermediary position between medium specificity and intermediality. Paradoxically, if gesture appears as a key element to define the medium specificity of film – cinema being the first art to reproduce gestures in motion – it also stresses the heterogeneity of the cinematic medium. In addition to dialoguing with other arts such as theatre, dance and painting, gestures also interconnect the various media components that constitute the cinematic art, especially in terms of image and sound. Secondly, by insisting on the relation between performance in film and performance in society, I have emphasised how gesture problematises, on the one hand, the tension between sociocultural conditioning and individual existence and, on the other hand, the intersubjective relationship between the individual and the collective. Thirdly, I have explored how gesture forges sensual, emotional and intellectual links between the filmmaker, the filmed subject and the audience. In this sense, the notion of gesture makes it possible to rethink the nature of the links between the practice of filmmaking, the craft of film performance and the process of reception by the spectator.

1 Citton, *Gestes d'humanités*, p. 28.

In the light of the arguments developed in this book, it could be argued that the cinematic medium does not exhibit a 'pure gesturality'[2] as Agamben claims, but rather transforms and impurifies the expression of gestures. While André Bazin regards cinema as an 'art impur' [impure art] that integrates other artistic forms such as literature and painting,[3] Alain Badiou adds that the impurity of the medium is not only aesthetic, but also results from exchanges with nonartistic forms: 'The cinema is a place of intrinsic indiscernibility between art and non-art.'[4] Due to these various processes of impurification, gesture in cinema proves fundamentally intermedial, hybrid, composite, heterogeneous, plural, at once human and technological.

The interaction between human gesture and film technology is made of mutual exchanges. By mediating the movement of gestures, the technology of the moving image conveys a vision of gesture that is bound to the specific expressive means of film. Camera angle, shot scale, lighting, sound effects, music, the processes of slow or fast motion, the size of the screen, the rhythm of the editing and the type of technology (analogue or digital) contribute to shaping the spectator's perception of filmed gestures. Framed, broken down and recomposed, gestures in film are endowed with a proper cinematic quality. They are at once performed by persons (whether actors or not) and conditioned by the media components of the cinematic machine, which contribute to moulding their potential meanings and mediating their emotional impact on the spectator.

If cinema transpires as a particularly pertinent instrument to reveal the impact of conditioning on the body, it also, simultaneously, makes it possible to see how the body resists sociocultural conditioning, homogenisation, standardisation and mechanisation. Significant in the analysis of all the films, the idea of gestural resistance manifests itself in various

2 Agamben, 'Notes on Gesture', p. 59.

3 See Bazin, 'Pour un cinéma impur. Défense de l'adaptation', in *Qu'est-ce que le cinéma?* (Paris: Les Editions du Cerf, 1987), pp. 81–106.

4 Alain Badiou, 'Considerations on the Current State of Cinema and on the Ways of Thinking this State Without Having to Conclude that Cinema Is Dead or Dying', in *Cinema*, ed. by Antoine de Baecque, trans. by Susan Spitzer (Oxford: Polity Press, 2013), p. 139. See also Rancière, *Malaise dans l'esthétique*, pp. 111–14.

forms: anxious resistance to self-conditioning in *Un homme qui dort*; slapstick resistance to gender norms in the domestic setting of Akerman's films; resistance to the dominant use of the audiovisual medium in Godard's cinema; resistance to the industrialisation and mass production of stereotypes in *Roberte*; resistance to predictability and Taylorist norms in *France/tour/détour*; and, finally, resistance to the isolation and invisibilisation of neurodiverse persons in Deligny's (net)work. In post-New Wave cinema, gestures of resistance are not heroic. On the one hand, they can express the characters' individuality through bodily reactions, pathological behaviours, clumsiness, unpredictable and indiscernible impulses as well as lines of flight. On the other hand, they can activate a political reflection on collaborative work, agency, communication, exchanges, communities, networks, heterogeneity, co-presence and co-existence. The existential density of gesture in cinema thus opens new ways of considering the links between aesthetics and politics. As discussed in Chapter 3, the notion of hypergesture proves particularly useful to analyse how, beyond their differences, gestures knot together and respond to each other.

While cinema conditions the expression and perception of gestures, I demonstrated that the transitional and liminal qualities of gesture reciprocally inform the nature of the cinematic medium. Gesture is indeed a transitory movement between the past and the future, between fluctuating corporeal and emotional states, and between different attitudes, postures and meanings. The fluidity of gestures – and their imperceptible transitions from one phase of movement to another – embraces the flow of the moving image. In its encounter with the human body in motion, the cinematic art integrates the dynamic, tactile, affective, relational and intersubjective qualities of human gesture in its own perceptual and expressive body. In Chapter 1, I discussed how the editing of *Un homme qui dort* activates a memory process, based on gestural shocks and replayed gestures. In Chapter 2, I highlighted how, by stressing the interval between the visual and aural qualities of gestures, Akerman's *L'Homme à la valise* creates effects of resonance and linkage between the image and the soundtrack, thus stimulating the spectators' kinesic intelligence. In Chapter 3, the study of *Prénom Carmen* revealed how the hypergestural quality of the editing interconnects the heterogeneous artistic and nonartistic components that compose the film. In Chapter 4, through an extended analysis of gesture in *tableau vivant*, I demonstrated how the plurality of the heroine's identities in *Roberte* and the ambiguity of her gestures mirror the dual and heterogeneous nature of the cinematic image, which is simultaneously the product of a mise-en-scène and the result of a performance experienced by the actors – in this context, film performance raises crucial ethical questions, especially when actors are subjected to violent acts. Finally, through the concept of gestural line, Chapter 5 expanded on the correlation between gesture and form, which lies at the heart of all of the chapters. When improvised, gestural lines can direct the movements of the camera, create changes of direction in the storylines and influence the form of the editing. In this sense, instead of imposing pre-programmed gestures, the cinematic apparatus records the complex intertwining of existential lines woven by human gestures.

This book develops several approaches to conceptualise gesture in post-New Wave cinema without claiming to provide an exhaustive view of this period. While I brought obscure authors such as Zucca and Deligny to light, I also referred to important, yet often little-known filmmakers, such as Cavalier, Moullet, Tanner, Ruiz, Stévenin, Garrel, Eustache, Straub and Huillet. This list, which could be continued, demonstrates the richness of the post-New Wave as well as the extent to which this period still remains underexplored in the French and Anglo-Saxon academic worlds. Furthermore, by studying Godard in two chapters, I gave this major filmmaker a pivotal position in the book. Godard's films problematise and crystallise some of the main features of the post-New Wave, notably the revival of silent cinema and the crucial role of gesture in the practice of filmmaking and the communication of images to the spectator. In the director's filmography, the post-New Wave represents a period of turmoil. From his post-May 1968 militant films and first video essays to his return to cinema in the late 1970s, not only did Godard question his approach to filmmaking and politics, he also experimented with new media and technologies. As discussed in Chapters 3 and 5, by using smaller cameras and video, Godard sought to free the filmmaker's hands from the constraints of classical shootings and open up the possibilities of experimenting with other styles and genres of filmmaking.

With the development of the camera Aaton, Godard anticipated the emergence of digital cameras in contemporary cinema. While the contemporary period is beyond the remit of my study, it is interesting to note that, at the turn of the century, the use of small DV (Digital Video) cameras reactivated the New Wave ideal of the *caméra-stylo*. Very easy to handle, DV cameras highlight the role of the filmmaker's gestures in the production of images. In the film essay and documentary *Les Glaneurs et la Glaneuse* (*The Gleaners and I*, 2000), Varda develops an ostensibly gestural style of filmmaking. Strengthening the links between the real and the imaginary, art and life, aesthetics and politics, she shows herself gleaning images with her small digital camera, connecting her practice of filmmaking with the elementary and ordinary gesture of peasant women gleaning a field, painted by Jean-François Millet in *Des Glaneuses* (*The Gleaners*, 1857) and performed by ordinary people every day in the modern world. Not only does she stress the role of her hands in the artistic process of the film's fabrication, she also shows how she politically engages her own body in the world she films.

Although Godard predicted the death of cinema in the early 1980s, the cinematic art and Godard both survived the digital revolution which occurred at the end of the twentieth century. Like other filmmakers of his generation, such as Varda, Cavalier and Marker, or his heir Leos Carax, Godard uses digital techniques less as a means to revolutionise cinema than an opportunity to meditate on the continuity of film history, from its origins to present time. In *3x3D* (2014) and *Adieu au langage* (*Goodbye to Language*, 2014), Godard experiments with 3D in order to reflect on the tension between the development of the illusion of depth through perspective since the Renaissance and the attraction towards flatness in modernity. Furthermore, in the same way that Godard and Miéville use video to revive the device of chronophotography in *France/tour/détour*, Carax experiments with digital cinema in *Holy Motors* (2012) to reveal the aesthetic and historical continuity between the most advanced film technologies, such as motion capture, and the origins of cinema, including pre-cinematic techniques like chronophotography. In line with the post-New Wave films examined in this book, *Holy Motors*, which is reminiscent of nineteenth-century motion studies, slapstick comedy and Louis Feuillade's serials, is a film haunted by the ghost of silent cinema. Beyond the postmodern melancholy caused by the technological metamorphosis of cinema in the digital age and the miniaturisation of cameras that seem to have infiltrated all areas of everyday life, the film proves essentially preoccupied with 'la beauté du geste' [the beauty of gesture], to refer to a line delivered by the main character Monsieur Oscar (Denis Lavant). 'On dit que [la beauté] est dans l'œil de celui qui regarde' [they say [beauty] is in the eye of the beholder], his interlocutor (Michel Piccoli) points out. For Carax, the beauty of cinematic art could thus be regarded as the encounter between gesture and the gaze – which in cinema comprises the eye of the camera, the filmmaker's vision and the spectator's look.

By way of conclusion, I will end by referring to a scene of *Les Glaneurs et la Glaneuse*, in which Varda films Marey's pictures of animal and human gestures with her digital camera. She moves her camera along a chronophotographic sequence that shows the broken down gesture of a man who falls on his feet after a jump. This playful shot not only stages the interaction between the digital camera and this pre-cinematic technique, but also shows the interplay between the gesture of the man filmed by Marey, the mobile eye of the camera manipulated by Varda's hand and, ultimately, the gaze of contemporary spectators who, more than a century later, watch Marey's pictures with pleasure and wonder. Ultimately, when incorporated into Varda's film, the ghostly movement of the man seems to gesture toward the future of cinema. Throughout the successive evolutions of cinema in film history, gesture occupies a paradoxical position. On the one hand, gesture manifests the historical continuity of film aesthetics from chronophotography to motion capture. On the other hand, the dynamism and ephemeral nature of gesture mirrors the ability of cinema to ceaselessly reinvent itself, not only through the contribution of new technologies and media, but most importantly through the emergence of singular styles of filmmaking and performance. For that reason, gesture remains a central preoccupation for contemporary filmmakers as well as an inexhaustible research area in film studies.

Bibliography

Agamben, Giorgio, 'Klossowski et la question de l'image', *Europe*, 1034–5 (2015), 59–60.

——, 'Kommerell, or On Gesture', in *Potentialities: Collected Essays in Philosophy*, ed. and trans. by Daniel Heller-Roazen (Stanford: Stanford University Press, 1999), pp. 77–85.

——, 'Notes on Gesture', in *Means Without End: Notes on Politics*, trans. by Vincenzo Binetti and Cesare Casarino (Minneapolis: University of Minnesota Press, 2000), pp. 48–59.

Agamben, Giorgio, and Thierry Tremblay, 'Un auteur messianique. Entretien avec Giorgio Agamben', *Europe*, 1034–5 (2015), 9–11.

Akerman, Chantal, *Chantal Akerman: Autoportrait en cinéaste* (Paris: Cahiers du cinéma, Centre Pompidou, 2004).

Akerman, Chantal, Danièle Dubroux, Thérèse Giraud and Louis Skorecki, 'Entretien avec Chantal Akerman', *Cahiers du cinéma*, July 1977, pp. 34–42.

Akerman, Chantal, and Elisabeth Lebovici, 'Losing Everything that Made You a Slave', in *Chantal Akerman: Too Far, Too Close*, ed. by Dieter Roelstraete and Anders Kreuger (Antwerpen: Ludion and M HKA, 2012), pp. 95–103.

André, Emmanuelle, *Le Choc du sujet: de l'hystérie au cinéma* (XIXe-XXIe siècle) (Rennes: Presses universitaires de Rennes, 2011).

Andrin, Muriel, 'Back to the "Slap". Slapstick's Hyperbolic Gesture and the Rhetoric of Violence', in *Slapstick Comedy*, ed. by Tom Paulus and Rob King (New York: Routledge, 2010), pp. 226–35.

Artaud, Antonin, *Le Théâtre et son double*, in *Œuvres complètes*, 26 vols (Paris: Gallimard, 1956–94), IV (1964).

——, *The Theatre and Its Double*, trans. by Mary Caroline Richards (New York: Grove Press, 1958).

Audin, Michèle, 'Mathématiques et littérature: un article avec des mathématiques et de la littérature', *Mathématiques et sciences humaines*, 178 (2007), 63–86.

Aumont, Jacques, *A quoi pensent les films* (Paris: Séguier, 1996).

——, 'Avant-propos', in *L'Invention de la figure humaine: Le Cinéma: l'humain et l'inhumain*, ed. by Jacques Aumont (Paris: Cinémathèque française, 1995), pp. 7–8.

——, 'La Traversée des ruines', in *L'Invention de la figure humaine: Le Cinéma: l'humain et l'inhumain*, ed. by Jacques Aumont (Paris: Cinémathèque française, 1995), pp. 25–35.

Auslander, Philip, *From Acting to Performance. Essays in Modernism and Postmodernism* (New York: Routledge, 1997).

Badiou, Alain, *Cinema*, ed. by Antoine de Baecque, trans. by Susan Spitzer (Oxford: Polity Press, 2013).

——, 'Considerations on the Current State of Cinema and on the Ways of Thinking this State Without Having to Conclude that Cinema Is Dead or Dying', in *Cinema*, ed. by Antoine de Baecque, trans. by Susan Spitzer (Oxford: Polity Press, 2013).

Baecque, Antoine de, 'Jean-Luc Godard et la critique des temps de l'histoire', *Vingtième Siècle*, 117 (2013), 149–64 <https://www.cairn.info/revue-vingtieme-siecle-revue-d-histoire-2013-1-page-149.htm> [accessed August 2018].

——, *La Nouvelle Vague: Portrait d'une jeunesse* (Paris: Flammarion, 1998).

Balázs, Béla, *Theory of the Film. Growth of a New Art*, trans. by Edith Bone (London: Dennis Dobson, 1952).

Balsom, Erika, *Exhibiting Cinema in Contemporary Art* (Amsterdam: Amsterdam University Press, 2013).

Barber, Stephen, *Projected Cities: Cinema and Urban Space* (London: Reaktion Books, 2002).

Barker, Jennifer M., 'Sonic Bodies. Listening as Acting', in *Theorizing Film Acting*, ed. by Aaron Taylor (New York: Routledge, 2013), pp. 243–55.

Barthes, Roland, 'Diderot, Brecht, Eisenstein', in *Image Music Text*, trans. by Stephen Heath (London: Fontana Press, 1977), pp. 69–78.

——, 'Listening', in *The Responsability of Forms: Critical Essays on Music, Art, and Representation*, trans. by Richard Howard (Berkeley: University of California Press, 1991), pp. 245–60.

——, *L'Obvie et l'Obtus. Essais critiques III* (Paris: Seuil, 1982).

——, *Œuvres complètes*, ed. by Eric Marty, 3 vols (Paris: Seuil, 1993–5), II (1994).

Bastide, Bernard, 'Correspondance François Truffaut-Fernand Deligny', *1895. Mille huit cent quatre-vingt-quinze*, 42 (2004), 77–110 <https://journals.openedition.org/1895/281> [accessed 19 August 2018].

Baudelaire, Charles, *Les Fleurs du mal*, ed. by Graham Chesters (London: Bristol Classical Press, 1995).

Bazin, André, 'Pour un cinéma impur. Défense de l'adaptation', in *Qu'est-ce que le cinéma?* (Paris: Les Editions du Cerf, 1987).

——, *Qu'est-ce que le cinéma?* (Paris: Les Editions du Cerf, 1987).

Beaune, Jean-Claude, *Le Vagabond et la machine: Essai sur l'automatisme ambulatoire, médecine, technique et société en France 1880–1910* (Seyssel: Champ Vallon, 1983).

Beauvoir, Simone de, *Les Belles Images* (Paris: Gallimard, 1966).

Bellos, David, *Georges Perec: A Life in Words* (London: Harvill, 1995).

——, *Georges Perec: Une vie dans les mots*, trans. by Françoise Cartano (Paris: Seuil, 1994).

Bellour, Raymond, '(Not) Just an Other Filmmaker', *Jean-Luc Godard, Son + Image 1974–1991*, ed. by Raymond Bellour and Mary Lea Bandy (New York: The Museum of Modern Art, 1992), pp. 215–31.

Benjamin, Walter, 'L'Œuvre d'art à l'époque de sa reproduction mécanisée', trans. by Pierre Klossowski, *Zeitschrift für Sozialforschung*, 5.1. (1936), 40–68.

——, 'On Some Motifs in Baudelaire', in *Walter Benjamin: Selected Writings. Vol. 4, 1938–1940*, ed. by Howard Eiland and Michael W. Jennings, trans. by Edmund Jephcott and others (Cambridge, MA: The Belknap Press of Harvard University Press, 2006), pp. 313–55.

——, *Understanding Brecht*, trans. by Anna Bostock (London: Verso, 1973).

——, 'The Work of Art in the Age of Its Technological Reproducibility. Second Version', in *Selected Writings. Vol. 3, 1935–1938*, ed. by Howard Eiland and Michael W. Jennings, trans. by Edmund Jephcott and others (Cambridge, MA: The Belknap Press of Harvard University Press, 2002), pp. 101–33.

Bergala, Alain, *Godard au travail, les années 60* (Paris: Cahiers du Cinéma, 2006).

——, *Nul mieux que Godard* (Paris: Cahiers du cinéma, 1999).

Bergala, Alain, Jean-Luc Godard and Jean-Pierre Beauviala, 'Genèse d'une caméra. Premier épisode', in *Jean-Luc Godard par Jean-Luc Godard*, ed. by Alain Bergala (Paris: Edition de l'étoile, 1985).

Bergson, Henri, *The Creative Mind*, trans. by Mabelle L. Andison (New York: Philosophical Library, 1946).

——, *Laughter: An Essay on the Meaning of the Comic*, trans. by Cloudesley Brereton and Fred Rothwell (New York: The Macmillan Company, 1914).

——, *The Two Sources of Morality and Religion*, trans. by R. Ashley Audra and Cloudesley Brereton (London: MacMillan and Co, 1935).

Bertharion, Jacques-Denis, *Poétique de Georges Perec: '… une trace, une marque ou quelques signes'* (Saint-Genouph: Librairie Nizet, 1998).

Blanchot, Maurice, 'The Laughter of the Gods/Le Rire des Dieux', in Pierre Klossowski and Maurice Blanchot, *Decadence of the Nude/La Décadence du nu*, ed. by Sarah Wilson and intro. by Alyce Mahon (London: Black Dog, 2002).

Bolens, Guillemette, *Le Style des gestes: Corporéité et kinésie dans le récit littéraire* (Lausanne: BHMS, 2008).

Bonitzer, Pascal, 'Le Silence extérieur', in *Pierre Klossowski*, ed. by Catherine Grenier (Paris: La Différence, Centre national des arts plastiques; Marseille: Ryôan-ji, 1990), pp. 37–41.

Bourdieu, Pierre, *La Distinction* (Paris: Minuit, 1979).

Brannigan, Erin, *Dancefilm: Choreography and the Moving Image* (New York: Oxford University Press, 2011).

Brecht, Bertolt, *Brecht on Theatre: The Development of an Aesthetic*, ed. and trans. by John Willett (London: Mehtuen Drama, 1990).

Bresson, Robert, *Bresson on Bresson: Interviews 1943–1983*, ed. by Mylène Bresson, trans. by Anna Moschovakis (New York: New York Review Books, 2016).

——, 'To Create Life without Copying It', in *Bresson on Bresson: Interviews 1943–1983*, ed. by Mylène Bresson, trans. by Anna Moschovakis (New York: New York Review Books, 2016).

——, *Notes on the Cinematograph*, trans. by Jonathan Griffin (New York: New York Review Books, 2016).

——, *Notes sur le cinématographe* (Paris: Gallimard, 1988).

Brook, Peter, *The Empty Space* (London: Penguin Books, 2008).

Brooks, Peter, *Melodramatic Imagination: Balzac, Henry James, Melodrama, and the Mode of Excess* (New Haven, CT: Yale University Press, 1976).

——, 'The Text of Muteness', in *Melodramatic Imagination: Balzac, Henry James, Melodrama, and the Mode of Excess* (New Haven, CT: Yale University Press, 1976).

Brookman, Philip, 'Helios: Eadweard Muybridge in a Time of Change', in *Eadweard Muybridge*, ed. by Philip Brookman (London: Tate, 2010), pp. 23–109.

Brun, Jean, *Les Vagabonds de l'Occident: L'Expérience du voyage et la prison du moi* (Paris: Desclée, 1976).

Bruno, Giuliana, *Atlas of Emotion: Journeys in Art, Architecture, and Film* (New York: Verso, 2002).

Buckland, Warren, 'Bodies in Filmic Space: The *Mise en Scène* of "Courtship Readiness", *The Big Sleep*', *Senses of Cinema*, 66 (2013) <http://sensesofcinema.com/2013/feature-articles/bodies-in-filmic-space-the-mise-en-scene-of-courtship-readiness-in-the-big-sleep/> [accessed 10 May 2017].

Burch, Noël, *Theory of Film Practice*, trans. by Helen R. Lane (London: Secker & Warburg, 1973).

Burgelin, Claude, *Georges Perec* (Paris: Seuil, 1988).

Butler, Judith, *Gender Trouble: Feminism and the Subversion of Identity* (New York: Routledge, 1990).

Butor, Michel, 'Souvenirs sur le théâtre de société', in *Pierre Klossowski*, ed. by Andréas Pfersmann (Paris: Centre Georges-Pompidou, 1985), pp. 27–9.

Campan, Véronique, *L'Ecoute filmique: Echo du son en image* (Saint-Denis: Presses universitaires de Vincennes, 1999).

Cavalier, Alain, and Jean-Louis Jeannelle, 'Alain Cavalier: le filmeur, la caméra et le spectateur', *Itinéraires*, 4 (2009), 175–91 <https://journals.openedition.org/itineraires/1282> [accessed 17 August 2018].

Certeau, Michel de, *The Practice of Everyday Life*, trans. by Steven Rendall (Berkeley: University of California Press, 1988).

Certeau, Michel de, and Luce Giard, 'Ghosts in the City', in *The Practice of Everyday Life. Volume 2: Living and Cooking*, trans. by Timothy J. Tomasik (Minneapolis: University of Minnesota Press, 1998).

Certeau, Michel de, Luce Giard and Pierre Mayol, *The Practice of Everyday Life. Volume 2: Living and Cooking*, trans. by Timothy J. Tomasik (Minneapolis: University of Minnesota Press, 1998).

Chamarette, Jenny, 'Between Women: Gesture, Intermediality and Intersubjectivity in the Installations of Agnès Varda and Chantal Akerman', *Studies in European Cinema*, 10.1 (2013), 45–57.

——, 'Burlesque Gestures and Bodily Attention: Phenomenologies of the Ephemeral in Chantal Akerman', in *Phenomenology and the Future of Film: Rethinking Subjectivity beyond French Cinema* (Basingstoke: Palgrave Macmillan, 2012).

——, *Phenomenology and the Future of Film: Rethinking Subjectivity beyond French Cinema* (Basingstoke: Palgrave Macmillan, 2012).

Chare, Nicholas, 'Gesture in *Shoah*', in *Gesture and Film: Signalling New Critical Perspectives*, ed. by Nicholas Chare and Liz Watkins (London: Routledge, 2017), pp. 46–58 (first publ. in *Journal for Cultural Research*, 19.1 (2015), 30–42).

Chastel, André, *Le Geste dans l'art* (Paris: Liana Levi, 2001).

Châtelet, Gilles, *Les Enjeux du mobile: Mathématique, physique, philosophie* (Paris: Seuil, 1993).

Chion, Michel, *Film, a Sound Art*, trans. by Claudia Gorbman (New York: Columbia University Press, 2009).

Citton, Yves, *Gestes d'humanités: Anthropologie sauvage de nos expériences esthétiques* (Paris: Armand Colin, 2012).

Comolli, Jean-Louis, *Corps et cadre: cinéma, éthique, politique, 2004–2010* (Lagrasse: Verdier, 2012).

——, 'L'Evadé. *Le Moindre Geste*, de Fernand Deligny, Jo Manenti et Jean-Pierre Daniel, 1959–1970', in *Voir et pouvoir: l'innocence perdue: cinéma, télévision, documentaire* (Lagrasse: Verdier, 2004).

——, 'Un cinéma hors de lui', in *Corps et cadre: cinéma, éthique, politique, 2004–2010* (Lagrasse: Verdier, 2012).

——, *Voir et pouvoir: l'innocence perdue: cinéma, télévision, documentaire* (Lagrasse: Verdier, 2004).

Coureau, Didier, 'Jacques Rivette, poétique des flux', in *Jacques Rivette : Critique et cinéaste*, ed. by Suzanne Liandrat-Guigues (Paris: Lettres modernes; Caen: Minard, 1998), pp. 47–66.

——, 'Jean-Luc Godard. Ouverture de l'ère de la complexité esthétique. 1979–1985', in *Jean-Luc Godard 2, au-delà de l'image*, ed. by Marc Cerisuelo (Paris: Lettres modernes, 1993), pp. 7–33.

Cowie, Elizabeth, *Representing the Woman: Cinema and Psychoanalysis* (Basingstoke: Macmillan, 1997).

——, 'The Time of Gesture in Cinema and Its Ethics', *Journal of Cultural Research*, 19.1 (2015), 82–95 (p. 83).

Cyrulnik, Boris, *La Naissance du sens* (Paris: Hachette, 1991).

Cyssau, Catherine, *Au lieu du geste* (Paris: Presses universitaires de France, 1995).

Damisch, Hubert, *Ciné fil* (Paris: Seuil, 2008).

Damour, Christophe, 'L'Influence de Delsarte sur le jeu de l'acteur de cinéma aux Etats-Unis', in *L'Acteur de cinéma: Approches plurielles*, ed. by Vincent Amiel, Jacqueline Nacache, Geneviève Sellier and Christian Viviani (Rennes: Presses universitaires de Rennes, 2007), pp. 19–31.

Dardigna, Anne-Marie, *Les Châteaux d'Eros ou Les Infortunes du sexe des femmes* (Paris: F. Maspero, 1980).

Darwin, Charles, *The Expression of the Emotions in Man and Animals* (Chicago: University of Chicago Press, 1965).

Decottignies, Jean, *Pierre Klossowski: biographie d'un monomane* (Villeneuve-d'Ascq: Presses universitaires du Septentrion, 1997).

Deleuze, Gilles, *Cinema 2. The Time-Image*, trans. by Hugh Tomlinson and Robert Galeta (Minneapolis: University of Minnesota Press, 1997).

——, *Francis Bacon: The Logic of Sensation*, trans. by Daniel W. Smith (London: Continuum, 2003).

——, 'Lettre à Pierre Klossowski', *Europe*, 1034–5 (2015), 61–2.

——, *L'Image-temps: Cinéma 2* (Paris: Minuit, 1985).

——, *The Logic of Sense*, trans. by Mark Lester (New York: Columbia University Press, 1990).

——, *Logique du sens* (Paris: Minuit, 1969).

Deleuze, Gilles, and Félix Guattari, *A Thousand Plateaus: Capitalism and Schizophrenia*, trans. by Brian Massumi (Minneaopolis: University of Minnesota Press, 2005).

Deleuze, Gilles, and Claire Parnet, *Dialogues II*, trans. by Hugh Tomlinson and Barbara Habberjam (New York: Columbia University Press, 2007).

Deligny, Fernand, *L'Arachnéen et autres textes*, postface by Bertrand Ogilvie (Paris: L'Arachnéen, 2008).

——, *Œuvres*, ed. by Sandra Alvarez de Toledo (Paris: L'Arachnéen, 2007).

Didi-Huberman, Georges, 'La Danse de toute chose', in Laurent Mannoni and Georges Didi-Huberman, *Mouvements de l'air: Etienne-Jules Marey, photographie des fluides* (Paris: Gallimard, Réunion des musées nationaux, 2004), pp. 177–316.

——, *Le Danseur des solitudes* (Paris: Minuit, 2006).

——, *L'Image survivante: Histoire de l'art et le temps des fantômes selon Aby Warburg* (Paris: Minuit, 2002).

Diderot, Denis, *Entretiens sur Le Fils naturel: De la poésie dramatique. Paradoxe sur le comédien*, ed. by Jean Goldzink (Paris: Flammarion, 2005).

——, *Essais sur la peinture: Salons de 1759, 1761, 1763*, ed. by Gita May and Jacques Chouillet (Paris: Hermann, 2007).

Didier, Béatrice, Antoinette Fouque and Mireille Calle-Gruber, eds, *Le Dictionnaire universel des créatrices* (Paris: Des femmes, A. Fouque, 2013). Ebook.

Doane, Mary Ann, *The Emergence of Cinematic Time: Modernity, Contingency, the Archive* (Cambridge, MA: Harvard University Press, 2002).

Dosi, Francesca, *Trajectoires balzaciennes dans le cinéma de Jacques Rivette: 'Out 1', 'La Belle Noiseuse', 'Ne touchez pas la hache'* (La Madeleine: LettMotif, 2013).

Douchet, Jean, 'Le Visage comme révélation, le geste comme signe, le corps découpé comme figure, le corps plein comme opacité', in *L'Invention de la figure humaine*, ed. by Jacques Aumont (Paris: Cinémathèque française, 1995), pp. 113–21.

——, *Nouvelle Vague* (Paris: Cinémathèque française, Hazan, 1998).

Dubois, Philippe, 'Video Thinks What Cinema Creates. Notes on Jean-Luc Godard's Work in Video and Television', in *Jean-Luc Godard, Son + Image 1974–1991*, ed. by Raymond Bellour and Mary Lea Bandy (New York: The Museum of Modern Art, 1992), pp. 169–85.

Duranty, Louis Edmond, 'Promenades au Louvre. Remarques sur le geste dans quelques tableaux', *Gazette des beaux-arts*, January–June 1877, pp. 19–37; 172–80; 281–9.

Durgnat, Raymond, *Franju* (Berkeley: University of California Press, 1968).

Dyer, Richard, 'The Role of Stereotypes', in *Media Studies: A Reader*, ed. by Paul Marris and Sue Thornham, 2nd edn (Edinburgh: Edinburgh University Press, 1999), pp. 11–18.

——, *Stars* (London: British Film Institute, 1979).

Ebbott, Mary, 'Marginal Figures', in *A Companion to Greek Tragedy*, ed. by Justina Gregory (Malden: Blackwell Publishing), pp. 366–76.

Eisenstein, Sergei, *Cinématisme: Peinture et cinéma*, ed. by François Albéra, trans. by Valérie Pozner and others (Dijon: Les Presses du réel, 2009).

——, 'Comment j'ai appris à dessiner', *Change*, 5 (1970), 21–3.

——, 'Dramaturgie de la forme filmique', trans. by Danièle Huillet, in *Cinématisme: Peinture et cinéma*, ed. by François Albéra (Dijon: Les Presses du réel, 2009).

——, 'L'Art de la mise en scène', *Cahiers du cinéma*, November–December 1970, pp. 29–42.

——, *Mise en Jeu and Mise en Geste*, trans. by Sergey Levchin (Montreal: Caboose, 2014). Ebook.

Epstein, Jean, *Ecrits sur le cinéma, tome 1: 1927–1953* (Paris: Seghers, 1974).

Estève, Michel, *Robert Bresson* (Paris: Seghers, 1974).

Fernandez, Carmen, 'Seyrig, Delphine', in *Le Dictionnaire universel des créatrices*, ed. by Béatrice Didier, Antoinette Fouque, and Mireille Calle-Gruber (Paris: Des femmes, A. Fouque, 2013).

Fieschi, Jean-André, Jean-Louis Comolli, Michel Mardore, André Téchiné, Gérard Guégan and Claude Ollier, 'Vingt ans après. Le cinéma américain, ses auteurs et notre politique en question', in *La Politique des auteurs: Les textes*, ed. by Antoine de Baecque (Paris: Cahiers du cinéma, 2001), pp. 122–42.

Fleischer, Alain, 'Retours, détours, contours', in *Pierre Klossowski, tableaux vivants*, ed. by Agnès de la Beaumelle (Paris: Gallimard, Centre Pompidou, 2007), pp. 45–61.

Flusser, Vilém, *Les Gestes* (Paris: Hors commerce Cergy, 1999).

Forbes, Jill, *The Cinema in France after the New Wave* (Basingstoke: Macmillan, 1992).

Fore, Devin, 'Gestus Facit Saltus: Bertolt Brecht's Fear and Misery of the Third Reich', in *Realism after Modernism: The Rehumanization of Art and Literature* (Cambridge, MA: The MIT Press, 2012).

——, *Realism After Modernism: The Rehumanization of Art and Literature* (Cambridge, MA: The MIT Press, 2012).

Formis, Barbara, *Esthétique de la vie ordinaire* (Paris: PUF, 2015).

Foucault, Michel, *Discipline and Punish: The Birth of the Prison*, trans. by Alain Sheridan (New York: Vintage Books, 1995).

——, *Surveiller et punir: Naissance de la prison* (Paris: Gallimard, 1975).

Fourastié, Jean, *Les Trente Glorieuses ou la révolution invisible de 1946 à 1975* (Paris: Fayard, 1979).

Fox, Albertine, *Godard and Sound: Acoustic Innovation in the Late Films of Jean-Luc Godard* (London: I.B. Tauris, 2018).

Frappat, Hélène, *Jacques Rivette, secret compris* (Paris: Cahiers du cinéma, 2001).

Freud, Sigmund, 'The Moses of Michelangelo', in *Writings on Art and Literature*, ed. by Werner Hamacher and David E. Wellbery (Stanford: Stanford University Press, 1997).

——, *Writings on Art and Literature*, ed. by Werner Hamacher and David E. Wellbery (Stanford: Stanford University Press, 1997).

Frodon, Jean-Michel, *Le Cinéma français de la Nouvelle Vague à nos jours* (Paris: Cahiers du cinéma, 2010).

——, 'Une nouvelle Nouvelle Vague ?', in *Le Cinéma français de la Nouvelle Vague à nos jours* (Paris: Cahiers du cinéma, 2010).

Gallagher, Shaun, 'Body Image and Body Schema: A Conceptual Clarification,' *The Journal of Mind and Behavior*, 7.4 (1986), 541–54.

Gheerardyn, Claire, 'Geste révélé, geste révélateur: Rilke face à Rodin', *Fabula / Les colloques*, Penser le mouvement (2015) <http://www.fabula.org/colloques/document2666.php> [accessed 15 April 2017].

Giard, Luce, 'Gesture Sequences', in *The Practice of Everyday Life. Volume 2: Living & Cooking*, ed. by Michel de, Certeau, Luce Giard and Pierre Mayol, trans. by Timothy J. Tomasik (Minneapolis: University of Minnesota Press, 1998).

Godard, Hubert, 'Le Geste et sa perception', in Isabelle Ginot, Marcelle Michel and Hubert Godard (postface), *La Danse au XXe siècle* (Paris: Larousse-Bordas, 1998), pp. 224–9.

Godard, Jean-Luc, *Jean-Luc Godard par Jean-Luc Godard*, ed. by Alain Bergala (Paris: Edition de l'étoile, 1985).

——, '*Prénom Carmen*: scénario', in *Jean-Luc Godard par Jean-Luc Godard*, ed. by Alain Bergala (Paris: Edition de l'étoile, 1985).

Godard, Jean-Luc, and Gideon Bachmann, 'The Carrots are Cooked: A Conversation with Jean-Luc Godard', *Film Quarterly*, 37.3 (1984), 13–19.

Godard, Jean-Luc, Guy Scarpetta and Dominique Païni, 'Jean-Luc Godard la curiosité du sujet', *Artpress*, pp. 4–18.

Godard, Jean-Luc, and Sylvie Steinebach, 'Les Signes du mal à vivre. Entretien avec Jean-Luc Godard', *L'Avant-scène cinéma*, March 1984, pp. 4–11.

Godier, Rose-Marie, *L'Automate et le cinéma: Dans 'La Règle du Jeu' de Jean Renoir, 'Le Limier' de Joseph L. Mankiewicz, 'Pickpocket' de Robert Bresson* (Paris: L'Harmattan, 2005).

Goffman, Erving, *Frame Analysis: An Essay on the Organization of Experience* (Boston, MA: Northeastern University Press, 1986).

——, *Interaction Ritual: Essays on Face-to-Face Behaviour* (New York: Pantheon Books, 1982).

Gordon, Rae Beth, *Why the French Love Jerry Lewis: From Cabaret to Early Cinema* (Stanford: Stanford University Press, 2001).

Grespi, Barbara, 'Mimismologie. Le geste cosmologique: Marcel Jousse et Jean Epstein', in *Geste filmé, gestes filmiques*, ed. by Christa Blümlinger and Mathias Lavin ([Milan] : Mimésis, 2018).

Guégo-Rivalan, Inès, 'Energie du geste et représentation: Denis Diderot, précurseur d'une "théâtralité" moderne?', *ATALA Cultures et sciences humaines*, 17 (2014), 337–49.

Guérin, Michel, *Philosophie du geste* (Arles: Actes Sud, 2011).

Harbord, Janet, *Ex-centric Cinema: Giorgio Agamben and Film Archaeology* (New York: Bloomsbury Academic, 2016).

Hirsch, Marianne, 'The Generation of Postmemory', *Poetics Today*, 29.1 (2008), 103–28.

Huvenne, Martine, 'Sound in Film as an Inner Movement. Towards embodied Listening Strategies', in *Moving Imagination: Explorations of Gesture and Inner Movement*, ed. by Helena De Preester (Amsterdam: John Benjamins, 2013), pp. 133–48.

I Don't Belong Anywhere: The Cinema of Chantal Akerman, dir. by Marianne Lambert (2015).

Ince, Kate, *Georges Franju* (Manchester: Manchester University Press, 2012).

Ingold, Tim, *Lines: A Brief History* (Abingdon: Routledge, 2007).

Irigaray, Luce, *An Ethics of Sexual Difference*, trans. by Carolyn Burke and Gillian C. Gill (London: The Athlone Press, 1993).

——, *Key Writings*, ed. by Luce Irigaray (London: Continuum, 2004).

——, *This Sex Which Is Not One*, trans. by Catherine Porter (Ithaca, NY: Cornell University Press, 1985).

——, 'The Wedding Between the Body and Language', in *Key Writings*, ed. by Luce Irigaray (London: Continuum, 2004).

——, 'Women's Exile', trans. by Couze Venn, *Ideology and Consciousness*, 1 (1977), 62–76.

Ishaghpour, Youssef, *Cinéma contemporain: de ce côté du miroir* (Paris: Ed. de la Différence, 1986).

——, 'La Télévision', in *Cinéma contemporain: De ce côté du miroir* (Paris: Ed. de la Différence, 1986).

——, 'Le Flux et le cadre: Chantal Akerman', in *Cinéma contemporain: de ce côté du miroir* (Paris: Ed. de la Différence, 1986).

Jacobs, Steven, *Framing Pictures: Film and the Visual Arts* (Edinburgh: Edinburgh University Press, 2011).

——, 'Tableaux Vivants 1: Painting, Film, Death and Passion Plays in Pasolini and Godard', in *Framing Pictures: Film and the Visual Arts* (Edinburgh: Edinburgh University Press, 2011).

James, Ian, 'Klossowski, Nietzche and the Fortuitous Body', *Romance Studies*, 19.1 (2001), 59–70.

——, *Pierre Klossowski: The Persistence of a Name* (Oxford: Legenda, 2000).

Jousse, Marcel, *L'Anthropologie du geste* (Paris: Resma, 1969).

Kandinsky, Wassily, *Point and Line to Plane*, trans. by Howard Dearstune and Hilla Rebay (New York: Dover Publications, 1979).

Kast, Pierre, 'Une fonction de constat. Notes sur l'œuvre de Buñuel', *Cahiers du cinéma*, December 1951, pp. 6–16.

Kendon, Adam, *Gesture: Visible Action as Utterance* (Cambridge: Cambridge University Press, 2004).

Klevan, Andrew, *Film Performance: From Achievement to Appreciation* (London: Wallflower, 2005).

——, 'Living Meaning, the Fluency of Film Performance', in *Theorizing Film Acting*, ed. by Aaron Taylor (New York: Routledge, 2012), pp. 33–46.

Klossowski, Pierre, 'Argument de 1966', in Pierre Klossowski and Pierre Zucca, *Roberte au cinéma*, special issue of *Obliques* (Paris: Borderie, 1978).

——, *La Monnaie vivante* (Paris: E. Losfeld, 1970).

——, *La Ressemblance* (Marseille: Ryôan-ji, 1984).

——, *Le Bain de Diane* (Paris: Gallimard, 1980).

——, 'Le Cinéma ne doit pas simuler la littérature', *Les Nouvelles Littéraires*, 15 March 1979, pp. 14–15.

——, *Les Lois de l'hospitalité* (Paris: Gallimard, 1995).

——, 'Decadence of the Nude/La Décadence du nu', in Pierre Klossowski and Maurice Blanchot, *Decadence of the Nude/La Décadence du nu*, ed. by Sarah Wilson and intro. by Alyce Mahon (London: Black Dog, 2002).

——, 'L'Idiome corporel est-il un simulacre de communication ?', in *La Ressemblance* (Marseille: Ryôan-ji, 1984).

——, 'L'Indiscernable', in *Pierre Klossowski*, ed. by Catherine Grenier (Paris: La Différence, Centre national des arts plastiques; Marseille: Ryôan-ji, 1990), pp. 184–8.

——, *Nietzsche and the Vicious Circle*, trans. by Daniel W. Smith (London: The Athlone Press, 1997).

——, 'Nietzsche, le polythéisme et la parodie', *Revue de métaphysique et de morale*, 63.2–3 (1958), 325–48.

——, 'Protase et apodose', in *Klossowski*, ed. by René Micha (Aix-en-Provence: L'Arc, 1970), pp. 8–20.

——, 'Questions aux romanciers. Pierre Klossowski', *Cahiers du cinéma*, December 1966, pp. 97–8.

——, *Sade mon prochain; précédé de Le Philosophe scélérat* (Paris: Seuil, 2002).

——, 'Simuler le simulateur (*Vincent mit l'âne dans un pré*)', *Cahiers du cinéma*, July–August 1976, pp. 83–4.

——, *Tableaux vivants: Essais critiques 1936–1983*, ed. by Patrick Mauriès (Paris: Le Promeneur, 2001).

Klossowski, Pierre, and Maurice Blanchot, *Decadence of the Nude/La Décadence du nu*, ed. by Sarah Wilson and intro. by Alyce Mahon (London: Black Dog, 2002).

Klossowski, Pierre, and Rémy Zaugg, 'Fragments d'une explication', in *Pierre Klossowski*, ed. by Catherine Grenier (Paris: La Différence, Centre national des arts plastiques; Marseille: Ryôan-ji, 1990), pp. 189–96.

Klossowski, Pierre, and Pierre Zucca, *Roberte au cinéma*, special issue of *Obliques* (Paris: Borderie, 1978).

Kornhaber, David, '"The Art of Putting Oneself on Stage before Oneself": Theatre, Selfhood, and Nietzsche's Epistemology of the Actor', *Theatre Research International*, 36.3 (2011), 240–53.

Kracauer, Siegfried, *Theory of Film: The Redemption of Physical Reality* (New York: Oxford University Press, 1960).

Král, Peter, *Le Burlesque ou morale de la tarte à la crème* (Paris: Stock, 1984).

Kristeva, Julia, 'Le Geste, pratique ou communication ?', *Langages*, 10 (1968), 48–64.

La Vie filmée. 1930–1934, dir. by Claude Ventura and Michel Pamart, written by Georges Perec (France Régions 3, 1975).

Laban, Rudolf von, *The Mastery of Movement*, rev. by Lisa Ullmann (Plymouth: Northcote House, 1988).

Lafont, Bernadette, *La Fiancée du cinéma* (Paris: Olivier Orban, 1978).

——, *Le Roman de ma vie: Souvenirs* (Paris: Flammarion, 1997).

Landsberg, Alison, *Prosthetic Memory: The Transformation of American Remembrance in the Age of Mass Culture* (New York: Columbia University Press, 2004).

Laurens, Stéphane, and Toshiaki Kozakaï, 'Pierre Janet et la mémoire sociale', *Connexions*, 80 (2003), 59–75.

Lederer, Jacques, and Georges Perec, *'Cher, très cher, admirable et charmant ami …' Correspondance Georges Perec-Jacques Lederer (1956–1961)* (Paris: Flammarion, 1997).

Lefebvre, Henri, *Eléments de rythmanalyse* (Paris: Syllepse, 1992).

——, *Everyday Life in the Modern World*, trans. by Sacha Rabinovitch (New York: Harper & Row, 1971),.

——, *La Vie quotidienne dans le monde moderne* (Paris: Gallimard, 1968).

Lefèvre, Raymond, 'Avant le nom (le langage) des enfants jouent à Carmen', in *Jean-Luc Godard* (Paris: Edilig, 1983).

——, *Jean-Luc Godard* (Paris: Edilig, 1983).

Lejeune, Philippe, *La Mémoire et l'oblique: Georges Perec autobiographe* (Paris: P.O.L, 1991).

Lenne, Gérard, *La Mort du cinéma: film/révolution* (Paris: Les Editions du Cerf, 1971).

Leroi-Gourhan, André, *Gesture and Speech*, trans. by Anna Bostock Berger (Cambridge, MA and London: The MIT Press).

——, *Le Geste et la parole I: Technique et langage* (Paris: Albin Michel, 1964).

——, *Le Geste et la parole II: La Mémoire et les rythmes* (Paris: Albin Michel, 1965).

Les Mystères de Paris: 'Out 1' de Jacques Rivette revisité, dir. by Robert Fischer and Wilfried Reichart (2015).

Leutrat, Jean-Louis, 'The Declension', in *Jean-Luc Godard: Son + Image, 1974–1991*, ed. by Raymond Bellour and Mary Lea Bandy (New York: The Museum of Modern Art, 1992), pp. 23–33.

Levaillant, Françoise, 'Des Moments suspendus. Aspects de la temporalité dans l'œuvre dessinée de Pierre Klossowski', in *Traversées de Pierre Klossowski*, ed. by Laurent Jenny and Andreas Pfersmann (Geneva: Librairie Droz, 1999), pp. 123–34.

Liandrat-Guigues, Suzanne, *Cinéma et sculpture: un aspect de la modernité des années soixante* (Paris: L'Harmattan, 2002).

Linhart, Robert, *L'Etabli* (Paris: Minuit, 1978).

Löffler, Petra, 'Gesturing the Image. The Chain-Linking of Gestures in Jean-Luc Godard's *Passion*', in *Gestures of Seeing in Film, Video and Drawing*, ed. by Asbjørn Grønstad, Henrik Gustafsson and Øyvind Vågnes (New York: Routledge, Taylor & Francis Group, 2017), pp. 31–43.

Loiperdinger, Martin, 'Lumière's "Arrival of the Train": Cinema's Founding Myth', *The Moving Image: The Journal of the Association of Moving Image Archivists*, 4.1. (2004), 89–118.

Lonsdale, Michael, *Abécédaire* (Paris: L'œil, 2012).

Lotman, Iouri, 'Le Problème de l'acteur de cinéma', in *Sémiotique et esthétique du cinéma*, trans. by Sabine Breuillard (Paris: Editions sociales, 1977).

——, *Sémiotique et esthétique du cinéma*, trans. by Sabine Breuillard (Paris: Editions sociales, 1977).

MacCabe, Colin, with Mick Eaton and Laura Mulvey, *Godard: Images, Sounds, Politics* (Bloomington: Indiana University Press, 1980).

——, 'Jean-Luc Godard. A Life in Seven Episodes (to Date)', in *Jean-Luc Godard: Son + Image, 1974–1991*, ed. by Raymond Bellour and Mary Lea Bandy (New York: The Museum of Modern Art, 1992), pp. 13–21.

Macé, Marielle, *Styles: critique de nos formes de vie* (Paris: Gallimard, 2016).

Mahon, Alyce, 'Pierre Klossowski, Theo-pornologer/Pierre Klossowski, Théo-pornologue', in *Decadence of the Nude/La Décadence du nu*, ed. by Wilson.

Margulies, Ivone, *Nothing Happens: Chantal Akerman's Hyperrealist Everyday* (Durham, NC: Duke University Press, 1996).

Marie, Michel, *The French New Wave: An Artistic School*, trans. by Richard Neupert (Malden, MA: Blackwell).

Mary, Philippe, *La Nouvelle Vague et le cinéma d'auteur: Socio-analyse d'une révolution artistique* (Paris: Seuil, 2006).

Matsuda, Matt K., *The Memory of the Modern* (New York and Oxford: Oxford University Press, 1996).

Mauss, Marcel, 'Les Techniques du corps', ed. by Jean-Marie Tremblay (Québec: Chicoutimi, 2002). Electronic edition (first publ. in *Journal de Psychologie*, 32 (1936), 271–93).

——, 'Techniques of the Body', trans. by Ben Brewster, *Economy and Society*, 2.1 (1973), 70–88.

Mazzola, Guerino B., 'Geometry of Gestures', in *Flow, Gesture, and Spaces in Free Jazz: Towards a Theory of Collaboration*, ed. by Guerino B. Mazzola and Paul B. Charlin (Berlin: Springer-Verlag, 2009).

Mazzola, Guerino B., and Paul B. Charlin, *Flow, Gesture, and Spaces in Free Jazz: Towards a Theory of Collaboration* (Berlin: Springer-Verlag, 2009).

McNeill, David, 'Introduction', in *Language and Gesture*, ed. by David McNeill (Cambridge: Cambridge University Press, 2000), pp. 1–10.

McQuire, Scott, 'Eternity's Hostage: The Camera and the Archive', in *Visions of Modernity* (London: SAGE, 1998).

——, *Visions of Modernity* (London: SAGE, 1998).

Mello, Marie-Hélène, 'Le Tableau vivant d'après Raoul Ruiz. Une esthétique de l'"inter-image"', in *La Circulation des images: Médiations des cultures*, ed. by Richard Bégin, Myriam Dussault and Emmanuelle Dyotte (Paris: L'Harmattan, 2006), pp. 139–51.

Merleau-Ponty, Maurice, *Phenomenology of Perception*, trans. by Colin Smith (New York: Routledge, 2005).

——, *Sense and Non-Sense* (Evanston, IL: Northwestern University Press, 1966).

Michaux, Henri, *Emergences-Résurgences* (Genève: Flammarion, 1972).

Millet, Catherine, 'Klossowski our Neighbour', in *Pierre Klossowski*, ed. by Anthony Spira and Sarah Wilson (Ostfildern: Hatje Cantz, 2006), pp. 42–57.

Mondzain, Marie-José, *Homo spectator* (Paris: Bayard, 2007).

——, *Images (à suivre): de la poursuite au cinéma et ailleurs* (Paris: Bayard, 2011).

——, 'La Shoah comme question de cinéma', in *Le Cinéma et la Shoah: Un Art à l'épreuve de la tragédie du 20e siècle*, ed. by Jean-Michel Frodon (Paris: Cahiers du Cinéma, 2007), pp. 29–36.

——, 'L'Auteur au risque de l'autorité de l'acteur', *Cahiers du cinéma*, July–August 2005, pp. 14–16.

Mondzain, Marie-José, and Pierre Lauret, 'Sans Image, il n'y a pas de *logos*. Entretien avec Marie-José Mondzain', *Cahiers philosophiques*, 113 (2008), 52–63 <https://www.cairn.info/revue-cahiers-philosophiques1-2008-1-page-52.htm> [accessed 18 August 2018].

Morisi, Eve Célia, 'The OuLiPoe, or Constraint and (Contre-)"Performance": "The Philosophy of Composition" and the Oulipian Manifestos', *Comparative Literature*, 60.2 (2008), 107–24.

Motte, Warren, 'The Work of Mourning', *Yale French Studies*, 105 (2004), 56–71.

Mouëllic, Gilles, *Improviser le cinéma* (Crisnée: Yellow Now, 2011).
——, 'Performance et improvisation dans *L'œuvre de l'art*', in *La Pensée esthétique de Gérard Genette*, ed. by Joseph Delaplace, Pierre-Henry Frangne and Gilles Mouëllic (Rennes: Presses Universitaires de Rennes, 2011), pp. 221–9.
Moullet, Luc, *Politique des acteurs* (Paris: Ed. De l'Etoile, Cahiers du cinéma, 1993).
Mowat, Hannah, 'Gesture and the *cinéaste*: Akerman/Agamben, Varda/Warburg' (unpublished doctoral thesis, University of Cambridge, Trinity Hall, 2015).
Mulvey, Laura, 'The Hole and the Zero. The Janus Face of the Feminine in Godard', in *Jean-Luc Godard: Son + Image, 1974–1991*, ed. by Raymond Bellour and Mary Lea Bandy (New York: The Museum of Modern Art, 1992), pp. 75–88.
——, 'Visual Pleasure in Narrative Cinema', in *Film Theory and Criticism: Introductory Readings*, ed. by Leo Braudy and Marshall Cohen (New York: Oxford University Press, 1999), pp. 833–44.
Nacache, Jacqueline, *L'Acteur de cinéma* (Paris: Nathan, 2003).
Nancy, Jean-Luc, *Listening*, trans. by Charlotte Mandell (New York: Fordham University Press, 2007).
Neefs, Jacques, and Hans Hartje, *Georges Perec: Images* (Paris: Seuil, 1993).
Naremore, James, *Acting in the Cinema* (Berkeley: University of California Press, 1988).
Nietzsche, Friedrich, *The Gay Science*, ed. by Bernard Williams and trans. by Josefine Nauckhoff (Cambridge: Cambridge University Press, 2001).
Noland, Carrie, *Agency and Embodiment: Performing Gestures/Producing Culture* (Cambridge, MA: Harvard University Press, 2009).
——, 'Introduction', in *Migrations of Gesture*, ed. by Carrie Noland and Sally Ann Ness (Minneapolis: University of Minnesota Press, 2008), pp. ix–xxvii.
Ogilvie, Bertrand, 'Vivre entre les lignes', in Fernand Deligny, *L'Arachnéen et autres textes* (Paris: L'Arachnéen, 2008).
Païni, Dominique, 'La Bonne Distance', *Artpress*, January 1985, pp. 52–5.
Paraskeva, Anthony, *The Speech-Gesture Complex: Modernism, Theatre, Cinema* (Edinburgh: Edinburgh University Press, 2013).
Pearson, Roberta E., *Eloquent Gestures: The Transformation of Performance Style in the Griffith Biograph Films* (Oxford and Berkeley: University of California Press, 1992).
Perec, Georges, *Entretiens et conférences: Volume I 1965–1978*, ed. by Dominique Bertelli and Mireille Ribière (Nantes: Joseph K., 2003).
——, *Les Choses: une histoire des années soixante* (Paris: Julliard, 1965).
——, *L'Infra-ordinaire* (Paris: Seuil, La Librairie du XXe siècle, 1989).
——, *Un homme qui dort* (Paris: Denoël, 1967).
——, *W or the Memory of Childhood*, trans. by David Bellos (London: Vintage, 2011).

Perec, Georges, and Bernard Queysanne, *Un homme qui dort* (Paris: La Vie est belle, 2007). DVD booklet.

Perivolaropoulou, Nina, 'Le Travail de la mémoire: dans *Theory of Film* de Siegfried Kracauer', *Protée*, 32.1 (2004), 39–48.

Pethő, Ágnes, *Cinema and Intermediality: The Passion for the In-between* (Newcastle upon Tyne: Cambridge Scholars, 2011).

Petrescu, Doina, 'The Indeterminate Mapping of the Common', *Field*, 1.1 (2007), 88–96.

Pierre Zucca, l'homme, le cinéaste, dir. Angela Romboni (Carlotta, 2007).

Pouillaude, Frédéric, 'Vouloir l'involontaire et répéter l'irrépétable', in *Approche philosophique du geste dansé: De l'improvisation à la performance*, ed. by Anne Boissière and Catherine Kintzler (Villeneuve-d'Ascq: Presses Universitaires du Septentrion, 2006), pp. 145–61.

Powrie, Phil, 'Godard's *Prénom Carmen* (1984), Masochism, and the Male Gaze', *Forum for Modern Languages Studies*, 31.1 (1995), 64–73.

Prieur, Jérôme, 'Hospitalité. Pierre Zucca: *Roberte*', in *Nuits blanches, essais sur le cinéma* (Paris: Gallimard, 1980).

——, *Nuits blanches, essais sur le cinéma* (Paris: Gallimard, 1980).

Queysanne, Bernard, 'Nous étions inspirés par la ville et la lumière', *Vertigo*, 35 (2009), 78–83 <http://www.cairn.info/revue-vertigo-2009-1-page-78.htm> [accessed 1 April 2016].

Queysanne, Bernard, and Cécile De Bary, 'Entretien avec Bernard Queysanne – Propos amicaux', in *Cahiers Georges Perec. Vol. 9: Le Cinématographe*, ed. by Cécile De Bary (Bordeaux: Castor Astral, 2006), pp. 109–26.

Rancière, Jacques, *Aesthetics and Its Discontents*, trans. by Steven Corcoran (Cambridge: Polity Press, 2009).

——, *Malaise dans l'esthétique* (Paris: Galilée, 2004).

Reader, Keith, *Robert Bresson* (Manchester: Manchester University Press, 2000).

Remy, Mathieu, 'L'évidente nécessité de la mémoire', in *Cahiers Georges Perec. Vol. 9: Le Cinématographe*, ed. by Cécile de Bary (Bordeaux: Castor Astral, 2006), pp. 41–54.

Reynolds, Dee, 'Empathy, Contagion and Affect. The Role of Kinesthesia in Watching Dance', in *Touching and Being Touched. Kinesthesia and Empathy in Dance and Movement*, ed. by Gabriele Brandstetter, Gerko Egert and Sabine Zubarik (Berlin: De Gruyter, 2013), pp. 211–31.

——, *Rhythmic Subjects* (Alton, Hampshire, England: Dance Books).

Richards, Thomas, *At Work with Grotowski on Physical Actions* (London: Routledge, 1995).

Rilke, Rainer Maria, *Rodin*, trans. by Jessie Lemont and Hans Trausil (London: Grey Walls Press, 1946).

Robert, Valentine, 'La Pose au cinéma: film et tableau en corps à corps', in *Entre code et corps: Tableau vivant et photographie mise en scène*, ed. by Christine Buignet and Arnaud Rykner (Pau: Presses universitaires de Pau et des pays de l'Adour, 2012), pp. 73–89.

Rodin, Auguste, and Paul Gsell, *Rodin on Arts and Artists*, trans. by Romilly Fedden (New York: Dover Publications, 1957).

Rohmer, Eric, *De Mozart en Beethoven: Essai sur la notion de profondeur en musique* (Arles: Actes Sud, 1998).

——, 'Le Cinéma, art de l'espace', in *Le Goût de la beauté*, ed. by Jean Narboni (Paris: Cahiers du cinéma, 2004).

——, *Le Goût de la beauté*, ed. by Jean Narboni (Paris: Cahiers du cinéma, 2004).

——, *The Taste for Beauty*, trans. by Carol Volk (Cambridge: Cambridge University Press, 1989).

Rosenbaum, Jonathan, '*Out 1* and Its Double', <https://www.jonathanrosenbaum.net/2017/05/out-1-and-its-double/> [accessed 9 May 2018].

Rossin, Federico, 'Marx au grand magasin. L'idiotie et le burlesque dans les films du groupe Dziga Vertov', trans. by Jean-Pierre Cometti and Andrea Paganini, *Vertigo*, 40 (2011), 73–9.

Ross, Kristin, *Fast Cars, Clean Bodies: Decolonization and the Reordering of French Culture* (Cambridge, MA: MIT Press, 1995).

Rouch, Jean, 'La Caméra et les hommes', in *Jean-Rouch ou le ciné plaisir*, ed. by René Prédal (Condé-sur-Noireau: Corlet; Paris: Télérama, 1996), pp. 42–5.

Ruiz, Raoul, *Poetics of Cinema*, trans. by Carlos Morreo (Paris: Dis voir, 2005).

Sayad, Cecilia, *Performing Authorship: Self-inscription and Corporeality in the Cinema* (New York: I.B. Tauris, 2013).

Scarpetta, Guy, 'Docteur, est-ce que l'âme a un corps ?', *Artpress*, January 1985, pp. 42–50.

Schefer, Jean-Louis, *L'Homme ordinaire du cinéma* (Paris: Cahiers du Cinéma, Gallimard, 1997).

Schilder, Paul, *The Image and Appearance of the Human Body: Studies in the Constructive Energies of the Psyche* (New York: International Universities Press, 1950).

Schmid, Marion, *Chantal Akerman* (Manchester: Manchester University Press, 2010).

Schmitt, Jean-Claude, *La Raison des gestes dans l'Occident médiéval* (Paris: Gallimard, 1990).

Sellier, Geneviève, *Masculine Singular: French New Wave Cinema*, trans. by Kristin Ross (Durham, NC: Duke University Press, 2008).

Shapiro, Meyer, *Theory and Philosophy of Art: Style, Artist, and Society* (New York: Georges Brazillier, 1994).

Sheer, Miriam, 'The Godard/Beethoven Connection: On the Use of Beethoven's Quartets in Godard's Films', *The Journal of Musicology*, 18.1 (2001), 170–88.

Sheets-Johnstone, Maxine, 'The Imaginative Consciousness of Movement: Linear Quality, Kinaesthesia, Language and Life', in *Redrawing Anthropology: Materials, Movements, Lines*, ed. by Tim Ingold (Abingdon: Routledge, 2011), pp. 115–28.

——, *The Primacy of Movement* (Amsterdam: J. Benjamins, 2011).

Sobchack, Vivian, *The Address of the Eye: A Phenomenology of Film Experience* (Princeton: Princeton University Press, 1992).

Sontag, Susan, 'Muriel ou le temps d'un retour', *Film Quarterly*, 17.2 (1963–4), 23–7.

——, *On Photography* (Harmondsworth: Penguin, 1979).

Spira, Anthony, 'A Pantomime of Spirits', in *Pierre Klossowski*, ed. by Anthony Spira and Sarah Wilson (Ostfildern: Hatje Cantz, 2006), pp. 62–77.

Smith, Daniel W., 'Klossowski's Reading of Nietzsche. Impulses, Phantasms, Simulacra, and Stereotypes', *Diacritics*, 35.1 (2005), 8–21.

Solomon, Maynard, *Beethoven Essays* (Cambridge, MA and London: Harvard University Press, 1990).

Stanislavski, Konstantin, *An Actor Prepares*, trans. by Elizabeth Reynolds Hapgood (London: Geoffrey Bles, 1937).

——, *Creating a Role*, trans. by Elizabeth Reynolds Hapgood (London: New English Library, 1970).

Steinberg, Leo, *Other Criteria: Confrontations with Twentieth-Century Art* (Chicago: University of Chicago Press, 2007).

——, 'Rodin', in *Other Criteria: Confrontations with Twentieth-Century Art* (Chicago: University of Chicago Press, 2007).

Stern, Lesley, 'Paths that Wind through the Thicket of Things', *Critical Inquiry*, 28.1 (2001), 317–54.

Sterne, Laurence, *Tristram Shandy* (London: Everyman's Library, 1991).

Sterritt, David, *The Films of Jean-Luc Godard: Seeing the Invisible* (Cambridge: Cambridge University Press, 1999).

Tchalgadjieff, Stéphane, 'Note du producteur Tchalgadjieff', in *Out 1 et son double/ Out 1 and its Double* (Paris: Carlotta, 2015), pp. 4–6. Booklet included in the box set of Jacques Rivette's *Out 1* [on DVD].

Thomas, Keith, 'Introduction', in *A Cultural History of Gesture: From Antiquity to the Present Day*, ed. by Jan Bremmer and Herman Roodenburg (Cambridge: Polity Press, 1991), pp. 1–14.

Toledo, Sandra Alvarez de, Patrick Leboutte, Jean-Louis Comolli, Josée Manenti, Jean-Pierre Daniel and Fernand Deligny, '*Le Moindre Geste:* Autour de Fernand Deligny', *L'Image, le monde*, 2 (2001), 33–65.

Truchot, Damien, 'Sur le temps faible: Akerman/Godard', in *Sur le geste*, ed. by Suzanne Liandrat-Guigues (Le Havre: De l'incidence, 2006), pp. 144–56.

Truffaut, François, 'Une certaine tendance du cinéma français', *Cahiers du cinéma*, January 1954, pp. 15–29.

Truffaut-Godard, scénario d'une rupture, dir. Claire Duguet (France Télévisions, 2015).

Valéry, Paul, *Degas Danse Dessin* (Paris: Ambroise Vollard, 1936).

Väliaho, Pasi, *Mapping the Moving Image: Gesture, Thought, and Cinema circa 1900* (Amsterdam: Amsterdam University Press, 2010).

Van Essche, Eric, 'Le Geste survivant. Mouvements de mémoire et mémoires en mouvement chez Georges Didi-Huberman', *DITS*, 12 (2009), 50–65.

Vera, Adolfo, 'Le Cinéma ou l'art de laisser revenir les fantômes: une approche à partir de J. Derrida', *Appareil*, 14 (2014) <https://journals.openedition.org/appareil/2115> [accessed 17 August 2018].

Vincendeau, Ginette, 'Introduction. Fifty Years of the French New Wave: From Hysteria to Nostalgia', in *The French New Wave: Critical Landmarks*, ed. by Peter Graham with Ginette Vincendeau (London: BFI, 2009), pp. 1–29.

Viviani, Christian, *Le Magique et le vrai: l'acteur de cinéma, sujet et objet* (Aix-en-Provence: Rouge profond, 2015).

Vouilloux, Bernard, *Ecritures de fantaisie: grotesques, arabesques, zigzags et serpentins* (Paris: Hermann, 2008).

——, 'La Pesanteur et la grâce du geste. Jean Starobinski dans l'espace des peintres', *Littérature*, 161 (2011), 33–50 <https://www.cairn.info/revue-litterature-2011-1-page-33.htm> [accessed 2 August 2018].

——, 'Le Geste dans le tableau vivant. Des arts de la scène à la photographie', in *Le Tableau vivant ou l'image performée*, ed. by Julie Ramos (Paris: Mare et Martin, Inha, 2014), pp. 121–34.

——, 'Le Geste ressassant', in *Le Geste, suivi de Le Geste ressassant* (Brussels: Lettre volée, 2001).

——, *Le Geste, suivi de Le Geste ressassant* (Brussels: Lettre volée, 2001).

——, 'Le Tableau vivant, entre genre et dispositif', in *Entre code et corps: Tableau vivant et photographie mise en scène*, ed. by Christine Buignet and Arnaud Rykner (Pau: Presses universitaires de Pau et des pays de l'Adour, 2012), pp. 91–103.

Wiazemsky, Anne, *Jeune Fille* (Paris: Gallimard, 2007).

Willett, John, *The Theatre of Bertolt Brecht: A Study of Eight Aspects* (London: Eyre Methuen, 1977).

Wilson, Sarah, 'Pierre Klossowski: Epiphanies and Secrets', in *Pierre Klossowski*, ed. by Anthony Spira and Sarah Wilson (Ostfildern: Hatje Cantz, 2006), pp. 12–29.

Witt, Michael, 'Altered Motion and Corporeal Resistance in *France/tour/détour/deux/enfants*', in *For Ever Godard*, ed. by James Williams, Michael Temple and Michael Witt (London: Black Dog, 2003), pp. 200–13.

Zucca, Pierre, 'Autour de la notion de signe unique', in *ça cinéma 14* (Paris: Albatros, [n.d.]), pp. 3–5.

——, 'La Double Nature de l'image', in Pierre Klossowski and Pierre Zucca, *Roberte au cinéma*, special issue of *Obliques* (Paris: Borderie, 1978).

——, 'La Photographie du plaisir', in *Images du cinéma: Photographies de plateau réalisées par Pierre Zucca* (Paris: Alain Moreau, 1980).

——, *Images du cinéma: Photographies de plateau réalisées par Pierre Zucca* (Paris: Alain Moreau, 1980).

Zucca, Pierre, Jean-Claude Bonnet, Philippe Carcassonne and Jacques Fieschi, '*Roberte*. Entretien avec Pierre Zucca', *Cinématographe*, June 1978, pp. 39–41.

Broadcasts

Akerman, Chantal, Philippe Langlois and Franck Smith, 'Marcher à côté de ses lacets dans un frigidaire vide', *Atelier de Création Radiophonique*, France Culture, 9 March 2008.

Bergala, Alain, *Godard-Tati, un burlesque erratique et discret*, online video recording, Cinémathèque française, 30 April 2009, <http://www.cinematheque.fr/video/132.html> [accessed 16 April 2017].

Cassard, Phillippe, Marc Chevrie and Jean Narboni, 'Jean-Luc Godard et Beethoven', *Le Matin des musiciens*, France Musique, 28 May 2014.

Klossowsi, Pierre, and Claude Rémusat, 'Entretiens avec Pierre Klossowski', *Les Nuits de France Culture*, France Culture, 12 May 2016 [1st broadcast 5–10 June 1972].

Perec, Georges, and Pierre Desgraupes, 'Georges Perec à propos de *Un homme qui dort*', *Lectures pour tous*, Office national de radiodiffusion-télévision française, 3 May 1967.

Perec, Georges, and Viviane Forrester, 'Le Belleville de Georges Perec', *Chemins*, Antenne 2, 22 March 1976.

Index

European Connections

Studies in Comparative Literature, Intermediality and Aesthetics

edited by
Hugues Azérad and Marion Schmid

European Connections: Studies in Comparative Literature, Intermediality and Aesthetics is a peer-reviewed series that publishes innovative research monographs, edited volumes as well as translations of key theoretical works. The series focuses on the literary and artistic relations that have shaped and continue to shape European cultures across national, linguistic and media boundaries, leading to vibrant new forms of artistic creation and aesthetic expression. It also wishes to explore relations with non-European cultures with a view to fostering more equitable models of cultural exchange and transfer.

The series promotes comparative, intermedial and interdisciplinary approaches, whether studies of specific writers, filmmakers and artists; critical re-evaluations of historical periods (from the medieval to the ultra-contemporary) and movements; or wider theoretical reflections within the fields of comparative literature, intermediality studies and aesthetics. In light of the urgent need to revitalize the idea of Europe along new lines of thought, the series encourages research that explores the rich connections within European artistic and cultural production as well as the participation of European cultures in what the great philosopher of relation Édouard Glissant has called the *Tout-monde*. The series publishes in English, French and German.

Volume 1 S. S. Prawer: W.M. Thackeray's European Sketch Books. A Study of Literary and Graphic Portraiture. 459 pages. 2000. ISBN 3-906758-68-0 / US-ISBN 0-8204-5081-2

Volume 2 Patricia Zecevic: The Speaking Divine Woman. López de Úbeda's La Pícara Justina and Goethe's Wilhelm Meister. 294 pages. 2001.
ISBN 3-906766-91-8 / US-ISBN 0-8204-5607-1

Volume 3 Mary Besemeres: Translating One's Self. Language and Selfhood in Cross-Cultural Autobiography. 297 pages. 2002. ISBN 3-906766-98-5 / US-ISBN 0-8204-5614-4

Volume 4 Michela Canepari-Labib: Word-Worlds. Language, Identity and Reality in the Work of Christine Brooke-Rose. 303 pages. 2002. ISBN 3-906758-64-8 / US-ISBN 0-8204-5080-4

Volume 5 Hugo Azérad: L'Univers constellé de Proust, Joyce et Faulkner. Le Concept d'épiphanie dans l'esthétique du modernisme. 474 pages. 2002.
ISBN 3-906769-61-5 / US-ISBN 0-8204-5873-2

Volume 6 Berry Palmer Chevasco: Mysterymania. The Reception of Eugène Sue in Britain 1838–1860. 284 pages. 2003. ISBN 3-906769-78-X / US-ISBN 0-8204-5915-1

Volume 7 Sabine Schmid: 'Keeping the Sources Pure'. The Making of George Mackay Brown. 310 pages. 2003. ISBN 3-03910-012-2 / US-ISBN 0-8204-6281-0

Volume 8 Walter Redfern: Writing on the Move. Albert Londres and Investigative Journalism. 266 pages. 2004. ISBN 3-03910-157-9 / US-ISBN 0-8204-6967-X

Volume 9 Johanna Marie Buisson: Lingua Barbara or The Mystery of the Other. Otherness and Exteriority in Modern European Poetry. 364 pages. 2012.
ISBN 978-3-03910-057-6

Volume 10 Karl Leydecker and Nicholas White (eds): After Intimacy. The Culture of Divorce in the West since 1789.
295 pages. 2007.
ISBN 978-3-03910-143-6

Volume 11 Patrick Crowley and Paul Hegarty: Formless. Ways In and Out of Form. 258 pages. 2005.
ISBN 3-03910-056-4 / US-ISBN 0-8204-6297-7

Volume 12 Susan Tridgell: Understanding Our Selves. The Dangerous Art of Biography. 234 pages. 2004.
ISBN 3-03910-166-8 / US-ISBN 0-8204-6976-9

Volume 13 Patsy Stoneman and Ana María Sánchez-Arce with Angela Leighton (eds): European Intertexts. Women's Writing in English in a European Context. 296 pages. 2005.
ISBN 3-03910-167-6 / US-ISBN 0-8204-6977-7

Volume 14 Daniel Hall: French and German Gothic Fiction in the Late Eighteenth Century. 294 pages. 2005.
ISBN 3-03910-077-7 / US-ISBN 0-8204-6893-2

Volume 15 Ana Gabriela Macedo and Margarida Esteves Pereira (eds): Identity and Cultural Translation. Writing across the Borders of Englishness. Women's Writing in English in a European Context. 282 pages. 2006.
ISBN 3-03910-67-2

Volume 16 Peter Wagstaff (ed.): Border Crossings. Mapping Identities in Modern Europe. 253 pages. 2004.
ISBN 3-03910-279-6 / US-ISBN 0-8204-7206-9

Volume 17 Katharine Murphy: Re-reading Pío Baroja and English Literature. 270 pages. 2005.
ISBN 3-03910-300-8 / US-ISBN 0-8204-7226-3

Volume 18 Elza Adamowicz (ed.): Surrealism. Crossings/Frontiers. 222 pages. 2006.
ISBN 3-03910-328-8 / US-ISBN 0-8204-7502-5

Volume 19 John Parkin and John Phillips (eds): Laughter and Power. 256 pages. 2006.
ISBN 3-03910-504-3

Volume 20 Humberto Núñez-Faraco: Borges and Dante. Echoes of a Literary Friendship. 230 pages. 2006.
ISBN 3-03910-511-6

Volume 21 Rachael Langford (ed.): Depicting Desire. Gender, Sexuality and the Family in Nineteenth Century Europe. Literary and Artistic Perspectives. 280 pages. 2005.
ISBN 3-03910-321-0 / US-ISBN 0-8204-7245-X

Volume 22 Elizabeth Russell (ed.): Loving Against the Odds. Women's Writing in English in a European Context. 222 pages. 2006.
ISBN 3-03910-732-1

Volume 23 Bruno Tribout and Ruth Whelan (eds): Narrating the Self in Early Modern Europe. 333 pages. 2007.
ISBN 978-3-03910-740-7

Volume 24 Viola Brisolin: Power and Subjectivity in the Late Work of Roland Barthes and Pier Paolo Pasolini. 307 pages. 2011.
ISBN 978-3-0343-0231-9

Volume 25 Gillian E. Dow (ed.): Translators, Interpreters, Mediators. Women Writers 1700–1900. 268 pages. 2007.
ISBN 978-3-03911-055-1

Volume 26 Ramona Fotiade (ed.): The Tragic Discourse. Shestov and Fondane's Existential Thought. 294 pages. 2006.
ISBN 3-03910-899-9

Volume 27 Annamaria Lamarra and Eleonora Federici (eds): Nations, Traditions and Cross-Cultural Identities. Women's Writing in English in a European Context. 185 pages. 2010.
ISBN 978-3-03911-413-9

Volume 28 Gerri Kimber: Katherine Mansfield. The View from France. 290 pages. 2008.
ISBN 978-3-03911-392-7

Volume 29 Ian R. Morrison: Leonardo Sciascia's French Authors. 179 pages. 2009.
ISBN 978-3-03911-911-0

Volume 30 Brigitte Gauthier (ed.): Viva Pinter. Harold Pinter's Spirit of Resistance. 258 pages. 2009.
ISBN 978-3-03911-929-5

Volume 31 Hilary Brown and Gillian Dow (eds): Readers, Writers, Salonnières. Female Networks in Europe, 1700–1900. 291 pages. 2011.
ISBN 978-3-03911-972-1

Volume 32 Nóra Séllei and June Waudby (eds): She's Leaving Home. Women's Writing in English in a European Context. 272 pages. 2011.
ISBN 978-3-0343-0167-1

Volume 33 Lorna Collins and Elizabeth Rush (eds): Making Sense. For an Effective Aesthetics. 250 pages. 2011.
ISBN 978-3-0343-0717-8

Volume 34 Bandy Lee and Lorna Collins (eds): Making Sense. Merging Theory and Practice. 280 pages. 2013.
ISBN 978-3-0343-0763-5

Volume 35 Jane Fenoulhet: Nomadic Literature. Cees Nooteboom and his Writing. 257 pages. 2013.
ISBN 978-3-0343-0729-1

Volume 36 Walter Redfern: Le Mort et le vif. Clichés/néologismes. 428 pages. 2014.
ISBN 978-3-0343-1754-2

Volume 37 Isabelle Chol and Jean Khalfa (eds): Les Espaces du Livre / Spaces of the Book. 269 pages. 2015.
ISBN 978-3-0343-1903-4

Volume 38 Julia Effertz: Songbirds on the Literary Stage. The Woman Singer and her Song in French and German Prose Fiction, from Goethe to Berlioz. 293 pages. 2015.
ISBN 978-3-0343-0734-5

Volume 39 Adrian Kempton: The Epistolary Muse. Women of Letters in England and France, 1652–1802. 374 pages. 2017.
ISBN 978-1-78707-488-0

Volume 40 Stephen Butler: The *Fausts* of Gérard de Nerval. Intertextuality, Translation, Adaptation. 300 pages. 2018.
ISBN 978-1-78874-183-5

Volume 41 Giovanni Pietro Vitali: Voices of Dissent. Interdisciplinary Approaches to New Italian Popular and Political Music. 364 pages. 2020.
ISBN 978-1-78874-204-7

Volume 42 Eva Franziska Pemmerl: Symphonie der Worte. Musikalisierung von Fiktion in ausgewählten Werken Irène Némirovskys. 270 pages. 2021.
ISBN 978-1-78997-602-1

Volume 43 Fabien Arribert-Narce, Fuhito Endo and Kamila Pawlikowska (eds): The Pleasure in/of the Text. About the Joys and Perversities of Reading. 176 pages. 2021.
ISBN 978-1-78997-700-4

Volume 44 Elizabeth Benjamin: Existentialist Comics. *Bande Dessinée* and the Art of Ethics. 232 pages. 2021. ISBN 978-1-80079-273-9

Volume 45 Flavia Bujor: Une poétique de l'étrangeté : Plasticité des corps et matérialité du pouvoir. 394 pages. 2023.
ISBN 978-1-78997-965-7

Volume 46 Sabrina Bouarour, « It's so queer ! » Les masculinités dans les films de Vincente Minnelli et de Jacques Demy.
360 pages. 2023.
ISBN 978-1-80079-285-2

Volume 47 François Giraud, Gesture in French Post-New Wave Cinema.
304 pages. 2023.
ISBN 978-1-80079-638-6

Volume 48 Roberta Capotorti, Entre mélancolie et connaissance: Réception créatrice de Proust en Italie.
266 pages. 2023.
ISBN 978-1-80079-301-9

www.ingramcontent.com/pod-product-compliance
Lightning Source LLC
Chambersburg PA
CBHW071449110726
47908CB00003B/562

* 9 7 8 1 8 0 0 7 9 6 3 8 6 *